£1.40

GW01393053

TOWARDS A POST-APARTHEID FUTURE

Also by Gavin Maasdorp

FROM SHANTYTOWN TO TOWNSHIP (*editor with
A. S. B. Humphreys*)
SOUTH AFRICA AND ITS NEIGHBOURS (*with R. I. Rotberg,
H. S. Bienen and R. Legvold*)

Also by Alan Whiteside

INDUSTRIALISATION AND INVESTMENT INCENTIVES IN
SOUTHERN AFRICA (*editor*)

Towards a Post-Apartheid Future

Political and Economic Relations in Southern Africa

Edited by

Gavin Maasdorp
Director and Research Professor
Economic Research Unit, University of Natal

and

Alan Whiteside
Senior Research Fellow
Economic Research Unit, University of Natal

M
MACMILLAN

Selection, editorial matter and Introduction © Gavin Maasdorp and
Alan Whiteside 1992
Chapters 2–12 © The Macmillan Press Ltd 1992

All rights reserved. No reproduction, copy or transmission of
this publication may be made without written permission.

No paragraph of this publication may be reproduced, copied or
transmitted save with written permission or in accordance with
the provisions of the Copyright, Designs and Patents Act 1988,
or under the terms of any licence permitting limited copying
issued by the Copyright Licensing Agency, 90 Tottenham Court
Road, London W1P 9HE.

Any person who does any unauthorised act in relation to this
publication may be liable to criminal prosecution and civil
claims for damages.

First published 1992 by
THE MACMILLAN PRESS LTD
Houndmills, Basingstoke, Hampshire RG21 2XS
and London
Companies and representatives
throughout the world

ISBN 0–333–53735–1

A catalogue record for this book is available
from the British Library.

Copy-edited and typeset by Povey/Edmondson
Okehampton and Rochdale, England

Printed in Hong Kong

Contents

Preface and Acknowledgements

The Economic Research Unit at the University of Natal has focused much of its attention over the past 25 years on economic relations among Southern African countries, especially those between South Africa and its partners in the Southern African Customs Union. This book is the latest product in a long line of research in this interesting and important field.

Much of the ERU's work has taken the form of confidential reports to sponsors, and some has appeared in journal articles or chapters in books. During the 1980s, however, the results of three large projects on the region were published in monograph or book form. In 1983–4 transportation policies in eight countries were examined (G. G. Maasdorp, *Transportation and Economic Development in Southern Africa* [Durban: Economic Research Unit, University of Natal, 1984]). From 1983–6 labour relations between South Africa and its neighbours were investigated, the results appearing in a two-part report by A. W. Whiteside under the general title of *Some Aspects of Labour Relationships Between the Republic of South Africa and Neighbouring States* (Pretoria: Human Sciences Research Council). *Part I – Legislation and Agreements* was published in 1985 and *Part II – Economic Aspects* in 1986. In 1985 the ERU commissioned a series of papers on government industrial policies from economists in the region. These were presented at a workshop in Swaziland in 1986, and were ultimately published in book form (A. W. Whiteside [ed.], *Industrialization and Investment Incentives in Southern Africa*, [Pietermaritzburg: University of Natal Press and London: James Currey, 1989]).

The project on which this book is based was launched in 1988. A notable lacuna in the discussion at the time on the post-apartheid economy concerned relations between South Africa and its neighbours both in the period leading up to the post-apartheid era as well as in the immediate period thereafter. This project was designed to examine likely relations in the region over the last decade of the twentieth century. A conference, at which the papers were presented, was held in

Maputo in December 1989, and the authors were subsequently given the opportunity to amend their papers.

Whilst this proved comparatively easy for the economists, the political scientists were thrown into considerable turmoil as a result of the rapidly changing events following the speech of President de Klerk in February 1990. Their conference papers consequently had to be substantially reworked. Professor F. van Zyl Slabbert was unable to find the time to revise his paper, and a new one by Professor Robert Schrire was commissioned. The papers by Schrire and Vale were finally submitted in October, by du Pisani in November, and by Patel in December 1990. Zulu's was completed in June 1990. The chapters by the economists were received during the first half of the year. We are grateful to all the authors for their cooperation throughout the project, and to all conference participants for their useful contributions to the debate.

The project was administered by a steering committee which consisted of the two co-editors, Professor Slabbert, Professor John Barratt, Professor Peter Vale and Mr Michael Spicer. We wish to thank the members of the steering committee for their assistance in this project.

The conference in Maputo could not have been held were it not for the assistance of the Mozambican Minister of Cooperation, Hon. Jacinto Veloso. Local arrangements in Maputo were handled by Mr Carlo Esposti of Gerencia Industrial Limitada who gave generously of his time and to whom we are greatly indebted. Mr Michael Spicer of Anglo American Corporation assisted in transport arrangements for delegates, notably in the form of an executive aircraft, for which we are most grateful. Other individuals whose assistance in the conference organisation was indispensable were Ms Sally Gallagher of Business Development Africa, Johannesburg, and Professor Agostinho Zacarias of the Institute of Foreign Relations, Maputo.

The project was made possible by a generous grant from the Friedrich Ebert Stiftung, Bonn, with which the ERU has enjoyed warm relations. Dr Werner Rechmann and Dr Winfried Feit of the FES were always helpful and full of encouragement, and we thank them for their role.

Finally, in the ERU, the skilful typing and patience of Sharon Horsman, Amanda Cooper, Kay Pedley and June Roberts, together with the administrative assistance of Mr Bruce Page, have been integral parts of the successful team work which characterised the project. At home, Jane Maasdorp and Ailsa Marcham have waited for the completion of this manuscript, and we appreciate their forbearance.

A note on terminology is necessary: in referring to race groups in South Africa, the word 'black' is applied to Africans, coloureds and Indians collectively.

Durban   GAVIN MAASDORP
                                                        ALAN WHITESIDE

List of Acronyms

In order to avoid repetition and save space in the text, the most common names of organisations and so forth are listed hereunder. In the case of political parties, the name of the country is given in brackets where this is not readily apparent from the name of the organisation.

AIDS	Acquired Immune Deficiency Syndrome
ANC	African National Congress (South Africa)
ASEAN	Association of South-East Asian Nations
AWB	Afrikaner Weerstandsbeweging (South Africa)
Azapo	Azanian People's Organisation (South Africa)
BDP	Botswana Democratic Party
BLS	Botswana, Lesotho and Swaziland
BMF	Black Management Forum (South Africa)
CMA	Common Monetary Area
COSATU	Congress of South African Trade Unions
CP	Conservative Party (South Africa)
DP	Democratic Party (South Africa)
EC	European Community
ECA	Economic Commission for Africa
EFTA	European Free Trade Association
EOI	Export-Oriented Industrialisation
Frelimo	Frente de Libertacao de Mozambique
GATT	General Agreement on Tariffs and Trade
GDP	Gross Domestic Product
GNP	Gross National Product
GSP	General System of Preferences
HIV	Human Immuno-virus
HNP	Herstigte Nasionale Party (South Africa)
IACs	Industrially Advanced Countries
IMF	International Monetary Fund
ISI	Import-substituting Industrialisation
ITC	Indigenous Technological Capabilities
LDCs	Less-developed Countries
MDM	Mass Democratic Movement (South Africa)
MPLA	Movimento Popular de Libertacao de Angola

NACTU	National Congress of Trade Unions (South Africa)
NAFCOC	National African Federated Chambers of Commerce (South Africa)
NATO	North Atlantic Treaty Organisation
NF	National Forum (South Africa)
NICs	Newly Industrialised Countries
NIDL	New International Division of Labour
NP	National Party (South Africa)
NRZ	National Railways of Zimbabwe
OAU	Organisation of African Unity
OECD	Organisation for Economic Cooperation and Development
PAC	Pan Africanist Congress (South Africa)
PF-ZAPU	Patriotic Front-Zimbabwe African People's Union
PTA	Preferential Trade Area for Eastern and Southern Africa
Renamo	Resistencia Nacional Mocambicana
RMA	Rand Monetary Area
SACP	South African Communist Party
SACU	Southern African Customs Union
SACM	Southern African Common Market
SADCC	Southern African Development Coordination Conference (note: The acronym SADCC is commonly pronounced 'Sadec'.)
SADF	South Africa Defence Force
SALC	Southern African Labour Commission
SDRs	Special Drawing Rights
SSA	Sub-Saharan Africa
SWAPO	South West African People's Organisation (Namibia)
TEBA	The Employment Bureau of Africa
UDF	United Democratic Front (South Africa)
UN	United Nations
UNHCR	United Nations High Commission for Refugees
UNIP	United National Independence Party (Zambia)
UNITA	Uniao Nacional para a Independencia de Total de Angola
ZANU (PF)	Zimbabwe African National Union-Patriotic Front

Notes on the Contributors

Ronald Bethlehem is Group Economics Consultant, Johannesburg Consolidated Investment Co. Ltd. He is the author of *Economics in a Revolutionary Society* (1988), chairs the economics committees of the South African Chamber of Business and the Consultative Business Movement, and edits the *Investment Analysis Journal*.

Anthony M. Hawkins is Professor of Business Studies at the University of Zimbabwe, writes for *The Financial Times* on African affairs, and is a consultant with the Business International group in London. He has written *Rethinking Corporate Strategy for Africa* (1990).

Raphael Kaplinsky is a Fellow of the Institute of Development Studies, University of Sussex. He lectured at the University of Nairobi from 1974 to 1977 and was an adviser to the PTA from 1986 to 1989. Consultancies for various United Nations and other international agencies have taken him to many developing countries.

Gavin Maasdorp is Research Professor and Director, Economic Research Unit, University of Natal, Durban. He has worked as a consultant, especially in transport, in Southern African countries for over 20 years and has published widely on development issues in South Africa and the region. He is a co-author of *South Africa and its Neighbours* (1985).

Hasu H. Patel is Professor of Political Science, University of Zimbabwe. His research has been concentrated on Uganda, Zimbabwe and Southern Africa, and he has published a number of books, co-authoring *The People's Storm: The Transfer of Power in Zimbabwe* (1991).

André du Pisani is Manning Director of Research, South African Institute of International Affairs, Johannesburg. He has lectured at the universities of Stellenbosch and South Africa, and has published widely on the politics of the Southern African region, particularly that of Namibia, his native country.

Robert Schrire is Professor of Political Studies and Director of the Institute for the Study of Public Policy, University of Cape Town. He has lectured at several universities in the USA, and has written widely on South African politics and foreign policy analysis. He has edited *Critical Choices for South Africa* (1990).

Peter Vale is co-director, Centre for Southern African Studies, University of the Western Cape. From 1984 to 1990 he was Research Professor and Director, Institute for Social and Economic Research, Rhodes University. He has published over 70 academic papers and writes extensively for the media.

Alan Whiteside is Senior Research Fellow, Economic Research Unit, University of Natal, Durban. He was an Overseas Development Institute Fellow in the Ministry of Finance and Development Planning, Gaborone from 1980 to 1982. He edited *Industrialisation and Investment Incentives in Southern Africa* (1989), and has written on labour migration and AIDS in Southern Africa.

Paulus Zulu is Senior Research Fellow, Maurice Webb Race Relations Unit, Centre for Social and Development Studies, University of Natal, Durban. He was a researcher at the University of Zululand from 1982 to 1984 and participated in the 'South Africa beyond Apartheid' project, contributing to *A Future South Africa: Visions, Strategies and Realities* (1988).

ZAIRE

DAR ES SALAAM

TANZANIA

LUANDA

ANGOLA

Lobito

ZAMBIA

LILONGWE

Namibe

LUSAKA

Blantyre

Nacala

MALAWI

HARARE

ZIMBABWE

Bulawayo

Beira

WINDHOEK

BOTSWANA

MOZAMBIQUE

Walvis Bay

(SA) NAMIBIA

GABORONE

Luderitz

PRETORIA

Johannesburg

MAPUTO

MBABANE

SWAZILAND

INDIAN OCEAN

Richards Bay

ATLANTIC

OCEAN

MASERU

LESOTHO

Durban

Saldanha

SOUTH AFRICA

East London

CAPE TOWN

Port Elizabeth

N

National boundaries

Railways

100 0   200   400 Miles

100 0   200   400   600 Kilometres

Southern Africa

1 Introduction

Alan Whiteside and Gavin Maasdorp

The 1980s have been described as 'a dismal decade' for Africa. It was a period in which real per capita incomes fell by 40 per cent to $350 at 1980 prices and the number of African countries classified as 'least developed' rose from 17 to 28. The decade saw a persistent and general decline in economic activity, social welfare and living standards. Only four African countries – Botswana, Burkina Faso, Cameroon and Mauritius – experienced income growth of more than 4 per cent per annum. Sub-Saharan Africa's (SSA) share of world GDP stood at 1.5 per cent in 1965, rose to 1.9 per cent in 1980 and fell back to 0.8 per cent in 1989.[1]

The problems of SSA have been well documented.[2] The World Bank notes that the continent is extremely diverse, but despite this there are surprising commonalities in the problems. These include high rates of population growth; low levels in investment and saving; inefficient resource use; weak institutional capacity and human resources; and a general decline in income and living standards.

The major problem is weak growth in the productive sector. Agriculture, generally the basis for all economic development, grew at only half the rate of population growth between 1970 85. To some extent this was due to environmental factors, but it also reflects government attitudes to farming, the policy being to keep farm prices low. Manufacturing, seen as the answer to development problems, grew by eight per cent during the 1960s but the overall growth rate from 1965–87 was about the same as that of total GDP. Mineral production grew at the same rate as the agricultural sector; only petroleum output expanded substantially.

In general, African countries also have poor export performances. Their share of world exports has stagnated or declined. Most African countries continue to rely on primary products for export earnings; however, not only has their market share declined but technological advances have reduced world demand and prices have fallen.

Declining export earnings have led many countries to resort to heavy external borrowing in order to maintain government expenditure. The effect of this has been to increase debt; SSA's total debt rose from $6 billion in 1970 to $134 billion in 1988. By the end of that period the region's debt was equal to its GNP and three-and-a-half times its export earnings. The debt of African countries has grown faster than that of other developing areas. The economic crisis has led to deteriorating social conditions. School enrolments have fallen and life expectancy is growing only slowly. The number of people with deficient diets has increased. High rates of open unemployment exist in virtually every country. The unemployed are increasingly qualified but their education is inappropriate. Governments appear to have become less efficient and politicians more corrupt. Africa, with a tenth of the world's population, accounts for a third of the officially recognised refugees and, in addition, there are another 12 million people who are displaced within their own countries. Previously world-class institutions such as Makerere University in Uganda now are in an appalling physical condition, and the physical and social infrastructure in general is deteriorating.

Africa is one of the areas worst hit by the AIDS epidemic with its social, economic and political implications. Although the continent has vast water and land resources with potential for growth, the ecology is fragile and there are signs of ecological degradation: population pressure has resulted in collapsing productivity of land, the demand for fuel wood gives rise to deforestation with consequent increases in erosion, and urban areas are increasingly polluted.

Perhaps the most worrying result of this litany of disaster and disappointment is the growing crisis of confidence. The World Bank notes that 'many people in and out of sub-Saharan Africa feel a growing sense of hopelessness. This crisis of confidence has been rein-forced by the adverse external image of Africa in the global media, which focuses mainly on Africa's economic, social, and political woes – famines, desertification, refugees, human rights violations, coup d'états, internecine violence, and health problems. The danger is that pessimism can become self-fulfilling; weak performance breeds disappointment, responsibility is shifted to others, inaction undermines self-confidence and performance sinks even further.[3] Of course, the changes in Eastern Europe have drawn the world's attention away from Africa; that and the Middle East conflict may lead to a growing neglect of the continent.

SOUTHERN AFRICA

The Southern African region shares many of the characteristics of the rest of Africa. Southern Africa contains the most successful and the

least successful countries in the world if growth in GNP per capita is a
measure of success. The countries are Botswana with a 6.7 per cent
annual growth rate between 1980–8 and Mozambique where the GNP
per head declined by 7.5 per cent per annum in the same period.

Table 1.1   Southern Africa – some salient statistics, 1988

	Area (mill. km²)	Population (mill.)	GNP Total (US$ mill.)	GNP Per capita (US$)
Angola	1.25	9.40	8000	850
Botswana	.58	1.20	1150	1000
Lesotho	.03	1.67	690	410
Malawi	.12	8.16	1320	160
Mozambique	.80	15.00	1550	100
Swaziland	.02	.74	580	790
Tanzania	.95	24.74	3780	160
Zambia	.75	7.49	2160	290
Zimbabwe	.39	9.26	6070	660
Namibia	.82	1.66	1840(a)	1100(a)
SADCC	5.71	79.32	26560	335
South Africa	1.22	36.65	77720	2120
Total	6.93	115.97	104280	899
South Africa %	16.6	31.6	74.5	235.8

Note: (a) 1989 figures
Sources: Rethinking Corporate Strategy for Africa (London: Business International, 1990); Namibia Country Profile 1990–91 (London: EIU, 1990); Development Bank of Southern Africa.

The 1980s were a period of uncertainty and conflict for Southern
Africa. The decade began on two optimistic notes. The first was the
independence of Zimbabwe and the second was the creation of
SADCC. The members of SADCC were Tanzania, Zambia, Angola,
Malawi, Mozambique, Zimbabwe, Botswana, Lesotho and Swaziland.
The organisation was set up to coordinate aid funds for regional
projects and to counter South Africa's economic dominance of the
region (which is reflected in Table 1.1).

By the middle of the decade, South Africa's townships were aflame and a state of emergency had been declared over the entire country. In Angola the war between the MPLA government and Unita, with support from the US/South Africa and the USSR/Cuba respectively, had intensified, and the question of Namibian independence was no nearer to resolution. In Mozambique the South African-backed Renamo rebel movement was locked in a bloody conflict with the Frelimo government. Transport systems were disrupted throughout the region, resulting in Malawi, Zambia and Zimbabwe having to route most of their overseas trade via South African ports at considerable extra cost. Studies undertaken by various organisations, including SADCC, the ECA and Unicef, estimate that the quantifiable costs of conflict and destabilisation have approached 25–40 per cent of GDP annually, and this has been even higher in Mozambique and Angola.[4] The conflict has led to increased expenditure on the military. Exports have suffered, not only because of transport difficulties but also because the production areas have been disrupted. Import costs have risen and this has resulted in mounting debt and higher prices. Refugees are a major burden, and schools, health facilities and infrastructure have been destroyed.

The 1990s have begun on an upbeat note. The withdrawal of South African and Cuban troops from Angola, the independence of Namibia (which almost immediately became the tenth member of SADCC), peace discussions in Angola and Mozambique, and a wider acceptance of multi-party democracy and economic liberalisation, have improved the international image of the region.

However, it is generally agreed that what happens in South Africa will have a major impact on the region. Without doubt, the continued existence of apartheid and the desire of the NP government to maintain control, both political and economic, has been a major cause of conflict and declining economic development in both the region and South Africa. The accession of F.W. de Klerk to the South African presidency, his release of imprisoned political leaders, unbanning of political organisations and statements about negotiation, brought a major change both to South African politics and to world attitudes to the region.

This book begins by examining political trends in South Africa and the region. It then goes on to deal with the issues of economic development and economic relations, before considering political relations. The overriding aim is to trace the future of South and Southern Africa in the 1990s and beyond.

Chapters 2–4 discuss political trends in the region. Although the authors – Robert Schrire on white politics and strategies in South Africa for the 1990s, Paulus Zulu on the extra-parliamentary opposition in South Africa, and Hasu Patel on the SADCC states - felt that the ground had been cut from under their feet, especially as regards predictions of future events, by the historic speech of President de Klerk in the Houses of Parliament in Cape Town in February 1990, and the events that followed from it, they make a brave attempt to predict the future course of events.

White politics will remain important in South Africa for the first part of the 1990s, if only because negotiations, and the speed at which they are carried out, are to a large extent dependent on white politicians. Schrire (Chapter 2) notes that, short of a successful revolution, it is rare for an established society to change course as rapidly and dramatically as has happened in South Africa. He looks at the dynamics of change in government policy, the challenges confronting President de Klerk and the NP, and various issues relating to negotiations. He concludes that the demands of transition will be enormous. The key parties will have to learn new rules: for the ANC the challenge will be to convert its revolutionary legacy into normal party politics, while the NP will need to accept that it will be only one of several major parties. Post-apartheid South Africa will be a fragile society, and Schrire speculates that the ruling elite may be inward looking, placing foreign policy issues low on their list of priorities. If this is the case, South Africa could be less active in the region for several years into the future.

Zulu (Chapter 3) examines the extra-parliamentary opposition prior to the unbanning of the ANC and explores the significance of this force in the struggle for political power. He argues that both the NP and the ANC control the nature and tempo of political power, albeit it from opposite directions, namely, control and resistance. He looks at the composition of the extra-parliamentary opposition, noting that it draws its support from a broad base: it is both a political movement and a product of specific issues. It will play an important part in determining the future of the negotiations, but its main role so far has been to bring about the shift in the government's policy towards apartheid and negotiations.

In Chapter 4, Patel examines the political environment in the SADCC countries, particularly from the perspective of its effect on the ANC. He traces the levels of support given for the ANC by the SADCC countries and notes that as support for the military aspect of

ANC activities declined, so support for diplomatic and political initiatives increased. He expects Swaziland and Lesotho to retain their constitutional monarchies, and Botswana its stable parliamentary democracy. Peace moves and constitutional reforms in Mozambique and Angola are discussed, as is the debate on one-party vs multiparty states in Zimbabwe, Zambia and Tanzania. Patel believes that Malawi's one-party system is likely to continue, but he finds favour with political developments to date in Namibia. He concludes his chapter by analysing changes in superpower attitudes to the region: specifically, they may work jointly for the successful resolution of the South African problem. Implicit in this will be dramatic changes for the rest of Southern Africa.

Following on from these political analyses, Chapters 5–9 are devoted to economic aspects, notably growth performance, development strategies, and present and future relations. Chapter 5, by Ronald Bethlehem, examines economic issues in South Africa. The main challenge is to achieve economic growth with redistribution of income and job creation. Bethlehem postulates three scenarios for South Africa's economic development in the 1990s. They are: conflict resolved, with sanctions lifted and political settlement; muddling on, where the NP continues to reform unilaterally but without the support of the opposition movements; and mandatory sanctions if reform stops. The effects of these scenarios on growth, employment, inflation, balance of payments, and economic policy are examined. Bethlehem warns that economic deterioration could result in a groundswell of opposition, even to a newly-mandated majority government. In the final reckoning, it is the extension of industrialisation that offers South Africa its best hope for the future.

A substantially different analysis to that of Bethlehem's is contained in Chapter 6. Raphael Kaplinsky examines the prospects for post-apartheid South Africa's manufacturing sector, and links this with regional trade. He attributes the stagnation in manufacturing in the the 1980s to the costs of apartheid; the impact of sanctions; the decline of commodity prices; and the great dependence on gold which meant that exchange rates were at a higher level than might otherwise have been the case. In attempting to construct 'a feasible and realistic industrial policy in the context of post-apartheid South Africa', Kaplinsky stresses the importance of technology transfer and productive process. Here he employs the Marxist notion of 'post-Fordism'. His analysis was strongly challenged by other economists at the Maputo workshop, but his views on industrial policy and the role of the State add another dimension to this book. In the final section of his paper, Kaplinsky suggests that post-apartheid South Africa might find more and longer-term opportunities in the PTA rather than SADCC. South Africa could rapidly come to dominate the PTA but would have to try not to alienate Zimbabwe and Kenya. Kaplinsky is cautiously optimistic about the prospects for South African manufacturing. Economic development in the SADCC countries is assessed in a detailed contribution by Anthony Hawkins (Chapter 7). SADCC, he notes, was established as an institution to foster economic development, but the rationale for its creation was more political than economic. As in the rest of Africa, the 1980s was a decade of stagnation for SADCC. Most worrying was the fall in agricultural production. In his assessment of the SADCC programme, Hawkins concludes that little progress has been made towards reducing external dependence, but this is hardly surprising given the nature of the development process. More important is his statement that little progress was made in reducing dependence on South Africa. Hawkins argues that SADCC has been bound together more by the cement of anti-South African sentiment than common economic interests. This means that in the 1990s, decisions will have to be taken concerning broadening and deepening the organisation. Deepening would imply member states giving away autonomy to a supra-national body; broadening would involve expanding the membership. The stage is set for controversial and divisive negotiations over the restructuring of regional economic relations into the next century but, as Hawkins notes, this may be determined by the pace of change in South Africa itself.

This question of future trade relations in Southern Africa is more fully discussed by Gavin Maasdorp (Chapter 8). He explores the main strands of future South African/regional relations in terms of institutional agreements concerned with trade. This is set against a background of emerging worldwide regional trading blocs, and the theory of economic integration. Maasdorp warns that the emergence of new trading blocs and the expected growth of investment by the West in East European countries might result in sub-Saharan Africa becoming marginalised. However, Southern Africa could be an exception. He examines the possibilities for economic integration in the region, analyses the various economic groupings (the SACU, CMA, SADCC and PTA), and considers possible changes in their membership and the implications for their future. He does not find economic integration demonstrably preferable to economic cooperation; however, the

present SACU/CMA groupings could be transformed into a common
market or perhaps even an economic union. Existing regional organisations might have to make considerable changes to their formats in
future.

Alan Whiteside (Chapter 9) looks at four topics: labour flows;
refugees; AIDS; and the environment. Migrant labour flows have
gone on for over a century. Today most of the labour moves from
Botswana, Lesotho, Swaziland and Mozambique to South Africa's
mines. However, the numbers of migrants have fallen and the origins
have changed; the 1990s will see further change and a consolidation in
the movement of labour in that fewer migrants will find work in South
Africa. This will increase unemployment and adversely affect foreign
exchange in the sending countries. The post-apartheid government will
find the employment of foreign labour one of the most difficult
problems with which to grapple. There are currently nearly two
million refugees from and in the region, the bulk being from Angola
and Mozambique. If political settlement can be achieved, the issue of
refugees would seem soluble. Whiteside notes that the implications of
AIDS and HIV infection could be dramatic; it could change the
demography of the region substantially and will affect economic,
political and social life. This will not, however, be felt until the middle
of the 1990s. Finally, the chapter suggests that environmental degradation is a potential source of concern and needs to be tackled now.

The chapters on future economic relations in the region are
complemented by André du Pisani's treatment (Chapter 10) of future
political relations between South Africa and SADCC states. He uses
both dependency approaches and regime theory to explain the
situation: however, he notes that 'one of the most enduring qualities
of the politics of Southern Africa is its cunning capacity to defy
regional "experts" '. Du Pisani draws up a chronology of South
Africa's political relations with the region. It is apparent that the
country has moved from the period of coercive incorporation to a new
neo-realist policy. He makes the constructive suggestion that, in the
period preceding the post-apartheid era, special multilateral mechanisms should be established in order to facilitate communication
between Pretoria and SADCC. He differs from Schrire (Chapter 2)
in that he believes South Africa will remain clearly dominant in the
region; in fact, he argues that South Africa might perhaps even
challenge Nigeria for political and economic leadership in Africa.

With all contributors agreeing that events in South Africa will
largely shape the future of the region, it is fitting that Peter Vale

(Chapter 11) should examine the external pressures for change in South and Southern Africa. In tracing the history of this pressure, he notes that South Africa was not regarded as an African issue – an important and often forgotten point. Vale seeks the 'least painful and most expeditious way to end apartheid'. He discusses negative pressures, such as sanctions, and then asks what positive pressures can be brought to bear by the international community on South Africa in the future. He suggests that one of the most important developments could be to bring South Africa back into Africa: if South Africa and South Africans can become a part of the African continent and feel at home as such, then the future could be very much brighter.

The concluding chapter brings together the various threads identified in the preceding chapters, but the editors also draw heavily on the discussions at various conferences on Southern Africa which they have attended during the last two years – in South Africa, Zimbabwe, Mozambique, the Soviet Union, Switzerland, Germany and Britain. Global and national factors are discussed, and political and economic influences identified. A matrix of possible scenarios for the region is developed.

It is clear that South and Southern Africa are entering an exciting decade. Decisions made in the next few years will determine the future of the people and the countries of the region. It is hoped that this book may influence some of those decisions and ensure that the region does indeed have a bright future.

Notes

1. Business International Ltd, *Rethinking Corporate Strategy for Africa: Opportunities and Risks in a Fast Changing Environment*, London, 1990.
2. World Bank, *Sub-Saharan Africa: From Crisis to Sustainable Growth*, Washington D.C., 1989.
3. Op.cit., p.23.
4. Op.cit., p.23.

2 White Politics and Strategies in the 1990s*

Robert Schrire

Short of a successful revolution, it is very rare for an established society rapidly and dramatically to change course and move in a fundamentally different direction. Yet this is exactly what is happening in contemporary South Africa. With a tempo which has caught all observers by surprise, the apartheid paradigm has been discarded by a National Party (NP) government, and all the associated political certainties have been relegated to the dustbin of history.

THE DYNAMICS OF CHANGE

These developments have been particularly dramatic because they were so unexpected. By the beginning of 1990, the NP was in its fifth decade of uninterrupted rule. In the leadership race the previous year to fill the vacancy created by the resignation of P.W. Botha as party leader, F.W. de Klerk, universally perceived to be the most conservative of the four contenders, squeaked in despite the almost universal opposition of party 'liberals'. The stage was clearly set for business as usual and a continuation of the equivocal limited reforms of the Botha era.

These expectations were shattered on 2 February 1990 when President de Klerk opened Parliament. South Africa's political destiny was changed fundamentally, for better or worse, by the announcement of the unbanning of the ANC, the PAC and the SACP, the forth-coming release of political prisoner Nelson Mandela, and the commit-ment to 'normal' politics and negotiations. What were the dynamics behind these decisions?

The Historical Legacy

The apartheid system,[1] erected in a complex set of measures over a four-decade period, remained viable as long as four conditions existed: (1) the international community was prepared to ignore South Africa's domestic structure and to incorporate it into the global economy;

(2) the domestic economic base remained dynamic and growth orientated; (3) black South Africans acquiesced to white rule and policies; and (4) the ruling group remained united and cohesive. During the years of Botha's rule all four conditions unravelled. The illusion of a 'normal' society was rudely shattered after 1984 by black-led revolts which began in the Transvaal and Eastern Cape and which spread nationally. Successive declarations of states of emergency failed to contain the violence completely. In reaction to this violence and especially to the often brutal response of the white-controlled State, action replaced rhetoric at the international level. Led by the Chase Manhattan Bank, the banking community lost confidence in the soundness of South African finances and this led to a banking crisis when creditors recalled their loans or refused to refinance or roll over existing debt. Several countries, including the United States, imposed selective sanctions against South Africa. In part the result of black unrest and global sanctions, and in part as a result of economic mismanagement and economically destructive domestic policies, the South African economy weakened dramatically: the currency declined to less than a third of its former value, per capita growth rates became negative, and unemployment increased significantly.

Partly in response to these pressures, and partly as a result of socio-economic forces which made Afrikanerdom less homogeneous, the ruling groups became increasingly divided. While the differences between English and Afrikaans-speaking whites narrowed, Afrikanerdom became increasingly divided on class lines with consequent conflicts over ideology and policy.

Botha the leader was both a victim of and a participant in these turbulent developments.[2] Although it was always clear that the foundations of the racially-based system – international incorporation, black acquiescence and economic vitality – would inevitably disintegrate, the timing of this collapse was the great imponderable. Botha's two immediate predecessors, Verwoerd and Vorster, were fortunate to have largely escaped the inevitable consequences of their legacy and policies. Both presided over periods of overall prosperity; both had to survive one period of insurrections; and both avoided the onset of major international boycotts and sanctions.

Time ran out during Botha's rule. To some extent despite his actions, to some extent because of his actions, the State became increasingly beleaguered. The fundamental racial bias of State structures and policies and the over-extension of State power, inherent in a system of government based upon the regulation of an extensive range of individual activities, produced its inevitable consequences: a politicised black population, economic weakness and international isolation.

The Rise of de Klerk

In early February 1989, P.W. Botha, after suffering a stroke, stunned his party by resigning as NP leader while remaining on as State President. The caucus, following his instructions, immediately proceded to elect a new leader. In the first ballot de Klerk obtained 59 votes, Barend du Plessis 30, Chris Heunis 25, and Pik Botha 16. In the second ballot de Klerk got 64 votes to 26 for Heunis and 40 for Barend du Plessis. In the final ballot de Klerk scraped home with 69 votes compared to du Plessis's 61.

The narrowness of de Klerk's victory was somewhat surprising, and the vote was strongly shaped by ideology. De Klerk was clearly perceived by his own party as the most conservative of all the candidates and most of the more liberal members voted for his opponents. Therefore, in the final round of voting, de Klerk won only 10 of the 71 votes which originally went to the 'liberals' – Heunis, du Plessis and Pik Botha.

What sort of man is de Klerk? He was born in 1936 into a prominent NP political family. His father was a leading member of Parliament, cabinet minister, and president of the Senate. De Klerk trained as a lawyer and turned down a chair of law at Potchefstroom University to go into politics in 1972; he joined the cabinet in 1978. His supporters claim that he is a shrewd and intelligent leader with a good sense of tactics. He is a personable man and fairly effective on television and in public, though lacking charisma. His critics argued after his election that he was too conservative and was a captive of his narrow Afrikaner background.

The Challenges Confronting de Klerk

De Klerk was absorbed throughout most of 1989 with the challenge of taking control over the National Party and State machinery and winning a mandate from his white electorate. After a lengthy power struggle with President P.W. Botha, de Klerk was able to unite his party behind his leadership and force his predecessor as party leader to retire from politics and government. His second challenge was to win a mandate from the white electorate.

The NP fought the 1989 elections under the worst of all possible circumstances: the white electorate was still reeling from the shock of P.W. Botha's resignation from the presidency and television attack on his successor, the Botha-Mandela meeting at Tuynhuys had confused the voters of the centre, inflation was running at over 15 per cent per annum, white real incomes were static or declining, and the South African Broadcasting Corporation, under new leadership and perhaps taking advantage of the power vacuum at the centre as a result of Botha's illness and the subsequent power struggle, gave more objective radio and television coverage to the campaign than in the past. The election results are shown in Table 2.1 and the distribution of votes between the parties in Table 2.2.

Table 2.1   Election results 1989 (pre-election situation in brackets)[3]

	NP	CP	DP	HNP	Other	Vacant	Total
Cape	42 (47)	2 (0)	12 (8)	0 (0)	–	0 (1)	56
Transvaal	34 (45)	31 (22)	11 (6)	0 (0)	1 (0)	0 (2)	76
Natal	10 (14)	– (–)	10 (5)	0 (0)	0 (1)	0 (0)	20
OFS	7 (14)	6 (0)	0 (0)	0 (0)	0 (0)	1 (0)	14
Total	93 (120)	39 (22)	33 (19)	0 (0)	0 (1)	1 (3)	166

Table 2.2   Voter support by party 1989 and 1987

	1987	1989
NP	1 083 575	1 053 523
CP	549 916	685 250
DP	343 017	451 544
HNP	62 888	5 536

The major results were that the NP lost 27 seats, the CP gained 17 seats and remains the official parliamentary opposition, the DP gained 14 seats, and the HNP did not win any seats and has effectively been eliminated as a political force.

Analysis of the detailed voting statistics indicates the following:

1. For the first time in three decades, the NP received fewer votes than its opponents and was supported by a minority of white voters,
2. The DP failed to make a decisive breakthrough amongst Afrikaans-speaking voters where its support remains at about five per cent – its support continues to be largely confined to affluent, urban and English-oriented areas,
3. The CP has broken out of its Transvaal strongholds and is now a nationwide party with parliamentary seats in three of the four provinces,
4. English-speaking voters were divided as follows: DP 70 per cent; NP 25 per cent; CP five per cent and Afrikaans-speaking voters were divided as follows: DP five per cent; NP 55 per cent; CP 40 per cent.

By the end of 1989 de Klerk was firmly in control. His predecessor had vanished from the political scene, he had created his own cabinet team filled with political loyalists, and won a strong parliamentary mandate if not a convincing vote of confidence from the electorate. De Klerk thus began a thorough re-evaluation of the options facing his government.

The Decision to Negotiate

As early as 1980, the Botha administration had come to the conclusion that grand apartheid had failed and that South Africa's destiny was to be a country permanently inhabited by whites, coloureds, Indians and Africans. Botha followed an unsuccessful policy of attempting the incremental and selective incorporation of black groups into the polity. Mass domestic violence, economic decline and growing international pressures were the inevitable result of the failure of this approach.

The conservatively-oriented de Klerk was forced to come to several painful conclusions. First, he recognised that an approach based upon 'business as usual' would probably cost the NP its parliamentary majority at the next election. Any policy which sought to adapt incrementally to changing circumstances would lead to an acceleration in the loss of support to groups on both the left and the right. Inevitably the NP would then be forced to enter a coalition with either the right-wing Conservative Party or the liberal Democratic Party. Both options would have catastrophic consequences for the NP.

Secondly, de Klerk gradually came to recognise the reality that the incremental reform policy had failed and could not be resurrected with better leadership and more sensitive management. Its continuation would lead inevitably to an 'eighty year war' between South Africa's peoples, economic decline and international isolation.

An evaluation of the political forces also convinced de Klerk that bold action was possible. The 1989 general elections convinced him that 70 per cent of whites favoured reform. The CP had not made the gains it had confidently expected. In addition, de Klerk's own intelligence agencies, supported by information provided by the United States and Great Britain, convinced the new president that the ANC was neither as monolithic nor as powerful as had been feared.

Global forces also made reform possible. Of major significance was the total and unexpected collapse of the Soviet Union and of Marxist ideology itself. This sudden removal of the long-feared total onslaught against South Africa greatly strengthened white confidence and propensity to take risks. In addition, the continued survival of conservative governments in the United States, West Germany and Britain created additional favourable external forces for domestic reform.

By the end of 1989, de Klerk, after consulting widely within and outside his party, in South Africa and abroad, had come to the conclusion that the 'big leap forward' would be less of a gamble than the failure to act decisively. Although the impetus for reform lies in socio-economic forces, de Klerk and his team recognised the inevitability of fundamental change and made a deliberate decision to seek to control the nature of change by acting proactively. In this, de Klerk was able to build upon the legacy of his predecessor. Despite the immobility of the last few years of the Botha era, the National Party had laid the foundations for the innovations of the 1990s by deciding, as early as 1986, to reverse its policy of ethnic partition and to accept in principle a common South African citizenship for all races. De Klerk began, in consultation with his closest advisers, to examine the consequences of this momentous decision. It was soon recognised that the decision to seek, for the first time in South African history, a negotiated solution to the problems created by race domination, would only succeed if the following major problem areas could be resolved: the historical barriers to negotiation would have to be overcome, the rules for negotiations determined, and the negotiations themselves concluded satisfactorily.[4]

Barriers to Negotiations

De Klerk was forced to accept several painful realities including the necessity of taking risky actions before it would even be possible to begin to negotiate. These included the unbanning of the ANC, the SACP and the PAC and the release of political activists. Charismatic political prisoners such as Mandela therefore would have to be released.

The process of making negotiations possible actually began under Botha's leadership during 1989 with the release of selected political prisoners, and the meeting between Botha and Mandela. It received its greatest impetus in de Klerk's historic February opening of Parliament speech in which most of the preconditions were announced. However, given the legacy of conflict and suspicion between the government and its black challengers since 1960, progress has been relatively slow. Issues such as the status of political prisoners, the question of an amnesty for those who had committed acts of political violence, and the continuing state of emergency, all created barriers to negotiations.

As a result, most of 1990 was taken up with the arduous task of resolving the pre-negotiation conflict issues. As 1991 approaches, there is reason to be optimistic that the fundamental issues have now been resolved. The state of emergency has been repealed and the ANC in turn has now officially suspended the armed struggle. Two successful meetings have been held between the government and the ANC in Cape Town and Pretoria. Although several issues have, as yet, not been fully resolved, the path appears to be clear for the next stage in the transformation process.

THE RULES FOR NEGOTIATION

Assuming that the pre-conditions for negotiations have been met by early 1991, the key political groupings will have to resolve the outstanding issues on the actual structure of the negotiations. Specifically, decisions will have to be taken on the following:

1. Who will be invited to the negotiations and on what basis?
2. Who will chair the negotiations and how will representation be structured?

3. What will be on the agenda?
4. How will final decisions be taken?
5. Who will rule the country during the negotiations?
6. How will the final proposals be implemented?

Who will be Invited?

The basic choice will be between inclusive and limited participation. If the negotiations are inclusive, all the key political factions from the left to the right would be included. This would have the advantage of incorporating all power groups into the process but would clearly make consensus impossible. Limited participation, for example bilateral talks between the government and ANC, would have the advantage of making the conduct of negotiations more manageable and would improve the probability of a final agreement. However, the exclusion of important interests would contribute to the dangers of violence and conflict, and would endanger the legitimacy of any pacts or agreements reached. It therefore seems probable that, in the end, the negotiations will be partially inclusive in their structure although extremist groups may choose not to participate.

Who will Chair the Negotiations and how will Representation be Structured?

Two key issues are involved here: who will control the structures of the negotiation processes and how will participants be chosen? The government is adamant that, as the legitimate and effective authority, it will control the negotiation process. The ANC and other opposition groups favour a neutral party or an outside adjudicator such as was used to manage the transition processes in Zimbabwe and Namibia. They stress the anomaly of a participant also acting as a judge during negotiations.

There is also no consensus on the choice of delegates. The government maintains that it is possible under the present circumstances to determine which groups have 'proven' support and genuine constituencies. The ANC, on the other hand, argues that only by electing a constituent assembly will it be possible to test the power bases of the contending factions.

Given the power of the NP government and its determination to retain a dominant voice in the structuring of the negotiations, it seems probable that the State President or his representative will chair the negotiations and determine the rules. However, actual negotiations may be conducted in several forums, both formal and informal. Thus there may be two or more tracks where negotiations take place simultaneously. Public attention may focus on the formal negotiations which will give the informal negotiations greater freedom and flexibility to create compromises.

No elections will be permitted for a constituent assembly and participants will be invited from the existing political groupings and parties. If the ANC wishes to participate, it will be forced to accept these conditions.

What will be on the Agenda?

It is almost universally recognised that the core of the South African dilemma is the political exclusion of African people from the institutions of government. Constitutional issues will therefore be at the heart of the negotiations.

In addition, many would argue that the proposed negotiations must also resolve the question of economic systems, specifically the issue of property rights. Although groups such as the ANC would prefer to restrict the deliberations to narrowly defined constitutional questions such as the nature of the franchise, a bill of rights, and the structure of legislative and executive power, the government will demand a more comprehensive approach.

It seems probable, therefore, that a comprehensive range of economic and political issues will be included in the agenda. This may produce, at a future stage, problems of legitimacy if the final agreements cover many substantive issues beyond constitutional structures. Indeed, many would argue that all that can be legitimately decided are the rules for political contestation. Substantive policy issues including economic structures and rights can only be resolved in the give and take of electoral politics.

How will the Final Decisions be Taken?

Despite the government's public commitment to negotiations, the actual mechanisms of proposed constitutional decision-making have been left vague. The government has maintained that decisions will be taken on the basis of consensus.

In the real world, a constitutional convention at which all the key groups, from the PAC on the left to the AWB on the right, are represented, will not be able to agree on a new constitutional formula. What the government therefore means by 'consensus' is that it will exercise a veto on constitutional proposals. It is important to recognise that the government has not been defeated. Despite the strains to which the political economy is being subjected, the State retains formidable capabilities of repression and patronage.

Decisions will not therefore be taken by consensus of all political factions in South Africa. If negotiations succeed, they will reflect a bargain struck between the NP and its most important challenger – the ANC. Although there will be enormous pressures on the NP to compromise, and the failure of negotiations would seriously damage the party, the present power realities will ensure that no new system will be adopted unless it enjoys the support of the present government.

Who will Rule the Country during the Negotiations?

South Africa differs from both the former Rhodesia and South West Africa in that an internationally recognised and effective government is voluntarily participating in a process which, if successful, will lead to its abdication from monopoly power. Thus the NP is determined to continue to control the instruments of the State throughout the process and not thereafter to fade from the scene.

Groups such as the PAC and ANC have claimed that a new transitional government or international presence similar to the Namibian UNTAG would be desirable. However, none have made this a precondition for negotiations. Although the present government regards its sovereignty as non-negotiable, it is flexible on the establishment of interim informal power-sharing arrangements. Indeed, in areas such as the joint monitoring of law and order, it has been argued that a power-sharing arrangement is already in place.

It is therefore possible that the government will make further compromises on this issue. De facto, although not de jure, the NP administration may be prepared to give other factions, specifically the ANC, an unofficial or non-statutory platform to make recommendations on budgetary matters, and to participate to an increasing extent in local administration and the implementation of law and order programmes.

How will the Final Proposals be Implemented?

South Africa is a sovereign state and therefore it is improbable that the government of the day will delegate to external forces administrative powers during the transition. At the same time the vast machinery of government is far from homogeneous and important elements within the State structures, especially in the police and security apparatus, may be less enthusiastic about the prospects for the post-apartheid society than some of the civilian politicians.

An inevitable tension must therefore exist between the role of the present State as the beneficiary of the status quo and the State as a source of conflict in political competition. The agents of the State have to administer a set of fundamental transformations which may in fact not be in their own interests.

However, the greater the legitimacy enjoyed by the final proposals, the more marginal will be the discretionary role of the State's administrative organs. De Klerk has already committed his government to the holding of a referendum to test the views of the present electorate on any new proposals. Other sections of the future electorate will no doubt exercise a similar testing right.

Should an unambiguous mandate for change be received, administrative structures composed of representatives of all the key power groups could be established to undertake the administration necessary to give birth to the new constitutional system. If, however, an important segment of the electorate rejects the proposals, the successful implementation of the proposals will become highly problematic.

THE NEGOTIATIONS

It seems probable that substantive negotiations on a new constitutional framework will begin late in 1991 or early in 1992. This will be a unique historical development in which the representatives of white and black aspirations, for the first time ever, will seek to reconcile demands which hitherto have been regarded as incompatible and irreconcilable. The stakes will be enormous: success would launch South Africa on a radically new path of multi-racial democracy, while failure would lead inevitably to renewed and intensified conflict and decline. The negotiations will inevitably be dominated by two topics: the structure of political power, and the type of economic system for a future South Africa. Reaching agreement on both these vital issues will be difficult and arduous.

At the beginning of 1990, a vast gap seemed to exist between the constitutional and economic policies of the two key groupings – the NP and the ANC. In the political sphere the NP remained committed to the concept of group rights and 'minority' protection. Although deliberately vague on the details, its basic position seemed to consist of the following: statutory groups would remain as the building blocks of the polity, separate voting systems for the racial groups, power-sharing at the top where the whites would enjoy a guaranteed power position, substantial decentralisation of power and autonomy to largely racially-defined local communities, and the retention of the homeland system for the so-called independent black states. The ANC remained committed to its long-standing demand for a one-person-one-vote polity based upon a common franchise and a centralised system of government in a unitary state with executive dominance.

However, during the dynamics of the transition process even in the absence of substantive negotiations, positions on both sides have changed significantly.[5] Already a consensus seems to be developing on several key issues such as the desirability of entrenching a strong bill of rights to protect individual and thereby also many so-called 'group rights', a non-racial franchise, a system of voting where all votes are of equal value, substantial political decentralisation to the regional and community level, and recognition of the need to explore the future position of the so-called independent homelands.[6]

In the economic field similar apparent incompatibilities existed at the beginning of 1990 between the NP and the ANC. The former began to stress with increasing fervour the presumed advantages of private property rights, the market system, economic freedom, limited government and privatisation. The ANC appeared committed to an activist government able to reduce the vast racially based economic inequalities and distortions through policies of nationalisation, increased taxation, high social expenditures and interventions in the systems of land ownership.

During 1990, the differences between the two key parties appear to have narrowed marginally. The NP administration, while remaining committed to a model of economic liberalism, has become more sensitive to the dangers posed by vast economic inequalities. In addition to accelerating the trend towards reduced inequalities in public expenditures between the racially defined groups, a special R2 billion fund has been created to assist the poor. Similarly, the ANC has become more flexible in its economic philosophy and has indicated that controversial policies such as nationalisation are 'negotiable'. Indeed, by the end of 1990 the ANC seemed to be in the process of dropping its commitment to nationalisation.[7]

Is a compromise between the conflicting political economy perspectives of the ANC and the NP possible? And what would such a compromise contain? Predictions about the outcome of these issues cannot be made by examining the detailed issues involved in a political vacuum. Clearly, the dynamics of the negotiations themselves and the pressures on the negotiators from their constituents will be of decisive importance.

If, however, we abstract the key issues from their political context, several compromise positions became possible. If we accept that any compromise pact will be a 'second-best' option for all the participants, then it is possible to predict several trade-offs between economic and political values. This would represent a considerable compromise on both sides. De Klerk is clearly hoping to convince the ANC leadership to accept a transitional period in which the NP would be permitted to retain control over the army and finances. The ANC in turn will seek to to achieve a majoritarian system with minimal constraints on the exercise of executive/legislative power.

Neither position appears to offer a basis for an accommodation. The ANC will not accept the principle of a phased transition, nor will the NP accept uncontrolled majority rule. However, it is possible that the NP will accept a limited majoritarian political system with statutory power-sharing in exchange for guaranteed property rights and a commitment to a market economy. In such a trade-off, whites would exchange a large measure of political power for a guarantee that their economic power would be protected. At the same time, a charter of socio-economic rights could be adopted pledging the new government to seek equality in the provision of public goods and services with all possible speed.

Indeed, it could be argued that of the three issues we have isolated – barriers to negotiations, the structure of negotiations, and the negotiations proper – the final issue is the most amenable to compromises. By the time the participants have resolved the two preceding issues, they will have developed some experience at working creatively together. In addition, domestic and foreign expectations may be so high that a failure could be politically disastrous to all the key players.

In addition, the actual choices to be made are finite. In fact, there are relatively few options in terms of economic and political principles. In every key area – the franchise, the structure of executive authority,

the contents of a bill of rights, the composition of the legislative, the
role of the judiciary, the status of private property rights – the choices
are limited. An analysis of the existing systems of political economy in
the contemporary world shows that only a few basic models with a
limited number of variations exist.

The task of reaching an accommodation may therefore be less
difficult and time-consuming than many observers, at present, are
predicting. If serious negotiations can begin by the end of 1991, it
should not pose insuperable difficulties to conclude them during 1993
or 1994. The key challenge then will be to win legitimacy among the
key power groups in society for what will clearly be a set of proposals
which will reflect major and often unsatisfactory compromises from all
the negotiating participants.

PROSPECTS

Transitions are, by their very nature, unique and rare. As such they
represent a series of steps towards an unknown destination. It is
precisely because of the discontinuities between normal politics and
transition politics, that considerable uncertainties characterise the
process of change.

Old-style 'white' politics was, in fact, 'national' politics. To a large
extent, blacks were the audience – the objects around which politics
revolved. In white politics, a disciplined and authoritarian National
Party, whose support was based upon the strong foundation of
mobilised ethnicity, dominated politics and policy. By excluding black
people from the franchise and by ensuring that its Afrikaner political
base remained united, the NP seemed to have a formula for the
retention of power in perpetuity.

All of this has now come to an end. Starting with community
organisations and exiled liberation movements, blacks have increasingly moved to the political centre stage. Afrikaners, and whites more
generally, are thoroughly divided on a wide range of issues. None of
the certainties of the past remain in place. This new dynamic creates, in
equal measure, opportunities and dangers, and it would be premature
to predict with confidence the outcome. However, it is possible to
isolate the obstacles as well as the favourable factors which will shape
the future.

One key obstacle to successful transformation is the response of the
masses to uncertainty and diminished State coherence. Expectations

change dramatically as new hopes and fears arise. The unbanning of the ANC has created enormous and largely unrealisable expectations of improved living conditions amongst many blacks, which the realities of the political economy doom to frustration. At the same time, the explosive potential of newly emergent feelings of relative deprivation is increased by the unwillingness or inability of the traditional repressive system of the State to retain the former high level of control.

In white ranks, the rapid pace of change has produced fears and confusion. Many of the government's traditional supporters have been stunned by the NP's rapid policy changes. After decades of virulent propaganda warning whites of the dangers of concessions, of the futility of attempting to negotiate with 'terrorist' groups such as the ANC, of the necessity for segregation and apartheid, the same party with many of the same leaders from the 1970s such as de Klerk, Magnus Malan and Gerrit Viljoen, has dramatically changed course. For many whites, it appears that either the NP is capitulating to external pressures or is no longer concerned with the interests of its traditional constituency.

Thus, reform has been accompanied by increasingly destructive spirals of violence. Within the white community, organisations with strong fascist tendencies and a potential propensity for violence are forming and reforming. Within black ranks, considerable violence with ethnic, ideological and criminal elements has already taken almost 1000 lives since the reform initiatives began in earnest.

From the perspective of socio-economic factors, the prospects for democracy are not encouraging.[8] Neither whites nor blacks have a genuine experience of democracy or any real attachment to its values. Historically repression and conquest, not voting or compromises, have been the means for resolving disputes. The vast inequalities within society, the intolerance of popular cultures and the high stakes of politics all create significant potential levels of conflict and violence. Given this socio-economic context, conflicts at the elite level can very easily spill over into destructive and uncontrollable mass violence.

Community violence poses two types of dangers to reform. Firstly, high levels of violence may so harden attitudes on all sides that it simply becomes impossible to conduct meaningful negotiations. Under these circumstances, either the ANC or the NP or both would refuse to continue with the search for peaceful solutions in an atmosphere of recriminations and hostility.

The second danger is that the violence will so polarise the communities that even if the ANC, NP and other key groups are successful in reaching a negotiated compromise, they will lose their constituencies in the process. Successful reform demands both a viable compromise and a legitimacy based upon the ability of the elites to deliver their constituencies. One possible danger lies in the frequently reiterated promise by the NP leadership to hold a referendum to test white opinion before implementing any new proposals.

Another key problem will be the difficulty in actually reaching an agreement which reconciles the white demand for security and the protection of their interests with the black demand for political power and economic justice. It cannot be assumed automatically that because the key participants have agreed to negotiate, a satisfactory outcome is inevitable. Nor do theoretical possibilities automatically translate into real-world agreements. The negotiations will be arduous and will require leadership skills of the highest order from all sides.

At the same time, several factors favour a successful series of negotiations. The power balance in South Africa is such that neither white nor black leaders are in a position to impose unilaterally their preferred solutions. A failure in negotiations would certainly be fatal to not only de Klerk personally, but to his party's ability to retain power in white politics. The ANC, too, would be hurt by a breakdown in the search for reconciliation although it would be in a better position to regroup than the NP.

Both the NP and the ANC have talented leaders, which greatly improves the prospects for accommodation. It is surely an historical irony that while P.W. Botha split his party in 1982 over the issue of marginal power-sharing with the minority coloured and Indian groups, de Klerk has revolutionised the party and its policies by opening its membership to blacks and accepting the principle of majority rule without losing a single parliamentary representative to the opposition!

Finally, the global environment for reform is favourable. The collapse of the Marxist empire has eliminated the major external source of instability. The generally conservative governments of North America, Japan and Western Europe have been supportive of even the modest reform measures in South Africa. Indeed, the role of the global community has probably become decisive. An end to sanctions, the reincorporation of South Africa into the Western political economy with renewed access to international capital, and a general return to international respectability epitomised by renewed sports and cultural links, would provide tangible proof to South Africas of the fruits of reform and liberalisation. All of this appears possible.

Within Africa and especially the Southern African region, the environment has become increasingly favourable. The conflict in Namibia has been settled and the remaining Cuban presence in Angola is no longer an issue of destabilisation. None of the so-called front-line states contain ANC military bases, and the armed struggle itself has been suspended. Economically weak countries such as Kenya and Zambia are taking advantage of the liberalisation measures adapted by South Africa to resume normal economic relations.

Within South Africa itself, opinion surveys seem to indicate that most people recognise that the apartheid system is irrevocably dead. Indeed, the role of new ideas may have been decisive in creating the reform impetus. Under Botha, most of the white elite groups began to recognise the impossibility of South Africa going it alone in an increasingly interdependent world. A racial polity was so clearly an anachronism that its legitimacy eroded with remarkable speed.

With varying degrees of enthusiasm, white and black South Africans generally accept the necessity of reform and the reality that there are no viable alternatives to democratisation and deracialisation. The greatest guarantee of the future of reform is the growing recognition that the present transition is not the result of de Klerk's choices but of an historical inevitability.

FINAL THOUGHTS

While progress in South Africa is not irreversible, the dynamics of change clearly are. Irrespective of the outcome of the negotiations and the de Klerk reform measures, the apartheid past cannot be resurrected. Negative possibilities such as a neo-fascist white-led takeover or a messy black dictatorship, would both represent a dramatic break from the status quo.

The demands of successful transition will be enormous. All the key players will have to learn from scratch the new rules of the transformed polity. The ANC will have to learn how to convert its revolutionary legacy into normal party politics. The NP will have to accept that, although in the new South Africa it will remain powerful because of the wealth and expertise of its largely-white constituency, it will be only one of several major players. Traditional relationships will have to be redefined – between the ANC and the SACP and trade unions. The NP, too, will have to redefine its relationships with the Broederbond, with Afrikanerdom, and with the traditional NP-supporting press. Opposition groups and the smaller factions will find it particularly difficult to redefine successfully their new roles. The most likely scenario is for the fragile process of deracialisation to continue. Indeed, if the earlier analysis is accurate, the speed with which the negotiations themselves will be concluded will surprise most observers. The outlines of the new political system are already becoming visible. The elections for a legislature will be on a colour-blind common voters' roll. However, the regional units upon which representations will be based will not all be of equal representativeness, so votes in one region – Johannesburg, for example – may count proportionately more than votes in Soweto. The president will not be directly elected, but will be elected by the legislature. The executive cabinet will be constituted on a proportional basis so that the major parties in the legislature will also be represented at the national cabinet level. A strong bill of rights will be entrenched which will include property rights, and the judiciary will be powerful and independent. The system will be decentralised and may include 'community' executive agencies such as local police forces and administrative agencies. Proportionality and community power-sharing will be built into the system at all levels.

What are the possible regional implications of these developments? It is perhaps an irony that white-dominated South Africa had the means but not the opportunity to act as the regional political leader and growth catalyst whereas a multi-racial South Africa will have the opportunity but not the means.

A post-apartheid South Africa will be a fragile society. Great and possibly unsustainable demands will be made upon limited resources for development and restructuring. It is probable that the ruling elites will be largely inward-looking and will place foreign policy issues low on their list of policy priorities. South Africa may therefore only rejoin the region as an active participant in the late 1990s when the post-apartheid order has had time to consolidate itself.

Notes

* The author wishes to thank Herman Giliomee and David Welsh for their comments on an earlier draft.
1. A huge literature on apartheid exists. For a recent synthesis see H. Giliomee and L. Schlemmer, *From Apartheid to Nation-building*, Cape Town: Oxford University Press, 1989.

2. The Botha era is analysed in detail in my book, *The Botha Era and the End of White Politics*, New York: Ford Foundation and Foreign Policy Association, forthcoming, 1991.
3. All the election statistics quoted in this section were kindly provided by Professor N.J. Olivier of the Democratic Party's research department.
4. An interesting analysis of many of these issues is contained in F. Cloete, 'A Hard Bargain: the Politics of Pre-Negotiation', *Indicator SA*, 7(2), Autumn 1990.
5. A growing literature on the politics of transition exists. See especially G. O'Donnell and P. Schmitter (eds), *Transition from Authoritarian Rule*, Baltimore: Johns Hopkins University Press, 1986.
6. The change in the NP position can be easily documented by comparing the 'Five Year Plan' prepared in 1989 as an election manifesto with de Klerk's detailed policy speech in Potchefstroom of 23 August 1990.
7. See especially the economics discussion paper published by the ANC in September 1990.
8. A good overview of these issues is contained in S. Huntington, 'Will More Countries Become Democratic?', *Political Science Quarterly*, 99, November 1984, pp. 193–218.

3 The Extra-Parliamentary Opposition in South Africa

Paulus Zulu

The reality of South African politics is that the NP and the ANC control both the nature and tempo of political power. They do this from opposite directions, namely, control and resistance. As Adam wrote in 1988: 'The reason for the increased presence of the African National Congress in South Africa lies in its legal absence'.[1] He went on to quote Tom Harris, a seasoned American analyst of South African politics: 'In a free election in South Africa, the now outlawed African National Congress could possibly win three fourths of the black votes as well as some white votes'.[2] This chapter is, however, not about the ANC but about the impact of its legacy, the politics of the extra-parliamentary opposition. In a way, it is a politics different from that of the ANC because even though the extra-parliamentary opposition has drawn its strength and ideology mainly from the ANC, it is not the ANC. This chapter examines the extra-parliamentary opposition prior to the unbanning of the ANC and explores further the significance of this force in the struggle for political power in a future South Africa.

MASS MOBILISATION

On 28 October 1989, approximately 85 000 people of all races (the vast majority of whom were Africans) gathered at a soccer stadium outside Johannesburg to welcome and pay tribute to seven members of the ANC who had been sentenced to life imprisonment for political offences in the early 1960s. Their release had come about as a result of increasing pressure on the State both from internal forces and the international community. The gathering was a response to the call by the MDM, a coalition of organisations, groupings and individuals which constituted the main thrust in the extra-parliamentary opposition to the apartheid State. Approximately a month later, on 26 November, another 65 000 people gathered in Umtata, the capital of 'independent' Transkei, to pay tribute to the same celebrities. Gatherings of this magnitude to welcome members of the ANC would have been inconceivable two years earlier in spite of what was then visible pressure on the State to speed up the process of change.

What was evident in the rallies that followed the release of the leaders, and also in the protests and marches subsequent to the ascendancy of President de Klerk in NP politics, was that 'the people' had effectively unbanned the ANC and other outlawed organisations. A new era had dawned in South African politics. And on 2 February 1990 President de Klerk announced the official unbanning of the ANC and other organisations, and the release of Nelson Mandela, the legendary hero of black South African politics.

The resounding welcome given to Mandela is now history: crowds of 80 000 in Cape Town, 130 000 outside Johannesburg, and 150 000 in Durban were unprecedented in South African politics and symbolised the 'success' of the extra-parliamentary opposition to apartheid, at least to the extent of contributing to the pressure on the State to acknowledge that it was prepared to start negotiations with its traditional enemy, the ANC.

The origins of the extra-parliamentary opposition can be traced to the dialectic between resistance and reform – resistance to the twin processes of domination and exploitation of blacks as a group by the super-ordinate white group, and reform by both the State and the private sector because of fear of losing political and economic power. The dialectic between resistance and reform, particularly the reform process in the 1980s, makes the politics of the extra-parliamentary opposition significant. This is so because, in addition to external pressures both political (diplomatic, military, and so forth) and economic, it is the refusal by the extra-parliamentary opposition to collaborate in the State's reform programme, and particularly the co-optive programme, that accelerates the pace of reform. In this chapter the focus is on the extra-parliamentary opposition as a social movement. The emphasis, therefore, is more on its capacity as a movement to sustain opposition to the State than on strength in numbers. This is particularly so because leadership in the constituent organisations may incur repercussions, from the State, in the form of harassment, detention and even imprisonment.

THE STATE'S PROGRAMME OF CO-OPTATION

Co-optation in this context refers to the mode of differential incorporation of specific segments or groups into the structures of political and economic power. It enables the elite from among those previously barred from participation to engage in the process of government or decision-making albeit on an unequal basis with the group in power. In co-optation the State hopes to broaden its social base of support in the belief that the co-opted elite will both 'manage' and influence the general masses from within their specific groups. At the macro or territorial level, homeland assemblies would legislate for and carry out the governing function among Africans while the Houses of Representatives and of Delegates would perform the same role with regard to 'coloureds' and Indians respectively.

The leadership in these institutions was vested with the same titles held in the white governing institutions. From this leadership the State created Chief Ministers, Chairmen of the Ministerial Councils and members of cabinets, vested them with the trappings of power (cars, high salaries and huge houses) and gave them the constitutional right to allocate and control resources within 'own affairs'. However, because this incorporation is no more than co-optive domination (actual power resides in the House of Assembly and in the Nationalist government as the executive organ of the State), the majority of the subordinated have continued to oppose participation in these institutions. This has given impetus to the politics of non-collaboration or non-participation expressed in the extra-parliamentary opposition.

Co-optation exists both at the territorial or national level as well as at the regional levels where it crystallises in local administrative structures. Even at this level there are problems: firstly, black local authorities do not have an independent source of revenue and therefore have no power to allocate resources, and secondly, in the case of Africans they were meant to act as substitutes for political expression at the national level. The policy of non-collaboration was thus extended to encompass any form of participation in the structures which operate at the local level as well.

The State opted for the strategy of co-optation, firstly, as a form of 'deracialisation' within apartheid, and secondly, as a mechanism of administration by proxy while retaining control. The tricameral parliament represents 'deracialisation' within apartheid. The occasional joint sittings by the white, coloured and Indian members is an innovation in South African terms yet the 4:2:1 ratio (4 whites to 2 coloureds and 1 Indian) underpins white control in the actual decision-making process. Excluding Africans from the tricameral arrangement gave further assurances to the conservative white voters that white hegemony would still be preserved. It is in this context that the politics of the extra-parliamentary opposition has to be critically appraised since, on the one side, it is the politics of reaction to co-optive dominance, and on the other, it has precipitated the reform process.

THE EXTRA-PARLIAMENTARY OPPOSITION

The extra-parliamentary opposition is a metamorphosis of the process of history and demonstrates the resilience and adaptability of the spirit of the subordinates in the face of a determined white oligarchy. As a movement, the extra-parliamentary opposition draws its intellectual, ideological, strategic and organisational strength mainly from the traditions of the Congress Alliance of the 1950s as well as from the Black Consciousness Movement of the late 1960s and early 1970s. It is this intellectual, organisational and ideological heritage which gives the extra-parliamentary opposition a sense of continuity with the past and consequently a sense of mission. Extra-parliamentary opposition to the State arises primarily out of three sources:

1. Material deprivation reflected in gross inequalities organised along racial lines.
2. Ideological arrangements which emanate from the correspondence between material well-being and political power, and the converse to that.
3. The national question, that is, who does the State actually represent? Here the State is conceived as a white regime representing the political and economic interests of whites. The struggle for political control thus assumes an assertion of a black nationalism fighting for inclusion in a single non-racial state through a majority decision.

Because of the coincidence between black political emasculation and material deprivation, the extra-parliamentary opposition, as champion of the black cause, commands a messianic appeal to the disenfranchised masses. This is a pertinent observation because without this appeal the mode of articulation of extra-parliamentary politics would probably have taken a different form. The extra-parliamentary opposition has both an empirical existence and a mystic, hegemonic influence which transcends both individuals and numbers. It is more or less like the kind of influence that the 'class struggle' has among Marxists or the Holy Ghost in Christian circles. Both make things happen yet both have no tangible existence except by effect.

Because the history of the extra-parliamentary opposition is well documented elsewhere,[3] the intention in this chapter is twofold: (i) to place the extra-parliamentary opposition within the politics of the 1970s and 1980s by demonstrating how it has influenced, and in turn has been shaped by, the reform policies of both the State and the private sector; and (ii) to present the extra-parliamentary opposition as a significant force for contributing to a future negotiated settlement for South Africa. In both instances it draws from the empirical as well as the spiritual attributes.

Social Composition

The extra-parliamentary opposition is both a political movement and a product of specific issues, for instance civic matters, educational issues and developments in the workplace. Such specifics may result in the creation of ad hoc or permanent organisations to deal with them. What is, however, common in all of the formations is the spontaneous rejection of State-created organs as mediators and the readiness with which newly formed structures seek assistance from, or affiliation with, existing organisations elsewhere. For instance, anti-removal committees or civic organisations formed to fight specific developments such as a hike in rent, service charges or transport fares, soon develop into civic associations affiliated to the UDF. The broad categories which constitute the extra-parliamentary movement are:

1. Youth organisations which are mainly located in educational institutions but which include a significant section of the unemployed and some of the youth affiliated to the unions.
2. Civic and community organisations with a cross-cutting membership which may include church, women's and even youth groups (most of the ad hoc groups such as rent, transport and anti-removal organisations fall within this category).
3. Worker and labour organisations mainly located on the factory floor but which are also involved in civic and community issues.
4. Professional and occupational associations sympathetic to, and co-operating with, civic and national organisations.
5. Institutional groups such as the churches.

As mentioned earlier, the extra-parliamentary opposition is both a movement and a metamorphosis of historical forces. This is evidenced in the strategic shifts that have taken place in the last few years. Since 1985 a number of influential organisations and personalities from inside South Africa have held consultations with the ANC in Lusaka and abroad on a wide variety of issues pertaining to the future of the country. It is these consultations, together with the *de facto* (and now *de jure*) internal presence of the ANC that have facilitated the metamorphosis in the extra-parliamentary opposition. In turn, this has brought about a mellowing in the strategies as well: hence, whereas non-collaboration formerly meant no contact with organisations and individuals 'working within the system', there is now a broad consultation and, at times, co-operation with such individuals and bodies.

Ideologically, the extra-parliamentary opposition falls into two broad strands, namely the charterist and the black consciousness elements. The main constituents in the charterist element are the UDF and COSATU while the black consciousness element is represented by Azapo, the NF combination and NACTU. Ideological differences between the two elements exist particularly with regard to the race question and the future economic arrangements in the country, but there are areas of mutual agreement. Indeed, there have been a number of instances where COSATU and NACTU have organised stayaways and consumer boycotts as if they were one unit, and where the UDF and Azapo-NF coalition have also co-operated in organising community-based resistance campaigns. There have been serious frictions as well but they seem to be overshadowed by the presence of a common enemy, the white regime, at least for the present.

The United Democratic Front

The UDF was formed in 1983 to oppose both the Tricameral Constitution and the 'Koornhof Bills'. The former sought to incorporate the coloured and Indian groups as junior partners in Parliament while the latter sought to entrench influx control in the guise of 'orderly urbanisation'. Material grievances such as problems in education, township civic matters and work led to an affiliation to the UDF by organisations involved in fighting these ills. Later, professional and other related associations also joined the UDF as either affiliates or working partners.

As the UDF is not a card-carrying organisation, it is difficult to estimate its strength in terms of numbers. What is significant, however, is that it is one of the driving forces behind the resistance to apartheid. It constitutes the electro-motive force of the resistance movement. While it may be difficult to locate the UDF and its strength in terms of structures, like the Holy Ghost it makes things happen, and the State attributes much of what is happening in resistance politics to the UDF. This intangible form is, therefore, both a source of strength and weakness in the UDF. The strength is its capacity to act, the weakness the difficulty to manage and organise effectively and to control its constituencies. Despite the weaknesses, however, the UDF is an effective mobilising force and has managed to survive the three-year state of emergency which resulted in most of its top leadership being detained, imprisoned, gagged or forced into hiding.

The biblical canon of the UDF is the Freedom Charter, and its policy is to isolate the State from popular and civil constituencies. Its strategy is non-collaboration with State-created institutions, a practice which sometimes becomes problematic in the face of the broad consultative tactics that the Front espouses.

The Azapo-NF Coalition

The Azapo-NF coalition represents the continuation of the Black Consciousness Movement. Unlike the UDF, Azapo is a card-carrying organisation and in 1987 claimed 'membership of 98 branches differing in size and spread throughout the country' and that it 'tends to attract only militant people, who are prepared to carry the consequences of being card-carrying members of a political organisation'.[4] In terms of numbers, the Azapo-NF coalition is much smaller than the UDF because its main areas of influence are the Western Cape and the Reef while the UDF commands a significant presence nationally.

Differences between the UDF and the Azapo-NF coalition lie in their interpretation of the national question in South Africa. The UDF, in line with the Freedom Charter, adopts a non-racial approach while the Azapo-NF line defines the oppressed as black where black is a political rather than an ethnic expression, but definitely refers to those who do not have the vote. This makes collaboration with white liberals and progressives difficult on the part of Azapo-NF while this does not pose any problems for the UDF.

Institutional and Professional Organisations

The Church

Perhaps the greatest problem for apartheid is not the existence of political organisations but rather the oppositional ethos it has generated in numerous institutions in the country. The organised church, through the South African Council of Churches and the Southern African Catholic Bishops' Conference, has acted as the spiritual benefactor of the extra-parliamentary opposition, not only by preaching against apartheid as a sin but also by providing the leadership and direction during mass action. Personalities like Dr Beyers Naude, Archbishop Tutu, ex-Reverend Alan Boesak, Archbishop Hurley and Reverend Frank Chikane have not only championed the cause of the underprivileged but have personally intervened or led peaceful protest marches, thus giving both dignity and restraint in situations where circumstances might precipitate conflict and disorder. Their presence has, in a number of instances, prevented the outbreak of physical conflict between protesting marchers and the police.

Professional Groupings

There are two factors which account for the inclination of black professionals to identify with the extra-parliamentary opposition, and, in a sense, these belie the strategy of a middle-class accommodation by the State and the private sector.

First, at an intellectual level apartheid does not resonate well with professional ethics. The material effects of discrimination alienate professionals from the State or State institutions. A number of young professionals are products of the black consciousness era and, therefore, are much more assertive in self expression and much more sensitive to discriminatory practices within the professions than has been the case with previous generations. Second, the dominance of the State's ideology in professional practice and within the services, for instance in social welfare, health and education, has encouraged the formation of organisations that espouse a different ethos.

Professionals in various spheres have formed alternative bodies whose main objectives are both to render a service and empower communities so that they do not become dependent consumers or rely on outside sources for the delivery of those services. Associations like the National Medical and Dental Association, the Black Management Forum, the Association of Black Accountants of South Africa, the

South African Black Social Workers' Association, the National Democratic Lawyers' Association, the National Educational Union of South Africa, the Union of Democratic University Staff Associations and many others constitute this category. They cooperate with community, worker and business organisations in the organisation of programmes designed to undermine apartheid.

Black Business
From about 1985 African businessmen, as represented by the National African Federated Chambers of Commerce (NAFCOC), have played an increasingly significant role in the extra-parliamentary opposition. This role has been complemented by the activities of blacks in professional and managerial positions as represented in the BMF. This complementarity has resulted in a number of consultations, by both groups, with both the ANC and MDM. Despite its heterogeneity (with membership including homeland-based affiliates, independent traders and incumbents in State-created structures), NAFCOC seems to have succeeded in identifying more with the extra-parliamentary opposition rather than pursuing an ideology in line with the structural determinants of its formation. By promoting a black middle class the State had hoped that it would increase its own support base, but NAFCOC's ideological associations, as well as its practical pursuits, belie these expectations.

Labour
The Wiehahn Commission, which recommended the legal recognition of African trade unions, ushered in a new era in extra-parliamentary opposition politics. Subsequent developments on the labour front resulted in the formation of two confederations – COSATU, with alignments to the Charterist principles, and NACTU, aligned to black consciousness. COSATU had approximately one million paid-up members and NACTU about 100 000 in 1989.

The principle of 'one industry one union' has further strengthened the federations such that a strike can almost paralyse the entire industry. What are of more significance, however, are firstly the captive constituency that unions command, and secondly the way in which unions advanced their political power from purely shopfloor to community issues. Webster argues that this has changed the political terrain such that the unions have not only pushed forward the visible frontiers of control but have also instituted a form of 'deracialisation' from below.[5] The emergence of African trade unions on the labour scene has thus brought in new challenges to racial capitalism and the ethnic State, and consequently strengthened the extra-parliamentary opposition. The fact that, in South Africa, worker and community politics coincide has facilitated cooperation between community-based organisations and the unions.

Unions have also injected organisation and a form of accountability to community politics, and have provided a leadership with a strong constituency. This has been noticeable in the organisation of stayaways and consumer boycotts as well as in the protest and celebration marches organised by the MDM. Whereas protest marches in the past assumed more of the form of mobilisation and were often difficult to discipline, more recent marches and celebrations were well organised and disciplined.

Strategic Logic

In broad terms, the extra-parliamentary opposition sees South Africa as a country where white people both dominate and exploit black people. This is an observation which is rooted in the empirical and, therefore, the existential situation of the black person in South Africa. The belief in a non-racial, democratic country is, therefore, a natural reaction to what prevails and has to be expected. Because the visible structures of inequality are predicated upon race, a number of black people see the dismantling of racial structures as a necessary precondition for democracy. The growth of trade unionism among black workers has, however, introduced a brand of worker politics into the scene, thus allowing for a class-based analysis of the South African social formation. African workers, in particular, have begun to attribute the South African social formation to capitalist forces where the State is an instrument of the ruling class. In this instance, democracy will come about when socialism replaces the present capitalist mode of production. Because of the composition of the extra-parliamentary opposition, the political vision of the future of South Africa hinges between a non-racial democracy and a non-racial socialist democracy.

Two visions – the political and the economic – dominate the conception of the future by the extra-parliamentary opposition which proposes a 'unitary, non-racial, democratic' South Africa. The vision has moved through historical periods and has encompassed the following:

1. Making South Africa ungovernable. This was to be achieved by refusing to cooperate with the State's programmes at every level, thus creating a legitimacy and administrative crisis for the State. Attempts to create 'alternative structures' in local government, education, etc., were part of this 'positive programme' of isolating the State from all popular constituencies.
2. Organising the masses around specific issues such as education, housing, rent, transport, health, and so forth, which would act as rallying points. Programmes would act as educational catalysts within a specific political context, thus acting further as conscientising agents.
3. Creating space within some official structures in order to advance the cause of liberation. Part of the reason for changing the slogan 'liberation first and education later' into 'people's education for people's power' or 'education for liberation' was to use schools as 'space' for organisation besides their pedagogical purpose.

In addition to the organisation and mobilisation of constituencies, the extra-parliamentary opposition engages in various forms of resistance to State-initiated activities. Such resistance includes either the withdrawal of support or active defiance manifested in boycotts, stayaways, or even 'breaking the laws' as has been the case in the defiance campaigns organised around hospitals, beaches and other separate amenities. The objective is to force the State either to change the laws and policies or to come to the negotiating table. However, the ultimate objective is to force the State to negotiate the future of South Africa, and to this end the extra-parliamentary opposition set specific preconditions:

1. Creating a climate which is conductive to free political participation – this could come about only through unbanning individuals and organisations, freeing all political prisoners and detainees, allowing political exiles to return and scrapping the state of emergency.
2. Following upon (1), calling a national convention of the representatives of the people to draw up a programme for negotiations.

Economic visions pertain to the future economic system for the country. To state that there is a uniform economic vision by the extra-parliamentary opposition would be an oversimplification of an otherwise complicated and contentious subject. The extra-parliamentary opposition is an alliance of otherwise heterogenous groups in terms of social origin. Support ranges from bodies such as NAFCOC and the BMF through to COSATU and NACTU. What unites them is the shared experience under apartheid and the commitment to an alternative political dispensation. There may, indeed, be different economic agendas. As Innes and O'Meara pertinently observed with regard to the African petit bourgeoisie: 'Given its position between capital and labour in the class struggle, the petit bourgeoisie tends to see the solution to its problems in purely political terms – reform in the political structures rather than changes in the relations of production'.[6] The Constitutional Guidelines drawn up by the ANC in 1988 are probably the most succinct document on the future economic system.

In terms of day-to-day pronouncements by significant sections from the extra-parliamentary opposition, there is strong support for nationalisation of the major industries or a significant portion of them; equality of opportunity in access to training and work as well as to rewards; a more equitable redistribution of the country's resources, that is, land and profits; and free access by all to the State's social security systems including medical services and social welfare.[7]

The above proposals, together with the ANC Constitutional Guidelines, point more to a social democratic alternative than either to a 'pure' capitalist or socialist economic vision. That is perhaps understandable given, first, the heterogeneity of the forces within the extra-parliamentary opposition, and second, the fact that until the recent ascendancy of the ANC, no faction had been able to command a hegemonic position within the movement.

Critique

The unbanning of the ANC, PAC, SACP and other organisations on 2 February 1990, and the growing prospects for negotiations, constitute a turning point in the history of the extra-parliamentary opposition. Until then, the politics of the extra-parliamentary groupings had been the politics of opposition where the reality of the prospects of forming an alternative government were remote. In essence, the extra-parliamentary opposition saw itself as the caretaker while the main organisations, particularly the ANC, were either outlawed or in exile. This became more apparent when the ANC won the organisational and ideological battle with black consciousness and the Unity Movement in the 1980s. The popularity of the UDF and of Congress politics after 1983 bears testimony to this. Mandela and Sisulu came out of prison to reassert this ideological and organisational hegemony.

The second weakness in the politics of the extra-parliamentary opposition prior to the unbanning of the ANC lay in the disjuncture between language, organisation and the conceptual apparatus of the constituent groupings. In a number of instances rhetoric triumphed over reality, and there was often a confusion between policy and strategy where the latter gained its own momentum and tended to dictate action. For instance, the strategies of non-collaboration or non-cooperation with the State, and the boycott of State-sponsored institutions, assumed the role of principles such that boycotts became the order of the day. This had a demobilising effect on the organisations as it crated impasses without substituting alternatives. This logjam was, in part, broken when organised labour joined the popular forces. It was at this stage that the concept of 'ungovernability' was replaced by the idea of 'creating and utilising spaces' in the enemy's own ambit. Despite this, the politics of the extra-parliamentary opposition continued to be mainly insurrectionist and reactive in character, an attribute which has implications for negotiations and a future settlement. Perhaps the unbanning of the ANC, PAC and SACP is a signal that the extra-parliamentary opposition has fulfilled its major task.

Prospects

This section includes the ANC as a key player and examines the extra-parliamentary opposition as constituted before the unbanning of the main organisations. Recent developments have brought the issue of negotiations for a future South Africa into the fore. Critical among such events are the unbanning of the ANC, PAC and the SACP which has tremendously altered the political landscape of South Africa, and a realignment in white politics including a change in the leadership of the governing NP. President de Klerk's pragmatic style of leadership has enabled the NP to shift position in order to seek new political alternatives.

It is against this background that both the government and the extra-parliamentary opposition are beginning to talk about the possibility of negotiations, at least within their own constituencies. Because the MDM is numerically the largest coalition within the extra-parliamentary opposition (it includes both the UDF and COSATU), and also because of its closeness both in terms of ideology and identification with the ANC, its position with regard to negotiations is particularly important.

The position of the MDM on negotiations is a shift from all positions taken by the extra-parliamentary opposition in the past. Because of this, the MDM has had to redefine negotiations through a reinterpretation of the 'terrain' of the struggle for democracy and, through this reinterpretation, incorporate negotiations into this terrain. The rationale for this is, first, that both internal and external pressures (the latter as manifested in the threat of sanctions, actual or threatened disinvestment as well as other forms of international isolation) have put South Africa on the defensive, and second, that because of this defensive position the government wants to regain the initiative, hence it has put negotiations on its agenda. This development, therefore, poses challenges to the forces that fight for democracy, for such development provides opportunities for a peaceful end to the conflict in the country. Consequently, if the MDM failed to respond to these developments it might miss a chance to contribute to the definition of a final settlement, and risk isolation from the popular democratic forces.

The MDM's position on negotiations is that they are part of the overall perspective of the national democratic struggle, part of the terrain of the struggle for liberation. After all, the MDM maintains, every liberation struggle in Africa since 1945 has ended with negotiations. Also, certain elements in the NP as representing the government, have come to recognise the need for negotiations. These reasons have led the MDM to question if their preconditions for negotiations still stand, particularly in the light of what they perceive as shifts in power positions between the State and popular forces. Accordingly, the precondition that all apartheid laws should go before the MDM negotiates with apartheid was dropped when it adopted the Harare Declaration. Currently, the movement insists on the assurance that the State creates a climate that is conducive to negotiations by allowing unrestricted political organisation. The MDM's proposed format for negotiation, that is, regular report-backs to the constituents both for briefing and for getting mandates on specific issues, mirrors the practice which prevails in the unions, thus reflecting COSATU's influence on the definition of democracy and accountability.

The unbanning of the ANC has altered tremendously both the tempo and prospects for negotiations. The extra-parliamentary opposition as constituted before this mammoth development is significant to the extent that the ANC has to take cognisance of the fractions as well as the role they have played when both the issues and the personalities in the negotiation process have to be constituted. Besides that, the extra-parliamentary opposition as constituted before February 1990 may have run its course and should probably disband.

CONCLUSION

The significance of the extra-parliamentary opposition lies more in its capacity to sustain opposition to the State against odds when considering its power relative to that of the State. The State has not been loath to use its coercive power when it felt its interests threatened beyond specific thresholds. This has created difficult conditions for planning on the part of extra-parliamentary organisations especially where, at the stroke of a pen, the State resorted to pronouncing their activities illegal. It is against these conditions that the extra-parliamentary opposition has demonstrated resilience and the capacity to be innovative. Further, the contribution by the extra-parliamentary opposition to the facilitation of the present political developments cannot be underestimated. Were it not for the pressure from organisations like the UDF, Azapo, COSATU, NACTU and others, together with the sympathy that the same organisations elicited from the international community, the shifts that have taken place in South African politics would not have materialised. The extra-parliamentary opposition created a political and economic crisis that even a powerful State could not overlook. Thus, the language of 'total onslaught' has been replaced by that of 'negotiation' and 'power sharing'. The first talks between the government and the ANC included leaders drawn from the internal extra-parliamentary opposition. That is a reflection of the contribution that this force has made to the shaping of South African history.

Notes

1. H. Adam, 'Exile and Resistance; the African National Congress, the South African Communist Party and the Pan African Congress' in P. L. Berger, and R. Godsell, (eds), *A Future South Africa: Vision, Strategies and Realities,* Boulder: Westview Press, 1988, p.95.
2. Ibid.
3. G. M. Gerhart, *Black Power in South Africa: The Evolution of an Ideology,* London: University of California Press, 1978; J. Leatt, T. Kneifel and K. Nurnberger (eds), *Contending Ideologies in South Africa,*

44   *Extra-Parliamentary Opposition*

Cape Town: David Phillip, 1986; T. Lodge, *Black Politics in South Africa Since 1945,* Johannesburg: Ravan Press, 1983; P. Zulu, 'Internal Resistance Movements' in Berger and Godsell (eds), op.cit.
4. V. Maphai, 'Resistance in South Africa: Azapo and the National Forum'. Research Paper Prepared for the South Africa Beyond Apartheid Project, 1987.
5. E. Webster, *Cast in A Racial Mould: Labour Process and Trade Unionism in the Foundries,* Johannesburg: Ravan Press, 1985, p.279.
6. D. Innes and D. O'Meara, 'Class Formation and Ideology: The Transkei Region' in *A Review of African Political Economy,* no. 7, 1976, p.83.
7. Zulu, op.cit., p.148.

4 The SADCC States, The International Environment and Change in South Africa

Hasu H. Patel

The last few years have witnessed important changes in the South African political scene, the liberation movement (especially the ANC), the SADCC countries, and the international environment.

SOUTH AFRICAN REFORMS AND THE LIBERATION MOVEMENT

The victory of the NP under its leader, F.W. de Klerk, in the South African general election of September 1989, evoked three broad responses. First, there was the view that South African white politics had undergone a profound change in favour of fundamental reform and that, therefore, there was a legitimately high expectation of immense change in the political/social landscape. Second, and contrary to the first response, was the view that de Klerk's victory might result in some moves to eliminate 'petty apartheid' but that 'grand apartheid', that is white domination, would be left untouched. Therefore there would be no real change from white minority to black majority rule. Third, the 'right wing' of white politics saw de Klerk's election victory as part of a continuing process of moving steadily 'left' and ultimately selling white survival to the black majority.

The release of Nelson Mandela in February 1990 was the culmination of a series of rapidly unfolding reforms following de Klerk's election victory. These reforms included the unbanning of the ANC, the PAC, the SACP and other elements of the liberation movement. The ANC in recent years has seized the diplomatic high ground but, while it is the dominant force in nationalist politics and without at least its agreement there cannot be a negotiated settlement in South Africa, organisations such as the PAC, Azapo and Inkatha cannot be ignored.

The escalating violence in 1990 indicates that peace/unity moves in black politics will be difficult and that the ANC-Inkatha relationship, in particular, is likely to continue to range from uneasy to hostile.

THE SADCC POLITICAL ENVIRONMENT

The political/diplomatic and military support given in the 1980s to the ANC in the SADCC region has been uneven. As support for the military aspect of the ANC's activities, especially in the form of military bases, declined, so support for its political/diplomatic activities increased. Additionally, the SADCC states have increasingly exhibited a preference for a peaceful negotiated end to apartheid, and internal/external pressures for the maintenance or implementation of political/economic pluralism.

Swaziland

Swaziland, which has a long-standing monarchy, and which has successfully gone through a political succession, is likely to remain a monarchy for the foreseeable future. Its then-secret security agreement with South Africa in February 1982 was directed against the ANC. Since 1981 ANC exiles in Swaziland have suffered harassment, raids, detentions, and deportations as a result of Pretoria's actions.[1]

Lesotho

The environment in Lesotho, long a haven for South African refugees, has been unfriendly to the ANC because of South Africa's destabilisation of that country, for example, its support for the Lesotho Liberation Army, the military raid in December 1982, and the January 1986 economic blockade which was an important factor in the subsequent military coup with a resultant diminution of the ANC's political/diplomatic presence. Lesotho's monarchy has been reduced to a figurehead position following the events in February 1990 when Major General Lekhanya, Chairman of the Military Council, stripped King Moshoeshoe II of his powers and vested the powers in himself following the latter's refusal to approve changes made in government by the Military Council. Later King Moshoeshoe who remained the Head of State, went into exile. But in November 1990, following disagreement between General Lekhanya and King Moshoeshoe concerning the latter's conditions for return, the latter's son was crowned as King Letsie III. Even if the Military Council's plans for democratisation by June 1992 are followed through (although in February 1990 the Military Council banned all political parties and refused demands for elections), Lesotho is likely to continue to have a constitutional monarchy.[2]

Botswana

In spite of repeated South African military attacks on Botswana, beginning with the June 1985 raid on Gaborone directed against the ANC, and South African pressure for a formal security agreement, Botswana has refused to sign such an agreement. Nonetheless, while Botswana has received South African refugees it has not allowed the ANC to have military bases nor permitted its territory to be used as an infiltration corridor by ANC guerrillas. Under the ruling BDP, the country has enjoyed multi-party (but one-party dominant), free enterprise, nationalist stability. The BDP won decisively the most recent elections in October 1989, and this stability is well set to continue for the foreseeable future.[3]

Mozambique

South Africa's repeated military attacks against Mozambique and support since 1980 of the activities of Renamo have pulverised Mozambique into becoming a country of destruction and death, of war and famine. The March 1984 Nkomati Accord – the 'Agreement on Non-Aggression and Good Neighbourliness' between Mozambique and South Africa – represented a major setback for the ANC throughout the SADCC region. The ANC's military operations through Mozambique were stopped and many cadres were flown out. But while Mozambique honoured its side of the agreement, South Africa did not honour its commitment to stop support for Renamo.

Mozambique's understandable basic concern now is peace and development. It has opened up to the West and South Africa, moved away from orthodox Marxism-Leninism (which was dropped at the Fifth Congress of Frelimo in July 1989), and encouraged a process of negotiations with Renamo, with Kenya and Zimbabwe acting as mediators. Mozambique's 12 principles for peace, Renamo's 16 principles and the USA's seven-point peace proposals for Frelimo-

Renamo talks, were gradually, during the first half of 1990, reduced to direct and unconditional talks between the opposing groups (which were part of the Kenyan-Zimbabwean document drawn up in December 1989).

During the latter half of 1990 a series of talks were held in Rome, Italy. The main stumbling blocks as of May 1990 were the venue (Frelimo proposing Malawi and Renamo wanting Kenya or Portugal) and the mediatory role of Zimbabwe's Robert Mugabe (which was preferred by Frelimo but objected to by Renamo). The November 1990 round of talks produced an agreement to restrict Zimbabwean troops to the Beira and Maputo Corridors, and the appointment of three Italians and the Catholic Archbishop of Beira as mediators, but there was no agreement on a ceasefire and Renamo's role in the first multi-party elections in 1991.

Additionally, President Chissano unveiled a draft constitution in January 1990, which has been under discussion to chart the course of the future political system for Mozambique. The draft constitution's proposals included: universal adult suffrage; a secret ballot, direct elections for the presidency of the country (for a maximum of three terms of five years each) and the National Assembly (candidates for the presidency and the National Assembly do not have to be Frelimo members); no mention of Frelimo's or the working class's 'leading role' (but a temporary maintenance of the one-party system); greater role for private enterprise; freedom of religion, expression, assembly and association being guaranteed by the outlawing of torture; an independent judiciary, and so forth. In early November 1990, Mozambique's parliament, the People's Assembly, unanimously approved a new constitution with effect from 30 November 1990, thus inaugurating an era of political/economic pluralism.[4]

Zimbabwe

While Zimbabwe has afforded a relatively high-profile political/ diplomatic presence to both the ANC and the PAC, it has refused to allow guerrilla bases or rights of transit to the liberation movement. Generally, even though Zimbabwe has continued a functional relationship with South Africa, this has been uneasy. Zimbabwe has been a very vocal critic of apartheid, and has also suffered through Pretoria's destabilisation activities, but its recent release from prison of a self-confessed South African spy was the result of a reappraisal of the regional political climate and an acceptance that South Africa had ceased its hostile acts. The country continues to pay a heavy price in money, material and people both because of its military support to Mozambique, since 1982, in the fight to secure the Beira and Maputo Corridors against Renamo attacks, and because of Renamo attacks along Zimbabwe's eastern border.

Generally, Zimbabwe's policy of internal reconciliation has been highly successful, though there have been significant and sometimes tragic hiccups. Racial representation in the Senate and the House of Assembly was abolished in 1987, and a unicameral Parliament was introduced in 1990. A successful conclusion to the unity talks between ZANU(PF) and PF-ZAPU was reached in December 1987. This represented a victory for reconciliation, assisted in a wider unity across ethnic/regional/linguistic boundaries, eliminated the dissident/ bandit problem in the south, assisted in checkmating South Africa's destabilisation activities, and brought peace and development in Matabeleland and the Midlands. The December 1989 Congress brought forth the united ZANU(PF), and the March 1990 general elections resulted in a massive presidential victory for Mugabe and a landslide parliamentary victory for the united ZANU(PF).

During the period 1980–90, Zimbabwe maintained a capitalist economy (with decisive moves towards trade liberalisation since 1989 and especially since July 1990) and a multi-party political system, although since December 1987 it has been a one-party- dominant system. Politically, ZANU(PF) remains committed to socialism, guided by Marxism-Leninism as applied to Zimbabwe's social, cultural and historical experience, and to a non-imposed one-party state. During the last few years, and especially during 1989–90, there has been a healthy debate on Marxism-Leninism and the one-party state with various bodies and important individuals arguing against a one- party state. The August 1990 ZANU(PF) Politburo meeting and the September 1990 ZANU(PF) Central Committee meeting decided against a legislated one-party state. Earlier, in July 1990, Zimbabwe lifted the countrywide state of emergency, in force since the mid-1960s, because of Zimbabwe's views on changes in South Africa, national unity and control of Renamo banditry in Zimbabwe, and the last detainee was deported to South Africa.

Malawi

Malawi is the only SADCC country to have formal diplomatic ties with South Africa, with consequent close economic and security relations and an inhospitable environment for the liberation movement. Since 1981 Malawi has allowed Renamo to mount raids into Mozambique. By 1985 there were many Renamo bases in southern Malawi, reportedly run with South African and Israeli advisers. At a meeting between Banda, Kaunda, Machel and Mugabe in September 1986, evidence of these bases in Malawi was given and Banda was threatened with economic/military reprisals. Malawi then switched course, and in December 1986 signed a security agreement with Mozambique and began providing troops to help guard the Nacala Corridor.

Malawi is host to over 800 000 Mozambican refugees and, in a meeting with Mugabe in March 1990, Banda agreed to assist the peace efforts in Mozambique. Malawi's one-party state has rested on the fulcrum of Life President Banda with visible support from women and Young Pioneers, and the one-party character has given Malawi a long-standing political stability. No political successor has been designated but reports often suggest John Tembo as a likely choice. Since 1989 there appears to be disaffection in the northern region (the traditional area of opposition) and among university students. Even after Banda, Malawi's one-party character is likely to continue, although the recent political pluralism in Eastern Europe/USSR and parts of Africa may well have an effect on Malawi.[5]

Zambia

Zambia has long been one of the most vocal critics of apartheid and a supporter of the liberation movement. The ANC in particular has had a high profile there, with its headquarters shifted from Tanzania in the early 1970s. Lusaka was one of the important centres for pilgrimages by white South African groups to meet the ANC, and Zambia was the location for the ANC's Second Consultative Conference held in Kabwe in June 1985. However, Zambia has long preferred and often searched for a peaceful end to apartheid. President Kaunda has met the last three South African Presidents, that is, Vorster, Botha and de Klerk. Additionally, the worsening economic situation, South Africa's destabilisation activities and some intra-ANC conflicts had all combined to produce a climate in which, in mid-1988, Zambia expelled about 2000 ANC cadres to Tanzania (mainly) and Uganda. This left the ANC with only a political/diplomatic presence in Zambia. Since late 1989, a treason trial involving a former Army Commander and three other senior Army officers, for allegedly planning a coup in

October 1988, has produced sensational revelations which have been lengthily reported in the local media. The alleged coup plotters, together with Lt. Luchembe, who tried an unsuccessful coup in June 1990, were later pardoned. Since 1973 Zambia has been a one-party state but in 1990 pressures for political pluralism gathered momentum. At the National Convention in March 1990 there was strong pressure for the introduction of a multi-party system. Both of Zambia's main newspapers, the trade union movement and the ruling UNIP's Central Committee had endorsed Kaunda's proposal of a referendum on a multi-party system. UNIP's National Council, the policy-reviewing body, initially sanctioned the proposed referendum with Kaunda indicating that he would campaign for the retention of the one-party system. However, the shock of the June 1990 coup attempt, food and price-rise riots, persistent massive demonstrations for multi-partyism and continuing agitation by the Movement for Multi-Party Democracy during 1990, resulted in the decision to cancel the referendum and agree to multi-party elections in 1991. In November 1990 the Parliament passed a Bill for multi-partyism in Zambia.[6]

Tanzania

Tanzania, like Zambia, has been one of the most important supporters of the liberation movement, providing a haven for both the ANC and PAC. Until the early 1970s the ANC's headquarters was in Tanzania, which continues to be the base for its educational training programmes. Until 1977 it was also the base for most of its military training. From early 1989 Tanzania became a haven for ANC cadres expelled from Zambia and Angola. Thus, in spite of Tanzania's economic difficulties, it continues to provide valuable political/diplomatic and military support to the ANC.

In terms of domestic politics, the 1984 constitutional amendment restricted the tenure of the President to a maximum of ten years. There has been some Zanzibari discontent, especially since 1988, with the continuing union between Zanzibar and mainland Tanzania. Since 1989 there has been discussion in the party, at the university and so forth, on the relevance of changes in Eastern Europe, and even former President Nyerere, then Chairman of the ruling Chama Cha Mapinduzi, questioned the wisdom of the one-party state in Africa. President Mwinyi has accepted, in principle, the idea of a multi-party system providing it is introduced gradually. In the November 1990 presidential elections Mwinyi massively won his second and last presidential term under the present one-party State system. Tied to the debate on political pluralism has been one on trade liberalisation and relations with the International Monetary Fund, with Tanzania increasingly and firmly committed to a mixed economy, although socialism still seems to be on the agenda.[7]

Angola

Angola, like Mozambique, has not known peace since independence, largely because of the continuing civil war between UNITA and the MPLA government. Nevertheless, Angola provided five military training camps to the ANC. In February 1984 Angola and South Africa signed the Lusaka Accord, basically a ceasefire agreement, which involved South African troop withdrawal from Angola and Angolan constraint of the SWAPO forces in southern Angola. After the military stalemate at Cuito Cuanavale in mid-1988, the United States mediated, with the USSR as an observer, an agreement between Angola, Cuba and South Africa which was signed in New York on 22 December 1988. This paved the way for South African troop withdrawal from Angola and Namibia's independence and resulted in the expulsion of ANC guerrillas from Angola. Since then, Angola and other African and non-African states have been engaged in trying to bring peace and development to the country by pursuing an agreement between the MPLA and UNITA; these efforts are continuing in spite of the failure of the Gbadolite Agreement of June 1989, mediated by Zaire.

Various proposals for peace in Angola have since been put forward, for example UNITA's twelve-point plan, President Mobutu Sese Seko's four-point plan, and President dos Santos' eight-point plan. The first direct and unconditional talks between low-level officials of the MPLA and UNITA took place in April 1990 near Lisbon. In spite of UNITA's offensive for the town of Mavinga (captured by Luanda forces in early 1990), the MPLA-UNITA negotiations process, with USA/USSR observers, continued during 1990. As of November 1990 there were disagreements on the timing of a ceasefire, recognition of UNITA and multi-party elections, and on issues such as a truce and integration of the two armies. Mobutu's role as the principal mediator (he has also used the nine-nation African Committee in the peace process) has come under fire, and the MPLA has also considered a referendum on a multi-party system. In October 1990, it was reported that the majority of the MPLA members favoured a multi-party system and that the MPLA Central Committee was debating a multi-party constitution which could be in place in early 1991, with presidential/parliamentary elections within three years (although UNI-TA wanted these elections within six months thereafter).[8]

Namibia

Namibia, with SWAPO's victory in 41 out of 72 seats (but not a two-thirds majority) in the November 1989 elections for the Constituent Assembly, became independent on 21 March 1990 as a multi-party democracy under President Nujoma. The constitution codifies a multi-party democracy, a strong Bill of Rights, a maximum of two five-year terms for the Head of State, and a mixed economy. Both the constitution and the independent government are testimony to the nationalism, reconciliation and pragmatism which are likely to be the hallmark of the future Namibia. However, its dependent status vis-à-vis South Africa (which controls the port of Walvis Bay and is owed nearly US$200 million), and the need to develop a dependable civil/military/security and technical/financial/economic apparatus, mean that Namibia cannot provide a suitable haven for the liberation movement, especially since South Africa could always use the 'Lesotho 1986' option against Namibia.[9]

Summary

The SADCC region exhibits a variety of political and economic systems; has been a region of war, especially because of South Africa's destabilisation policies since the mid-1980s; and has been subject to internal and external pressures both for peace and for the maintenance or implementation of political and economic pluralism. Additionally, the SADCC rearbase of the South African liberation movement, especially the ANC, has undergone drastic change with, at one level, disadvantages to the ANC. In large measure this has been because of South Africa's military, economic, and psychological destabilisation policies. Some idea of the staggering cost endured by the SADCC states as a result of South Africa's destabilisation policies may be gained from a recent UN study which concluded that the costs for the period 1980–8 were about US$60 billion, approximately 1.5 million dead (of whom about 925 000 were infants and children), and millions of refugees and displaced persons.[10]

Even though its rearbase has shrunk in the SADCC region, paradoxically, the ANC has achieved a highly visible political and diplomatic status in the region: its constitutional proposals (in the form of the Harare Declaration of August 1989) were endorsed by the Non-Aligned Movement in Belgrade in September 1989 and largely adopted by the UN General Assembly in December 1989. And the roots of the SADCC's preference for a peaceful negotiated settlement of the South African problem, enshrined in the Harare Declaration, go back at least to the Lusaka Manifesto of 1969.[11]

THE INTERNATIONAL ENVIRONMENT

The international environment, like the SADCC regional environment, has been both a burden and a blessing to the liberation movement. The cataclysmic changes in recent years in the USSR and Eastern Europe have had and will continue to have a profound impact on South African liberation. Beginning with perestroika and glasnost, the USSR and Eastern Europe have seen an avalanche of political, economic and social changes which include the following: (i) greater political debate and participation; (ii) the elimination of the leading role of the Communist Party, with replacement of long-standing leaders and power-sharing between different political forces; (iii) demands for greater adherence to human rights; (iv) greater latitude for market forces or private enterprise, thus a loosening or abandonment of central planning; (v) social/national upheavals in the form of demonstrations, strikes, violence and claims by various ethnic groups/nationalities to protection, exclusivity and self-determination.

Even though the various versions of perestroika and glasnost are, at the official level, meant to refurbish and strengthen socialism and may well do so in some instances, nevertheless the very idea of socialism is increasingly under question. From the perspective of East-West relations and superpower positioning in the international system, it appears that socialist systems are not only being questioned but are in retreat. The post-Second World War international power system, as reflected in the European theatre, is disappearing: what some call the Soviet Empire is disintegrating, the Brezhnev Doctrine concerning the right of socialist states to intervene in order to protect socialism is dead, the economic communities of the East and West are coming together, the East-West military blocs are exhibiting their redundancy, the bipolar system is evaporating, and the Cold War was officially proclaimed to be over at the November 1990 Paris Summit of the Conference on Security and Cooperation in Europe.

The above changes, detonated in the USSR and exploding in Euro-America, are pathways to the development of Gorbachev's common European home stretching from the Atlantic to the Urals. In an important way, they represent a socialist retreat in the international power system. This retreat, also in terms of non-support for revolutionary violence for decolonisation and independence, may be gleaned from the USSR's New Political Thinking. The Soviet (and, therefore, presumably Eastern Europe's) preference is for the peaceful resolution, through compromises and a balance of interests, of all international and regional conflicts, including that in South Africa.

In foreign policy terms, the New Political Thinking views the world, which includes a common European home, as an interdependent, interconnected, integral community of people with universal human values. The basic threat is the annihilation of the human race, but there are limits to confrontation, especially between the two superpowers, because of the threat of nuclear annihilation. Therefore all international/regional conflicts must be settled peacefully, through compromises and a balance of interests with an understanding by the superpowers of each other's vital interests, and also through the creation/use of an international legal order, especially the United Nations, with democratisation of the international political system.[12]

In many ways the USSR's New Political Thinking is breathtaking, but in terms of its rejection of revolutionary violence, and as this applies to the liberation movement in South Africa, it represents both a burden and a blessing. The burden is in the fact that it undercuts the armed struggle in South Africa. The blessing is that, paradoxically, it has enhanced the possibility of a negotiated settlement in South Africa and, therefore, it has strengthened the political/diplomatic status of the liberation movement, especially the ANC with which the USSR has had both direct and (through the SACP) indirect relations.[13]

The New Political Thinking's emphasis on the peaceful resolution of all international and regional conflicts points to the USSR's preference for majority rule with minority guarantees in South Africa. This may also be gleaned from the writings of some Soviet scholars; while these writings are not official USSR policy, it is also true that Soviet scholars have an enhanced role in policy-making in the Gorbachev era. One often-quoted scholar is Starushenko who, in 1986, called on the ANC to avoid broad nationalisation of property, to provide comprehensive guarantees for whites, and proposed a parliament with proportional

representation involving equal representation for the four racial
groups with the right of veto.[14]

Another recent scholarly view is that of Tikhomirov, whose premises
for a political settlement in South Africa are: (i) recently, South Africa
has entered a crisis spiral, resulting in reformism giving way to
authoritarianism; (ii) key positions in the economy are held by
whites, many of whom are turning to ultra-right positions; (iii) the
example of other African countries shows that independence results in
the flight of skilled personnel and capital, and sometimes sabotage of
industrial projects; (iv) radical economic reforms will produce a deep
economic crisis in South Africa with negative socio-political consequences because of multi-nationality, ideological disunity and reac-
tionary and conservative traditions; (v) racial discrimination and
political inequality must go – a view supported by all black social
groups and many whites, providing whites are guaranteed safety; (vi)
therefore, possibilities exist for 'a compromise political settlement'.[15]

Based on the above premises, Tikhomirov argues for a possible joint
USSR-USA role in arriving at a peaceful resolution of the South
African crisis, based on a declaration of principles and objectives:

- Apartheid must be eliminated.
- Africans should be granted political rights.
- Neither the USSR nor the USA intend to establish domination in
  Southern Africa.
- South Africans themselves should determine the character and
  structure of the future state.
- Neither the USSR nor the USA intend to interfere with the process
  of settling this conflict in South Africa and they believe that this
  settlement should be of a peaceful nature. The two powers are
  ready to do their utmost for the achievement of this settlement if so
  requested by the South Africans.
- The USSR and USA reject all attempts to establish priority of an
  external force in Southern Africa and express their readiness to
  recognise the future democratic South Africa as a non-aligned
  nation and to maintain broad political economic, cultural and
  other relations with it.
- The USSR and USA declare the inadmissibility of interference by
  any country and, therefore, express their readiness to act as
  guarantors of the security system in Southern Africa.
- The USSR and USA could also co-sponsor an international
  scientific conference attended by leading organisations and move-

ments of South Africa. This conference could draft a settlement
and a programme of action of the future democratic government.
The two powers could also offer 'good offices' in talks between
various political forces in South Africa with a view to reaching a
political settlement of the conflict.[16]

Thus, the ground has been prepared for a major initiative on South
Africa in which the two superpowers will have a decisive role in the
search for a compromise political settlement. While it will be a joint
initiative involving common superpower positions, in practice the
USSR will have conceded the USA's – and therefore the West's –
'vital interest' in the future of South Africa. It appears that a new
partition of Africa is in the offing with the USSR collaborating in
making Africa, and especially Southern Africa, the West's sphere of
influence in which the West's (and especially the USA's) hegemony is
assured. An influential view is that this agreement dates from the 1986
Reykjavik Summit, and that the USSR is now concentrating on
political and diplomatic alliances rather than military ones.[17]
    The hegemonic position of one superpower in Africa has also meant
that the USA is the major 'external' actor in Southern African affairs,
thus emphasising the relative success of American policy objectives in
the region, stretching back at least to the National Security Study
Memorandum 39 (NSSM 39) of 1969, the Nixon/Kissinger strategy on
Southern Africa (commonly known as the Kissinger study). The
NSSM 39's objectives included improving America's position in
Africa, reducing violence, reducing the influence of the USSR/China,
encouraging moderation in racial/colonial policies of white regimes,
and protecting economic/scientific interests. Option Two of the NSSM
39 proposed closer contact with black/white states in Southern Africa
to encourage white moderation, reduce cross-border tension/violence,
and improve interstate relations. It was based on the beliefs that blacks
could not gain political power through violence, whites needed
persuasion and assistance to make the needed changes, and the white
South African state was the dominant power in Southern Africa.[18]
    The Reagan doctrine of rolling back communism through armed
support of 'anti-communist freedom fighters', such as UNITA in
Angola, and the 'linkage' policy of tying Cuban troop withdrawal
from Angola with the independence of Namibia – part of the policy of
'constructive engagement' which gave the South African government
more time to 'reform'[19] – may be seen as way-stations in the unfolding
of the basic tenets of the NSSM. At least since the 1987 speech by

George Shultz, then USA Secretary of State, weight is also given to the aspirations of the black majority, but in a future democratic and capitalist system which will protect basic rights and which will devolve power, thus also ensuring continuity of emphasis on the 'white factor'. According to Jeffrey Davidow, a former USA Ambassador in Zambia and presently US Deputy Assistant Secretary of State for Africa, 'a new constitutional order with equal political, economic and social rights for all' arising after a negotiated settlement would include:

- A democratic, multiparty electoral system with a universal franchise.
- Effective institutional safeguards for basic human and civil rights.
- Safeguards for the rule of law and an independent judiciary.
- An allocation of power between the national government and regional and local authorities.
- An economic system that guarantees economic freedom while allocating governmental, social and economic services fairly.[20]

Thus South Africa is poised on the threshold of a possible negotiated settlement because of the confluence of a number of factors. According to Mafeje:

South Africa is reaching a turning point, primarily because of the maturation of its internal contradictions. But, every now and then, this is amplified by regional and international events. The latter two act like detonators which trigger off different impulses. For instance, rapprochement between the USA and USSR favours conservative forces and confronts revolutionary forces with difficult tactical and strategic questions. This is especially true of liberation movements based outside their own country who have to rely on sympathetic states also concerned about their own survival.... Insofar as states seek to reproduce themselves and consolidate their given power base, they cannot be revolutionary but at best be progressive.... The prospects for a negotiated settlement are good because a number of states desire it and the South African state needs it. There are those within the liberation movement who, because of their class aspirations, are strongly attracted by it and by the possibility of a quick solution in their lifetime.[21]

CONCLUSION

A confluence of internal, regional and international factors has meant that the moment for a possible negotiated settlement of the South African crisis has arrived. Such a confluence of factors has influenced the ANC and the NP, with both increasingly coming to occupy the middle ground in South African politics.

While a negotiated settlement will require the agreement of at least the ANC and the NP, organisations such as the PAC, AZAPO and Inkatha, each representing a significant black constituency, cannot be ignored as non-persons in a political settlement; nor can be dismissed the actual/potential destructive role of the right-wing elements in white politics, for example the CP, HNP, AWB and other groups which favour geographic partition and oppose de Klerk's reform process. The potential for violent resistance by the white right remains a threat to peaceful negotiated settlement, and also has implications for the development of the region as a whole. For such action

will be resisted vigorously by the black majority and a nightmarish spiral of violence and chaos will engulf not only South Africa but the SADCC region as well. Thus, all democratic forces both inside and outside South Africa should do all they can to avoid such a catastrophe.[22]

Notes

1. R. Ajulu and D. Cammack, 'Lesotho, Botswana, Swaziland; The Captive States', in P. Johnson and D. Martin (eds), *Destructive Engagement: Southern Africa at War*, Harare: Zimbabwe Publishing House, 1986, pp.158–69.
2. Ibid., pp.139–59; K. A. Maope,'The Military and Constitutionalism in Lesotho', *Southern Africa Political and Economic Monthly* (SAPEM) (Harare), 3(1), 1989, pp.25–7.
3. Ajulu and Cammack, op.cit., pp.151–9; A. Molokome, 'The Multi-Party Democracy in Botswana', *SAPEM*, 2(12), 1989, pp.9–10, and various articles on Botswana in *SAPEM*, 3(8), 1990.
4. See, for example, D. Martin and P. Johnson, 'Mozambique: To Nkomati and Beyond', and 'Zimbabwe: Apartheid's Dilemma', in Johnson and Martin, op.cit.; A. Isaacman 'Mozambique', *Survival* (London), 30(1), 1988, pp.14–38; H. H. Patel, 'Zimbabwe', *Survival* (London), 30(1), 1988, pp.38–58; H. H. Patel and J. R. N. Shave-Mutenje, 'Frontline States' Security: The Zimbabwean Case', in *Security and Defence of Non-*

Aligned Countries, Belgrade: Centre of the Armed Forces for Strategic Research and Studies, 1989, pp.448–69; and H. H. Patel, 'No Master, No Mortgage, No Sale: The Foreign Policy of Zimbabwe', in T. M. Shaw and Y. Tandon (eds), *Regional Development at the International Level, Vol. II: African and Canadian Perspectives*, Lanham, MD: University Press of America, 1985, pp.219–63.
5. Isaacman, op.cit., pp.26–7, 31.
6. T. Lodge, 'State of Exile : The African National Congress of South Africa, 1976–86', *Third World Quarterly* (London), 9(1), 1987, pp.4–5, 18–19.
7. See, for example, ibid., pp.6, 10–13, 18–19.
8. See, for example, ibid., pp.6, 18; and J. Marcum, 'Angola', *Survival* (London), 30(1), 1988, pp.3–14.
9. H. Campbell, 'Namibia; What Kind of Independence?', *Monthly Review* (New York), 41(44), 1989, pp.9–23.
10. United Nations, *South African Destabilisation: The Economic Cost of Frontline Resistance to Apartheid*, New York: UN, 1989, pp.1–56.
11. For some comments on the Lusaka Manifesto of 1969, see H. H. Patel, 'Race and International Relations', *Zambezia* (Harare), 3(1), 1973, p.74.
12. M. Gorbachev, *For a 'Common European Home', for a New Way of Thinking*, Moscow: Novosti Press, 1987, pp.1–31; M. Gorbachev, *On the Basis of Full Equality, Independence and Mutual Respect*, Moscow: Novosti Press, 1988, pp.1–16; and D. Nabudere, 'Current Reforms in the USSR and their relation to Africa', and V. Sokolov, 'Soviet Foreign Policy: A reply', in *SAPEM*, 11, 1988, pp.3–7 and 7–9, respectively.
13. Lodge, op.cit., pp.16–17; and W. P. Esterhuyse, 'The International Political Status of the African National Congress', *Africa Insight* (Pretoria), 19(1), 1989, pp.34–5.
14. Esterhuyse, *op.cit.*, p.35; Nabudere, op.cit., p.6; A. Mafeje, 'Whither South Africa', *SAPEM*, 2(8), 1989, p.6; and I. Mandaza, 'Movements for National Liberation and Constitutionalism in Southern Africa', *SAPEM*, 2(9), 1989, p.23.
15. V. I. Tikhomirov, 'South Africa: Is a Political Settlement Possible?', *SAPEM*, 2(8), 1989, pp.10–11.
16. Ibid., p.12.
17. *Africa Confidential* (London), 30(5), 1989, p.1.
18. I. Mandaza, 'Southern Africa: US Policy and the Struggle for National Independence', in B. Magubane and I. Mandaza (eds), *Whither South Africa?*, Trenton, NJ: Africa World Press, 1989, pp.122–4, 129.
19. Ibid., p.119; H. Cohen, 'Constructive Engagement at Work in South Africa: A View From The Inside', *SAPEM*, 2(10), 1989, pp.12–16; and H. H. Patel, 'South Africa's Destabilisation Policy', *The Round Table* (London), 303, 1987, p.304.
20. J. Davidow, 'Southern Africa at the Crossroads', *SAPEM*, 2(12), 1989, p.48.
21. Mafeje, op.cit., p.7; also see Mandaza, op.cit., in ref.15, pp.21–3.
22. H. H. Patel, 'SA: The Continuing Long March to Liberation', *The Sunday Mail* (Harare), 18 February 1990, p.5.

Editors' Note
In addition to the above references, extensive use was made of a number of journals and newspapers. The main ones were: *The Herald*, (Harare); *Africa Insight* (Pretoria); *Moto* (Gweru); *Financial Gazette* (Harare); *Sunday Mail* (Harare); *Parade* (Harare); *Time* (New York); *Africa Confidential* (London); and *Africa South* (Harare). The full references are obtainable from the author.

5 Economic Development in South Africa[1]
Ronald Bethlehem

South Africa has conflicting long-term needs. Domestically, because of its rapid population growth and urbanisation, it requires job creation. Externally, its dependence on a high level of export earnings means that it needs to maintain its competitiveness in the global market economy. The two needs conflict as job creation requires investment in labour-intensive projects, whereas maintaining competitiveness in export markets requires largely capital-intensive development. These are generalisations, and it is necessary to guard against their pitfalls. Not all labour-intensive investment necessitates higher unit-cost production and not all capital-intensive investment necessarily promotes greater efficiency. Some development involves an intensity of investment also in human capital. However, as generalisations they remain true and may, therefore, serve as useful post-apartheid policy guidelines.

BACKGROUND

The importance of economic growth for South Africa is illustrated by a comparison of the growth of real GDP and the economically active population since 1950. During the first three decades of this period, the growth of the economy substantially exceeded that of the workforce. Thus, industrialisation was broadened and its benefits were extended. During the 1980s, however, real GDP grew at a mean rate of only 1.8 per cent per annum compared with approximately 2.5 per cent per annum in the case of the economically active population. In the main, the difference between these growth rates was reflected in growing structural unemployment (although even in the 1960s when the rate of real GDP growth was at its highest, structural unemployment increased because much of the growth achieved was of a capital- rather than a labour-intensive kind). However in the 1980s real gross domestic fixed investment slumped to the point where the total stock of capital, adjusted for inflation, began to contract in per capita terms. This was serious not only for current employment but also for the future performance of the economy. Because so much of South Africa's domestic economy depends on foreign trade, the nature of the economy needs to be viewed in a global perspective. Foreign trade equals approximately 55 per cent of GDP, and this makes the country's economic performance highly sensitive to changes in the world economy. The prices at which imports are bought and exports are sold are determined by demand and supply conditions in the world over which neither the government nor local producers have any control. This applies as well to the exchange rates at which external trade contracts are settled. Since the emergence of the floating exchange-rate system in the 1970s, a new element of uncertainty has had to be confronted by planners in both the public and private sectors. The instability of world commodity prices and exchange rates requires that South Africa itself maintains a domestic system that is quick to adapt to change in the global economy.

Price and exchange-rate instability, however, are but one aspect of the global economy. They reflect the mechanisms through which adjustment is effected to new demand/supply conditions, but the global economy is also in the process of restructuring, and this too is of concern to South Africa. Three important aspects of this restructuring are: (i) the consolidation of the trading system into new regional groupings; (ii) the relative decline of the United States despite the maintenance of its central role in the world financial system; and (iii) the Third World debt problem and the emergence of the US, the Soviet Union and also Eastern Europe as competitive debtors vis-à-vis developing countries.

Each of these aspects is of importance to South Africa albeit for different reasons. The consolidation of regional groupings, notably the European Community (EC), threatens to exclude South Africa from regional participation. The relative economic decline of the US is a problem for the stability of the world financial system and is of particular concern to South Africa because of the sensitivity of the gold price to inflation, exchange-rate changes and developments on world financial markets. Events surrounding the collapse of stock markets in October 1987 and October 1989 are a warning that all is not well with the world financial system, which furthermore is threatened by other aspects of global imbalance such as the trade deficit of the US and the huge debt of Third World countries which emerged in the wake of the oil crises of 1973–4 and 1979–80. Any default of a major world debtor would seriously affect the banking systems of the US and all principal Western industrialised countries. The former East Bloc countries would also be affected for they are bound into the world system through their own indebtedness and trade dependence. All this, however, describes only part of the background against which South Africa's economic development has to be viewed. No less important is the power struggle which continues to dominate the country's internal politics. If it carries on interminably, escalating in intensity, the result for the economy could be catastrophic. If emergence into a post-apartheid era can be quickly achieved, the impact on economic development could be positive, even dramatic. It is a matter of balancing-off a threat of increasing structural unemployment and removing the constraints that have for so long inhibited the economy's growth.

Economic growth in recent decades, disappointing though it has been, has occurred more in spite of apartheid than because of it. Particularly impressive has been the resilience shown by the economy during the 1980s when it was buffeted not only by a collapse of the gold price and extremely adverse climatic conditions but also by unrest and sanctions. It should not be doubted, therefore, that South Africa's potential for sustained economic growth exists.

STRUCTURE OF THE ECONOMY

Table 5.1 provides a broad perspective of the South African economy.

Sectoral Aspects

Only about 11 per cent of employment was accounted for by agriculture and 10 per cent by mining in 1988. The single most important sector from an employment point of view is manufacturing, but commerce and services together account for by far the largest proportion of the workforce. Nevertheless the economy continues to straddle two worlds. That described above is the modern economy (the First World sector); that not shown is the Third World sector, made up of subsistence agriculture and informal activities. More than 50 per cent of the country's population is still dependent on these for survival, and this proportion has increased with the weak performance of the economy in the 1980s.

Table 5.1 SA economy in domestic perspective, 1988 (at 1985 prices)

Sector	FCS Amount (R bn)	%	GDP Amount (R bn)	%	Employment Amount (000s)	%	Performance Ratios FCS/Employment (R/worker)	GDP/Employment (R/worker)	GDP/FCS %
Agriculture	18.0	4.5	7.3	6.0	923.4	11.3	19 479	7 882	40.5
Mining	33.4	8.4	16.4	13.6	793.8	9.7	42 020	20 710	49.3
Manufacturing	44.8	11.2	28.7	23.7	1503.3	18.3	29 803	19 071	64.0
Electricity	39.5	9.9	5.4	4.5	94.3	1.2	418 594	57 642	13.8
Construction	2.5	0.6	3.9	3.2	387.9	4.7	6340	10 032	158.2
Wholesale & retail	18.5	4.6	14.0	11.5	1073.8	13.1	17 265	13 019	75.4
Transport	56.2	14.1	10.4	3.5	493.3	6.0	113 877	21 005	18.4
Other	186.0	46.6	35.1	29.0	2926.8	35.7	63 536	12 002	18.9
Total	398.8	100.0	121.2	100.0	8196.5	100.0	48 649	14 785	30.4

Notes: FCS = Fixed capital stock; GDP = Gross domestic product (real)
Sources: South African Reserve Bank; National Manpower Commission

Table 5.1 also shows sectoral contribution to national production and the relative productivities of sectors. Electricity and transport evidence the greatest capital intensity, but their importance in total GDP is less than that of mining, the capital intensity of which is also high. The sectors of greatest labour intensity are agriculture, wholesale and retail distribution, and construction, in that order of importance. It is clear from the category 'other' that the capital intensity of the service sector is well above average, but caution is necessary when considering these general data because of variations in capital and labour intensities within sectors.

Demographically, South Africa is in transformation. The total population is growing by about 2.5 per cent, whites by under one per cent and Africans by 2.9 per cent per annum. However, the urban African population has been growing at over 7.5 per cent per annum – the consequence of natural increase and migration from the rural areas. Although this rate will fall, Africans will comprise just over 70 per cent of the urban population by the end of the century as against just over 50 per cent in 1980. These figures imply much more than a formal restructuring of population: they point also to a social, cultural and economic transformation. White resistance to political change is directly concerned with the Africanisation of urban society, or put another way, with its de-Europeanisation.

The economic restructuring of South Africa is occurring also in the areas of production, income and expenditure. For example, the contribution of agriculture to GDP has continued to decline in the post-war period. It averaged 15.2 per cent in the 1950s, 10.9 per cent in the 1960s, 7.9 per cent in the 1970s and only six per cent in the 1980s. The main sectors of growth have been mining (helped in particular by the increase in the gold price in the 1970s and early 1980s), manufacturing and financial services.

In 1970 the African share of non-agricultural income was 20.1 per cent. It had risen to 29.6 per cent in 1984 when publication of racially classified data in the mining sector was ended. By comparison, Africans accounted for 70.4 per cent of the total population in 1970 and 72.7 per cent in 1985. While differences between African and white per capita incomes remain large, this significant rise in the African share of total non-agricultural income is important. It reflects a fundamental shift and has already made itself felt in expenditure patterns. Higher propensities to consume among lower-income compared with higher-income groups have resulted in proportionately higher African consumption levels. Thus, the retail expenditure of

Africans, coloureds and Asians together (excluding expenditure on motor vehicles) is believed already to exceed such white spending – a trend which is bound to continue.

The Central Government's share of aggregate expenditure has risen noticeably, the public sector share of total gross domestic expenditure averaging 18.3 per cent in the 1950s, 21.3 per cent in 1960s, 28.5 per cent in 1970s and 27.7 per cent in 1980s. This expansion of government expenditure has been directed at health care, education, housing and general welfare as well as defence, law enforcement and public-debt servicing. Together, protection services, social services and State debt costs accounted for 73.1 per cent of total government expenditure in 1988–9.

South Africa's increased dependence on gold mining is due largely to the rise in the gold price following the breakdown of the fixed exchange-rate system in the early 1970s. Higher gold prices made the mining of lower-grade ores possible, but this in turn has given rise to problems. A particular difficulty has been the recent instability of the price of gold. Although South Africa benefited from a higher price once the official fixed price was abandoned, higher gold mining revenues quickly resulted in a general raising of the country's cost structure as competition through the economy for participation in the gold price windfall increased.

However, the general cost structure has not been amenable to downward adjustment when the gold price has fallen. This has necessitated a painful internal correction accommodated essentially by a collapse of the rand exchange rate, disrupting attempts to keep the country's economy on an even development path. South Africa has experienced demand-pull inflation pressures when the gold price has risen strongly and cost-push inflation pressures when it has fallen, thus adding to its balance-of-payments difficulties.

Such problems will be of particular concern to any post-apartheid government especially since, in a broader democratic system, the pressure on the mines and government to accommodate wage demands when the gold price is high and rising can be expected to be as great, if not greater, than has been the case until now. Likewise, in periods of a declining gold price, resistance to cuts in incomes is likely to remain and to be given added force by political action on the part of constituency interests.

While the rise in the gold price has brought important benefits to South Africa, it has also been retrogressive beyond the problems of instability associated with the metal's price. The greater dependence on gold and the greater weight thus given to gold in fluctuations of the rand exchange rate, have adversely affected other industries. In gold mining, South Africa has ceased to be a low-cost producer. Four factors have been at work, namely, the increase in labour costs, the shift towards the exploitation of lower grades, the mining of ores at ever-greater depths necessitating more costly infrastructure (including ventilation and haulage systems), and declines in labour efficiency. To counteract these forces, more capital-intensive methods of production, of, which trackless mining has been the most outstanding example, have had to be introduced. The result has been a significant decline in mining employment.

Finally, account must be taken of the fact that minerals are diminishing assets. In the ultra long term, earnings from metals and minerals exports will have to be replaced by earnings from secondary and tertiary industries if import levels and growth are to be maintained. Failure to effect an appropriate adjustment could have a retarding effect on future development.

Capital/Labour Intensity of Production

In terms of the need to create jobs in South Africa, the evidence relating to capital investment is not encouraging. Table 5.2 shows that the capital/labour ratio for the economy as a whole has risen consistently and significantly in each of the last three decades. In the 1980s, the ratio was 2.5 times that in the 1950s. Table 5.2 also shows a secular decline in the ratio of fixed capital stock to GDP at constant prices, that is, the production of a given unit of GDP has required an increasing input of capital and a declining quantum of labour over the years. Why has this occurred? Is it the consequence of changing technological circumstances? Or has it been the result of policies adopted by successive South African governments? Evidence suggests that policies such as cheapening capital relative to labour in order to reduce white dependence on blacks (achieved mainly through tax incentives and a manipulation of interest rates and the rand exchange rate)[2] and narrowing interracial wage gaps, have been the more important factors, although technological change, the higher costs of new productive methods and the need to maintain competitiveness in export markets have also played a part. It is ironical that policies to reduce wage gaps, reinforced by trade union demands for wage increases unrelated to productivity improvements, have contributed

Table 5.2   Productivity and employment

	1950–9	1960–9	1970–9	1980–8
Averages				
GDP (R mill., 1985 prices)	39 154	63 836	100 017	125 327
FCS (R mill., 1985 prices)	80 407	131 447	243 137	369 876
Employment (000s)	4 263	5 337	6 798	7 909
Ratios:				
GDP/FCS	48.7	48.6	41.1	33.9
GDP/TE	9.2	12.0	14.7	15.8
FCS/TE	18.9	24.6	35.8	46.8

Notes: GDP = Gross Domestic Product; FCS = Fixed Capital Stock; TE = Total Employment
Sources: South African Reserve Bank; National Manpower Commission

significantly to the relative cheapening of capital and, thus, also to an aggravation of unemployment.

The economy's dismal growth performance has aggravated structural unemployment. Table 5.2 suggests that, were the growth of real GDP to be reduced to an average of only one per cent per annum in the 1990s, unemployment could increase by as much as two million over and above what it would have been had growth averaged between three to four per cent per annum.

Income and Wealth Distribution

In terms of income and wealth distribution, South Africa is an unequal society. Its inequality also is skewed according to race. This has serious implications for social and political stability as well as for economic development.

The Gini coefficient measures income inequality on a scale from nought to one, independent of population size or average income level. In 1975, the latest year for which data are available, South Africa had a Gini coefficient of 0.68 compared with coefficients in Western industrialised countries of between 0.35–0.41[3] and in most semi-industrialised countries of between 0.50–0.60.[4] In 1975 a minority of five per cent of the population (mainly whites) owned 88 per cent of all personal wealth.[5]

The skewing of inequality by race has serious implications for the economy of South Africa for two reasons. Firstly, it directly affects entrepreneurial participation, expenditure patterns and the extent of the domestic market. Second, it feeds back negatively into the struggle for political power. Not surprisingly, the deprived majority has come to see the winning of political power as the best means for redressing economic grievances. If the State can be captured, its authority can be used to redistribute income and wealth either by expropriating from the rich and giving to the poor directly or by making transfers from rich to poor through the fiscus. Alternatively, the State can be used as an agent of the poor, asserting its ownership through nationalisation of the means of production, distribution and exchange.

The case for redistribution may appear overwhelming on pragmatic or moral grounds, but there are equally plausible reasons why it should be approached cautiously. No purpose would be served in expropriating land, for example, were the consequence to be a decline in food production. If nationalisation has the effect of damaging economic performance because it aggravates a flight of capital or of skilled manpower, the job, equally, might be ill done.

It is for this reason that alternatives to State-sponsored redistribution need to be found. Some measure of State action is probably inevitable. Even the present government has found itself driven in the direction of greatly increased welfare expenditure in the face of African needs in housing, education, medical and social support. However, State action has to be carefully considered and should not obstruct other redistributive processes, especially where these can be shown empirically to be effective and powerful.

An alternative to State-sponsored redistribution is economic growth itself, but this too needs to be examined critically and its shortcomings acknowledged. McGrath has stressed, for example, the need to avoid a direct linking of increases in real GDP and welfare, the true matter at issue.[6] In South Africa, the real problem resides in the improbability of even very high rates of real GDP growth reducing poverty in absolute terms because of the sheer numbers of unemployed involved. Policy, thus, would need to be directed not at the elimination of poverty but rather to its minimisation.

In a final reckoning, however, inequality, poverty and redistribution will be powerful political issues facing a post-apartheid government. For this reason it is essential that the business community, whose interests could be profoundly affected, accepts that these issues cannot be left only to government to tackle and that it gives attention to the matter of corporate ownership and to a widening of African participation generally in the entrepreneurial sector of the economy.

Manpower

Manpower poses a major constraint on South Africa's industrial growth. The economy is confronted simultaneously with a severe shortage of skilled personnel and a surfeit of unskilled workers. Unless the imbalance between these categories can be corrected, hopes of achieving the required real GDP growth rate are likely to be disappointed. Much will depend on better use being made of existing educational facilities, that is, opening available facilities to people of all races, a radical restructuring of the present educational system, and action being taken by the business sector to improve the literacy and technical competence of employees already beyond school-going age. An aggravating factor in the shortage of skilled manpower is the emigration of qualified people caused by concerns about the security situation and the country's longer-term social and political stability.

Industrial Concentration and Monopoly

McGregor has focused criticism on the degree of industrial concentration in South Africa and in particular on the concentration of ownership in the hands of a few major companies.[7] This criticism is linked to the wider issues of inequality and the struggle against white domination. Whatever the validity of the criticism, concentration has occurred for particular reasons. Amongst these have been the need to diversify risks, reduce costs and generally exploit economies of scale within a strictly limited domestic market. In this, South Africa has not been alone although, compared with North American and West European countries, its domestic market is small.

However, there are disturbing aspects of industrial concentration in South Africa from an economic as well as from a political or ideological standpoint. Competition in the economy has suffered especially when imports, which could have served to preserve the free choice of consumers, have had to be restricted for balance of payments purposes. Monopolistic tendencies, therefore, have been encouraged and these, it is feared, have also made the control of inflation more difficult.

Nevertheless, none of these problems would be solved by switching instead to a generalised State ownership of industry. On the contrary, such a policy could compound the problems of monopoly and bureaucratic inefficiency. The solution to the problem needs to be sought elsewhere: in increasing efficiency and competition; widening consumer choice; exposing the economy to more, not less, international trade; and in privatisation and deregulation. These things can only be fully done if a new constitutional order is instituted and the country's relationship with the outside world and its neighbours is normalised.

Sanctions

Like other developing countries, South Africa has a deficiency of domestic savings relative to its need for the financing of new capital formation. Such a deficiency should logically be made good through an importing of savings from developed countries. In South Africa's case, however, this ceased to be possible from 1985–6 when first financial and then trade sanctions were imposed. If sanctions continue to be applied, and are successful, their effect will be to further retard economic development. Given the imperative for growth already discussed, it is essential that sanctions be removed at an early date. On this point, both advocates and opponents of sanctions are agreed. Differences, however, continue to exist over the efficiency of sanctions as a political weapon to bring about a change in the government's policies.[8]

Table 5.3 shows the extent of South Africa's dependence on imported savings. During the 1950s, 1960s and 1970s this dependence was maintained but the position changed dramatically after 1985 when financial sanctions were imposed. Since 1984, capital outflows have exceeded R24 000 million (or approximately $10 000 million). Such a rate of capital export cannot be sustained without serious damage to the growth of the economy. This became especially clear in the closing years of the 1980s when, after a limited recovery from the 1985–7 recession, monetary and fiscal policy had again to be tightened to maintain the surplus on the current account of the balance of payments required for purposes of debt repayment. The excess of domestic savings over domestic investment, which such debt repayment involves, is given added perspective in Table 5.4. In the 1980s both personal and government savings fell sharply, leaving the main burden of savings on the corporate sector. The coincidence of the fall in personal and government savings and the cutting off of imported savings, is the single most serious threat posed to the future development of the country.

Table 5.3 Financing gross domestic investment (R million, current prices)

	1950–9	1960–9	1970–9	1980–9
Averages				
Gross domestic investment	900	1 931	7 439	28 764
Gross domestic saving	818	1 921	7 246	30 544
Current a/c surplus (deficit)	(82)	(10)	(193)	(1 780)
Financed by:				
Net capital inflow (outflow)	93	81	87	(2 197)
Decrease (increase) in reserves	(11)	(72)	106	417

Source: South African Reserve Bank

Table 5.4 Gross domestic saving

	1950–9	1960–9	1970–80	1980–8
Averages (R million):				
Personal saving (PS)	201	613	1 727	2 636
Corporate saving (CS)	108	205	1 388	7 676
Government saving (GS)	102	280	650	(372)
Provision for depreciation	406	824	3 481	18 601
Total	818	1 921	7 246	28 541
Personal disposable income (PDI)	n.a.	5 382	16 820	67 944
Corporate disposable income (CDI)	n.a.	1 925	7 816	39 216
Government current income (GCI)	n.a.	1 463	5 783	29 737
Gross domestic product (GDP)	3 638	7 949	26 621	117 857
Percentage of total saving (TS):				
Personal saving	24.6	31.9	23.8	9.2
Corporate saving	13.3	10.6	19.2	26.9
Government saving	12.5	14.5	9.0	– 1.3
Provision for depreciation	49.7	42.9	48.0	65.2
Total	100.0	100.0	100.0	100.0
Ratios:				
PS/PDI	n.a.	11.4	10.3	3.9
CS/CDI	n.a.	10.6	17.8	19.6
GS/GCI	n.a.	19.1	11.2	– 1.3
TS/GDP	22.5	24.2	27.2	24.2

Source: South African Reserve Bank

ROLE OF THE STATE

The role of the State, and the interaction of the State and the market, constitute the central issues of political economy.[9] Given the mixed nature of the South African economy, four main aspects of the State's role may be identified: (i) as regulator of social process; (ii) as provider of essential goods and services; (iii) as entrepreneur; and (iv) as macroeconomic stabiliser.

Ideological differences between the main protagonists in the power struggle are to be found with respect to each of these functions. The approach of the ruling National Party (NP) has traditionally been to place considerations of the State and national interest (narrowly defined in terms of the interests of whites or of Afrikaners) above those of market forces. In this, it has shared much in common with socialist critics for whom conflicts of class and the struggle against exploitation have been key issues. In contrast, liberals have viewed the South African economy as essentially forming part of the global economy, and have advocated policies which promote an international division of labour and the principles of free trade and comparative advantage. For nationalists and socialists, an optimising of the State's role has been the primary objective; for liberals, limiting the size and the authority of the State, and providing the greatest scope to market forces, have been overriding.

Although differences of ideology have complicated the search for a consensus on the role of the State in South Africa, recent developments in the country and in the world economy have helped to modify differences between the parties and to identify greater areas of common ground between them. The NP now accepts the error of Verwoerdian ideology and has moved closer to the liberal position regarding the importance of market forces and economic efficiency. Socialists have come to accept the errors of central planning and to recognise that market forces cannot be ignored in a global economy where no central authority exists to control prices and to which all national economies are inextricably bound.

In both the capitalist West and the socialist East, disillusionment with State interventionism has become manifest. The importance of these developments to South Africa cannot be overstated. In its own way it has experienced disillusionment with macroeconomic stabilisation. The history of the last twenty years is a chronicle of disappointment with government attempts to intervene beneficially in the economy. Quite aside from the unreality of Verwoerdian policies with respect to the reversal of African urban influx and the effects of apartheid laws on economic growth, South Africa has come to experience as well the limits of monetary and fiscal fine-tuning. Managing the economy in the context of world cyclical developments has not been easy, and has been complicated further by adverse exogenous developments regarding the gold price, climatic conditions and sanctions. As in Western Europe and North America, the trade-off between unemployment and inflation has ceased to operate, necessitating an acknowledgement of market efficiency.

As in other countries, an expansion of the State sector has been directly linked to a deterioration of economic performance. Growth has suffered because of the crowding-out effects on the surplus-earning private sector while both inflation and the balance of payments have been adversely affected by excessive Exchequer spending and the rise in the deficit before borrowing. Because the difference between gross domestic saving and gross domestic investment is equal to the external current account deficit, a large proportion of corporate saving has had to be directed towards the repayment of debt.[10]

It is against this background of overseas and domestic experience regarding the public sector that the government has accepted some measure of privatisation and deregulation. In economic terms, privatisation has three main objectives: (i) to reduce the size of the State sector relative to that of the private sector so as to increase the scope for the latter's expansion; (ii) to reduce the size of the State sector's borrowing requirement and so reduce the finance burden of the State and inflation; and (iii) to improve efficiency through the replacement of bureaucratic administration by entrepreneurial management. Deregulation is intended to remove restrictions which needlessly discourage entrepreneurial initiative.[11] Privatisation and deregulation are necessarily complementary because, without deregulation and the increased competition that it assures, improving the efficiency of privatised former State enterprises could be frustrated.

It is regrettable, therefore, that both privatisation and deregulation have attracted criticism as being instruments for the maintenance of apartheid and white domination. Two main arguments have been advanced. It is argued with respect to privatisation that its purpose is to shift racial segregation from the public sector, where its enforcement is becoming untenable, to the private sector, where its enforcement can be defended on grounds of free association and the right to privacy. In the case of deregulation, it is argued that its effect will be to expose blacks, handicapped by historical legacies, to unequal competition from whites. While a grain of truth in these criticisms has to be acknowledged, they clearly do not represent the whole truth. Clearly, neither privatisation nor deregulation should be used as obstructive mechanisms in creating a new and more just society, but their benefits to such a society need also to be remembered, and the reasons for their adoption as policy in other countries should not be lost sight of. Even social democratic governments in the West, and more doctrinaire socialist countries elsewhere, have found it necessary to implement such programmes because these have advanced the objectives both of economic efficiency and social democratisation.

SCENARIOS 2000

Three scenarios regarding the course of South Africa's economic development in the 1990s are specified. These are broadly described below.

Conflict resolved. Here the damage to the economy is minimised; sanctions are lifted and punitive action on the part of the State is restrained so as to ensure a maintenance of business confidence. The growth path is determined exogenously by favourable export market conditions, renewed capital inflows and an expansion of domestic manufacturing industry uninhibited by apartheid constraints and controls. This scenario implies a negotiated constitution supported by all important parliamentary and extra-parliamentary parties or groups.

Muddling on. Unilateral NP reform is still rejected by the ANC. Economic sanctions continue to be applied and are intensified as time passes. The growth of the economy, therefore, is impaired and structural unemployment increases. This scenario implies that a narrowing of the political gap between the NP and the ANC is checked by, for example, a strengthening of conservatives as opposed to reformers in the de Klerk government or growing radical pressure on the ANC leadership.

Mandatory sanctions. It is assumed that reform stops. The present policy of relative openness in economic management would be abandoned by the government. The policy of reform would be discredited and reformers would be replaced by conservatives in the NP leadership. This could even involve a rapprochement between the NP and the CP, or a CP assumption of power through a splitting of the NP into reform and conservative factions. This would lead the international community to adopt mandatory sanctions against the country.

It is not possible to quantify these scenarios econometrically. However, an attempt at a schematic quantification is made in Table 5.5 with respect to all of the variables mentioned.

Table 5.5   Scenarios 2000

	Scenario 1: *Conflict* *Resolved*	Scenario 2: *Muddling* *On*	Scenario 3: *Mandatory* *Sanctions*
Growth	3 to 6% p.a.	0 to 3% p.a.	−3 to +3% p.a.
Employment	3 to 6% p.a.	−1 to +2% p.a.	−5 to +3% p.a.
Inflation	7.5 to 15% p.a.	12.5 to 20% p.a.	10 to 30% p.a.
BoP (Rand billions):			
Cur. A/C	(2.5 to 5)	2.5 to 5	0 to 2.5
Cap. A/C	3.5 to 6	(2.5 to 5)	1 to 3.5
Net reserves	On balance. rising	On balance: unchanged	On balance: falling
Policy	Market related Exchange control scrapped	Market related Exchange control retained	Direct controls prices and incomes

Growth

Clearly, the best growth scenario is *Conflict Resolved*. Per annum increases in real GDP could be expected to average between three to six per cent compared to a *Muddling On* growth rate of nought to three per cent, the range experienced in the 1980s. In a *Mandatory Sanctions* scenario the range of possible growth widens considerably because uncertainty increases markedly, but rates of absolute decline (perhaps to the extent of three per cent per annum) are possible.

Employment

In a *Conflict Resolved* scenario, the growth of employment would probably match that of real GDP because tendencies towards capital intensity could be expected to be offset by considerable labour-intensive investment, that is, the rising trend in the capital/labour ratio, evident throughout the period 1950–89, would be modified or even checked. With employment growing at a rate faster than the average increase in population, a start would be made to rolling back poverty. In the short-to-medium term, structural unemployment would continue to rise but this would taper off and eventually be reversed provided a GDP growth rate averaging 4.5 per cent per annum in real terms is sustained into the long term. In a *Muddling On* scenario, employment growth is unlikely to exceed about two per cent per annum, and the same is true of a *Mandatory Sanctions* scenario although here, provided sanctions can be circumvented, a growth rate of employment equal to population remains possible.

Inflation

During the 1980s inflation, as measured by annualised changes in the CPI, averaged 14.6 per cent. There is reason to believe that the level of inflation could be significantly reduced under a *Conflict Resolved* scenario, notwithstanding a likely increase in State welfare expenditures, provided inflation in the major industrial countries remains low, capital inflows are resumed, and monetary and fiscal policy is kept appropriately tight (see below). However, it would probably be too much to expect that inflation could be brought down as low as that in the economies of the country's leading trading partners. A *Muddling On* scenario implies more of what has already been experienced in the 1980s, while a *Mandatory Sanctions* scenario would most likely result in a far higher level of inflation because the balance of domestic demand and supply would be biased towards an increase of the former and a reduction of the latter. An effective prices and incomes policy would be needed to prevent inflation surging, but in such a case the underlying causal imbalance would remain uncorrected.

Balance of Payments

The outstanding feature of a *Conflict Resolved* scenario is South Africa's return as a net importer of foreign savings. The country would return to a position of deficit on the current account but this deficit would be more than offset by inflows of capital. As a consequence the net reserves would rise. During the 1980s South Africa was forced into being a net exporter of capital, the average current account surplus being offset by capital outflows. Under a *Mandatory Sanctions* scenario, the size of the external sector could be expected to shrink but, on balance, capital outflows, now officially restricted as a retaliatory measure against sanctions, and made necessary to check capital flight, would be likely to exceed whatever surplus was earned on current account.

Policy

The monetary and fiscal policy needed to counter the inflationary pressures inherent in a *Conflict Resolved* scenario would of necessity have to include: (i) a relaxation of exchange control so that real interest rates are kept positive and competitive with those in the US, Britain, Germany and Japan, (ii) a tightening of exchequer financing to keep increases in welfare expenditures balanced by increases in taxes, and (iii) the maintenance of the rand exchange rate at a market clearing level so that the balance between the current account and the capital account of the balance of payments is maintained. If interest rates are kept artificially low, not only is malinvestment encouraged but the capital account is weakened relative to the current account, putting strain on the net reserve position. *Muddling On* implies a continuing need for exchange controls. It also implies that South Africa is denied the benefit of capital inflows when sentiment in money and capital markets vis-à-vis the country improves. Under *Mandatory Sanctions*, existing exchange controls have to be augmented by direct controls on imports, credit extension, prices and incomes as the only way to check capital flight and prevent a runaway inflation. There is little empirical evidence, however, that such controls are able to sustain the level of domestic entrepreneurial confidence against such adverse background circumstances as those assumed.

CONCLUSION

It is widely acknowledged that South Africa is in the process of a major transformation. This is being driven by demographic change and by economic and political pressures which make restructuring of the country's economic and political system essential. The need for economic and political restructuring is linked. Without economic growth there is little chance of meeting the demographic challenge. Economically, restructuring will have to address the matter of income and wealth inequalities and particularly the under-participation of Africans in the entrepreneurial sector of the economy.

This under-participation has contributed to a tendency among Africans to associate capitalism with apartheid and to prefer some type of socialist economy. In a sense, the choice between socialism and capitalism is meaningless in today's world. Neither system is unchanging and therefore amenable to satisfactory definition. However, a market economy is able to accommodate economic institutions that are both socialist and capitalist in character and, therefore, is in a position to serve a purpose in reconciling ideological differences. It is also the system of the global economy of which South Africa is part and to which it is bound constantly to adjust.

Linked to the conflict between socialism and capitalism in South Africa is the matter of black (especially African) economic empowerment. If exploitation is seen to be the usual consequence of a juxtapositioning of weak and strong elements in a social context, it is not the elimination of capitalism per se, but rather that of black economic weakness, which is required if the exploitation of blacks is to be overcome. Moreover, the strengthening of blacks economically should not require a concomitant economic weakening of whites; any such suggestion would reflect a mercantilist view of power, that is, that what is gained by one must necessarily be taken from another. Just as the principles of free trade gave the lie to mercantilist ideas in the context of international trade, so Keynesian theory has been able to show that interdependence in the domestic economy is the dominant characteristic of contemporary industrial society. One individual's expenditure must necessarily be seen as another's income, and so the circular flow of interdependence is extended.

A factor of particular importance to South Africa is the close link between the cycles of business and socio-political turbulence. In almost every instance since the NP came to office in 1948, serious unrest in the townships has been preceded by significant economic deterioration. This has been the case even where the economic deterioration has been caused by exogenous developments for which no first-instance blame can be placed at the door of the government.

The economic deterioration which took place ahead of the Soweto uprising of 1976 and that which occurred prior to the unrest of 1983–6, were both the result of a major fall of the gold price. In each instance the position was made worse by policy errors and misjudgements concerning the course of external developments. Nor is South Africa alone in such experience. In other countries (Zambia and Poland are but two), economic decline, accompanied by governmental attempts to apply corrective measures, has resulted in social unrest. To this even a future non-racial, democratic government in South Africa would have to pay heed. Were such a government to come to office and implement policies which met its ideological agenda but had the effect also of causing the economy to falter or decline, it could itself be confronted by a rise in popular dissatisfaction that spilled over into violence.

In a final reckoning, it is the extension of industrialisation in South Africa which offers the country its best hope for the future. It is in industrialisation that the greatest possibilities of reduced population growth, increased production and a closing of the wage gap reside. As industrialisation proceeds, inequalities generally tend to diminish. This certainly has been the experience of the rest of the world. The greatest income and wealth differences, in terms of broad statistical averages, are to be found in the underdeveloped, not the industrialised countries.

Notes

1. Much of this paper is based on the author's *Economics in a Revolutionary Society*, Johannesburg: Ad. Donker, 1988.
2. S. Terreblanche, 'SA Economy Still on the Decline', *Democracy in Action,* April 1989.
3. M.D. McGrath, 'An Overview of the Effects of Apartheid on Economic Growth and on Income Distribution'. Unpublished paper presented to Idasa seminar, June 1989.
4. M.D. McGrath, 'Economic Stagnation, Economic Strategy and Income Distribution in the South African Economy'. Paper presented to the Biennial Conference of the Economic Society of South Africa, September 1989.
5. Ibid.
6. Ibid.
7. R. McGregor, *The Mechanics of The Johannesburg Stock Exchange*, Cape Town: Juta & Co, 1989.
8. See, for example, C. Meth, 'Sanctions and Unemployment' in M. Orkin (ed.), *Sanctions Against Apartheid*, Cape Town: David Philip, 1989; K. Overden and T. Cole, *Apartheid and International Finance: A Program for Change*, Victoria: Penguin Books, 1989; and two papers by C.J. van Wyk:

'The Effects of Sanctions and Disinvestment on the South African Economy', paper delivered to a seminar on 'South Africa and the International Community', Vaal Triangle Technikon, 1989, and 'Facing the Nineties: The South African Business Scene Amidst Sanctions and Disinvestment', Trust Bank, 1989.

9. R Gilpin, *The Political Economy of International Relations*, New Jersey: Princeton University Press, 1987.

10. R. Gouws, 'Economic Challenges of the 1990s'. Address to the Hollandia Forum, Vereeniging, 1989.

11. L. Tager, 'Deregulation in the South African Context: The Dismantling of Socio-Economic Apartheid'. Unpublished paper, Trust Bank, 1988.

6 The Manufacturing Sector and Regional Trade in a Democratic South Africa

Raphael Kaplinsky

This paper considers the context in which industrial policy can be formulated in a democratic South Africa.[1] It reviews South Africa's past manufacturing performance, identifying its relative failure by comparison with other middle-income economies; considers the causes for this poor performance; discusses the context in which industrial policy can be formulated after transition to democratic rule; and isolates four major factors which will have to be considered. These are the role to be played by the State, the importance of a small-unit focus to strategy, the necessity of embracing specific policies to foster the growth of indigenous technological capability, and the new opportunities opened in developed-country export markets. This is followed by a more detailed discussion of trade prospects in regional markets, especially within the PTA.

A REVIEW OF SOUTH AFRICA'S MANUFACTURING PERFORMANCE

By the mid-1970s it had become clear that the industrially advanced countries (IACs) were experiencing a significant slowdown in growth rates. After almost three decades of historically unprecedented expansion (accompanied by an even faster growth in economic integration), the trend rate of GDP, productivity and trade growth was moving to a lower path.[2] However, this change in trajectory was uneven, and the slowdown was felt most acutely during the 1970s in the 'old industrial centre' (North America and Europe), and during the 1980s in Africa, South America and parts of Asia. Through most of this period, growth rates in Japan and the Asian 'newly industrialised countries' (NICs) remained high.

83

From Table 6.1 it can be seen that, compared to the performance of economies with similar per capita incomes, South Africa both grew less rapidly between 1965–80 and experienced an even more marked slowdown after 1980. Although its rate of economic expansion exceeded that of the IACs between 1965–80, its contraction after 1980 was also more acute. Table 6.2 shows a continued – and indeed precipitous – decline in South African growth rates between 1960–87. Coupled with a high population growth rate, this has led to a significant fall in real per capita incomes.

Table 6.1   GDP growth rates, 1965–85 (percentages)

	1965–80	*1980–87*
Korea	9.5	8.6
Brazil	9.0	3.3
Mexico	6.5	0.5
Zimbabwe	4.4	2.4
Greece	5.6	1.4
Israel	6.7	2.2
Upper middle-income countries	6.7	3.4
Industrial market economies	3.7	2.6
South Africa	4.1	1.0

Source: World Bank (1989).

Table 6.2   Average GDP growth in South Africa, 1960–87

Year	*Percentage*
1960–5	6.1
1965–70	5.5
1970–5	4.0
1975–80	2.7
1980–7	1.0

Sources: Knight (1986); World Bank (1989).

There are many dimensions to this decline in South African growth rates and real per capita incomes. Most relevant to this discussion of medium- and long-term opportunities in the manufacturing sector is the pattern of sectoral specialisation which has emerged: between 1965–87, the share of agriculture in GDP fell from ten to six per cent, that of 'industry' rose from 42 to 44 per cent, and that of manufacturing remained stable at 23 per cent. Manufacturing's stable share contrasts with the experience of the more dynamic middle-income economies in two respects (Table 6.3). First, its share is lower in South Africa, even by comparison with other mineral exporters such as Brazil, and second, it expanded in most of these economies.

Table 6.3 Share of manufacturing in GDP (percentages)

	1965	1987
Korea	18	30
Brazil	26	28
Mexico	20	25
Zimbabwe	20	31
Greece	16	18
Industrial market economies	20	NA
South Africa	23	23

Source: World Bank (1989).

The judgement that South Africa's manufacturing sector has performed poorly by comparative standards is borne out in a recent study of the economy's capital-goods sector.[3] The contrast is particularly striking with Korea and Brazil: exports exceeded imports in both these countries in the mid-1980s, whereas in South Africa exports were valued at only 11.1 per cent of imports in 1986.

One unusual feature of South African manufacturing is the poor export performance of those traditional subsectors which have generally been the platform on which a dynamic manufacturing sector has been built. Two subsectors – shoes and garments – stand out in particular since South Africa is strongly endowed with the determinants of export competitiveness, namely, cheap labour and domestic raw materials.

EXPLANATIONS FOR SOUTH AFRICA'S DECLINING GROWTH RATES

Although there has been a widespread global slowdown over the past two decades, each country's experience also reflects specific factors.

What were these specific factors affecting South Africa's performance – especially the relative decline of its manufacturing sector – and what implications do these have for this sector in a post-apartheid society? Clearly, this is a complex discussion which can only be addressed at the most general level here. Four potential explanations suggest themselves: the costs of apartheid; the impact of sanctions; the decline in commodity prices; and the impact of what has come to be called the 'Dutch Disease'.

The Costs of Apartheid

Until the end of the 1960s, apartheid proved to be functional to growth. The pattern of accumulation was extensive, based upon the intensification of work. In this period, 'efficiency' and 'profitability' were based upon low efficiency wages.[4] Racial separation benefited this type of economic growth by allowing the rural areas to subsidise the costs of reproducing the labour force for the modern sector. In addition, the migrant labour system allowed the reserve army of labour to be brought into operation, thereby keeping wage rates low. Political domination contributed to the rate of accumulation by limiting worker resistance, both on the shop floor and in the wider political domain.

As South Africa's economy changed in the 1970s to a more technology-intensive structure,[5] so this system of labour supply (which was arguably the structural underpinning for the political system of apartheid) became increasingly dysfunctional. Instead of a high-turnover, unskilled labour force, South Africa's economy required a more stable and more highly skilled set of workers. The authoritarian work structures and broader political conflict characteristic of apartheid made it impossible for management to reap the creative potential of the workforce, as has increasingly been the case in Japan and the dynamic sectors of the European economies. Moreover, the superstructural costs of apartheid were becoming significant and the military burden on fiscal budgets and scarce resources (particularly in armaments production) has had large opportunity costs. It is perhaps not surprising, therefore, that it was during this period that a *verligte* tendency began to emerge in white politics – enlightened capital had concluded that apartheid was no longer merely morally objectionable, but was also increasingly economically inefficient.

The Economic Impact of Sanctions[6]

The success of sanctions has only belatedly come to be recognised. Most clearly, it is apparent that the financial sanctions imposed during the mid-1980s played a major role in preparing the ground for the political liberalisation which emerged in white politics during and after the 1989 election.

Sanctions have also had significant economic costs. Investments in capital goods for military production and the diversion of scarce resources from more economically (and of course socially) productive uses are only one part of the story. Another is the fiscal, and especially the foreign-exchange, cost involved, particularly as a consequence of the oil embargo. This was estimated (by ex-President Botha) to have cost $25 billion between 1973–84, almost equivalent to South Africa's current accumulated foreign debt.[7]

Historically, and in almost all environments, sanctions have been most effective when targeted at a country's exports rather than its imports. Thus, aside from the military embargo, South Africa has experienced little difficulty in obtaining technology.[8] Indeed, the short-term consequences of the disinvestment campaign may even have had positive effects, transferring ownership to South African enterprises. Transnational corporations (TNCs) have responded to divestment pressures by using a variety of non-equity channels to transfer technology. However, sanctions directed against South Africa's exports have been significantly more effective. Nine key countries alone (USA, Denmark, Canada, Finland, Norway, Sweden, France, Australia and New Zealand) reduced their imports from South Africa between 1983–7 by $1.25 billion, a reduction equivalent to 12 per cent of South Africa's non-gold exports and seven per cent of total exports.[9]

These aggregate figures mask important implications for the regional nature of South Africa's trade. Clearly, sanctions have had little impact on trade within SADCC. It is even possible that, because the maintenance of apartheid has been accompanied by the destruction of transport infrastructure in the SADCC region, the net effect has been to consolidate South Africa's share of these regional markets. However, the wider African trading hinterland, especially in the non-SADCC PTA region, has been largely closed to South African exporters. This has had important – but as yet unquantified – negative implications for the economy, including in relation to the low rate of accretion of indigenous technological capability.

Perhaps one of the most significant economic costs of apartheid is one which is inherently difficult to measure. It concerns investor confidence and the impact which this has on manufacturing in general, and technological capability in particular. Long-term manufacturing growth depends upon the time horizons of investors. The shorter these time horizons, the less likely they are to invest in technological development. In addition, when time horizons are short, investors also tend to move into speculative rather than productive activities. It is clear that many sectors of South African manufacturing are blighted by political uncertainty which has led to a relative neglect of manufacturing. This is partly the reason why South Africa was a net (re-)exporter of numerically controlled capital goods in the mid-1980s,[10] and why the manufacturing sector is relatively poorly developed. Again, a contrast with the NICs highlights these deficiencies in industries such as capital goods, automobiles and electronics where investments in long-term technological development are a necessary condition for successful development.[11]

It is thus clear that the overall economic cost of sanctions has been high. A variety of attempts have been made to measure this economic impact. For example, the Trust Bank estimated that during 1985–90 alone, sanctions and disinvestment will have cost South Africa around $20 billion and will have reduced per capita incomes by 10 per cent more than they would have otherwise been.[12] This ignores the opportunity cost of resources diverted to strategic uses.

Decline in Commodity Prices

Whatever the long-term trends may be, there is little doubt that from the late-1970s until the end of the 1980s, many less developed countries (LDCs), particularly those in sub-Saharan Africa (SSA), have been hard-hit by a fall in commodity prices. South Africa has not been immune to these trends and, despite the diversity of its commodity exports, the fall in the gold price during the 1980s has led to a larger fall in its terms of trade than in most of the NICs. Between 1980–7, South Africa's terms of trade fell to 71, whereas those of all middle-income countries fell to 88, Korea's rose to 105, and Brazil's and Mexico's fell respectively to 97 and 73.[13] This falling trend is not restricted to the 1980s, however, and since 1973 there has been an overall fall in South Africa's terms of trade (both if gold is excluded or included) by around 30 per cent.[14]

There are two basic reasons for this relatively large fall in South Africa's external terms of trade. First, it reflects a fall in the price of the commodities which South Africa exports. But second, it is one of the consequences of the poor performance of the economy's manufacturing sector. If South Africa had exported manufactures successfully, this would have diversified the export base, making it less vulnerable to the change in price of particular commodities. Moreover, since most manufactures have seen a rise in price relative to primary commodities, this would have arrested the fall in South Africa's terms of trade. Thus, Brazil's relatively good external terms of trade resulted more from the expansion of manufactured exports than the mix of its commodity exports, while Korea's improving terms of trade reflected the growth of manufactured exports.

It is difficult to assess whether this fall in the terms of trade will continue. But the fact that world gold production is on a sharply upward curve, and that South Africa is losing its position as a low-cost supplier, does not bode well for the future of its international terms of trade. Moreover, insofar as exports predominantly comprise commodities, the general trend towards what has come to be called the 'dematerialisation of production' (that is, a lowering of the natural commodity content in products) suggests the danger of relying on a commodity-based strategy for development.

The Dutch Disease[15]

The significance of gold and other precious metals in South Africa has made it vulnerable to what is called the Dutch Disease, and this has had adverse implications for its manufacturing sector. The Dutch Disease takes the following form. When a country has a natural resource providing a high rent component (such as gold in South Africa), the effect is to raise the exchange rate to a greater level than it would have been in the absence of this natural resource. This reduces the domestic currency receipts of exporting and makes imports more attractive than domestic production. The economic consequence has tended to be a decline in the supply of internationally tradeable commodities (such as manufactures) relative to those of non-tradeables (such as construction and many services).

Countries possessing these natural resources – such as Iran, Nigeria and the UK with oil, and Holland with natural gas – have often experienced difficulty in expanding their manufacturing sectors to reflect their standards of per capita incomes. Thus they display a tendency for incomes to arise from rentier rather than from directly productive activities, and experience great difficulty in maintaining economic growth when the natural resources are depleted (Holland's natural gas) or when its prices fall (Nigeria's oil revenue). However, deindustrialisation is not an inevitable consequence of possessing rich resources since 'the severity [of the Dutch Disease] appears to depend more on the nature of accompanying macroeconomic policy than on the size of the booming primary sector'.[16] Macroeconomic policy in South Africa clearly does not seem to have met the challenge.

AFTER THE END OF APARTHEID: THE CONTEXT FOR POLICY

Specific assumptions will have to be made concerning the political context in which industrial strategy is to be formulated. It is assumed that South Africa will make the transition to a democratic status within a time-horizon of three to ten years so that political barriers to international trade and technology transfer are effectively removed. These assumptions are necessary preconditions for the success of industrial strategy and hence a regeneration of economic growth. It is further assumed that the alleviation of unemployment and the eradication of poverty will be at the top of the policy agenda of a democratic government. To some extent these objectives represent a conflict with the expansion of the manufacturing sector, since both compete for scarce resources. But industrial policy can be fashioned in a variety of ways: these will have differential impacts on employment and income distribution, and this will obviously have to be borne in mind. So, too, will the problem of time preference. There is a long history in policy design (specifically in relation to the choice of techniques) focusing on the time horizon of employment generation. It has generally been argued that there is a direct trade-off between employment- and output-maximisation, and between the growth of output and employment over time, although recent evidence suggests that this choice may be significantly less acute than has previously been believed.[17] Nevertheless, there is no doubt that it remains one of the most crucial dilemmas in industrial policy formulation in economies experiencing high unemployment.

There is increasing evidence that the basis of competitive production is changing from one in which standardised products were produced on a mass-production scale utilising special-purpose machinery, to one in which more flexible patterns of production prevail. It is now common to refer to this transition as that between Fordism and post-Fordism. There are three major characteristics to this transition. First, the pattern of competitive production is becoming increasingly systemic in nature, involving a more organic perspective on enterprise behaviour, closer links between firms, a more organic labour process in which the hierarchical patterns of Fordism and Taylorism[18] are no longer effective, and the introduction of flexible automation. Second, the basis of competition is changing from one in which cost minimisation was the major objective function in production to that in which innovation and product characteristics dominate. Third, whereas labour in Fordism was seen as a cost which had to be minimised, in post-Fordism its role is that of a resource whose potential has to be maximised.

These changes in the nature of capitalism have important implications for policy formulation in three areas.

Import-Substituting Industrialisation

The adoption of flexible perspectives in production is associated with a reorientation of production control towards small-batch production and (at the more advanced stages) the adoption of flexible automation technologies. In many sectors this leads to a change in the scaling factors inherent in manufacturing, and this is often associated with a reduction in optimum plant size.[19]

This reduction in optimal production has important implications for ISI. Briefly, a recounting of the past experience of ISI has been that high rates of growth are possible in the early stages in which import replacement occurs, particularly in consumer goods production. But once this process of replacement draws to an end, production expansion is limited by market growth; in addition, ISI in the intermediate- and capital-goods sectors is more difficult to achieve for technological reasons. But perhaps most significantly, many sectors have experienced minimum plant sizes which make production for small domestic markets inherently high-cost.

In all these respects the transition to post-Fordist production presents new opportunities for ISI. This is not to suggest that all constraints towards ISI are thus removed, partly because there are some sectors in which the scale economies of plants are increasing, and partly because reduced plant size is often associated with enlarged firm size. Thus, it is in the context of these complex and sometimes contradictory changes in the scaling parameters of production, that policies towards ISI need to be constructed.

Changing Principles of International Location

The increase in economies of scale during Fordism reached its high point in the late 1970s and early 1980s when 'best practice' was defined by the price-competitive production of 'world products' in 'world factories'. This was one of the factors which provided the opportunity for export-oriented industrialisation (EOI) in many of the NICs, since their cheap labour (especially women employed in export processing zones) was a major source of comparative advantage. Yet it was not only the NICs which saw a growth in the trade/GDP ratio; the level of international integration grew in many parts of the global industrial economy.[20]

Post-Fordism seems to be associated with significant alterations in the global siting of production because of changes in both the politics and the economics of location. The unevenness of transition to post-Fordism is reflected in growing differentials in productivity growth rates and trade imbalances, and this has spilled over into neo-protectionism. Increasingly, market access is becoming conditional upon locating production (at least the assembly stages) in final markets. More significantly for South Africa, there appears to be a growing trend towards the regionalisation of market access, and there are signs that a series of regional trading blocs (Europe, North America and the Pacific Zone) will come to be the major organising principles for global trade. This represents a substantial change from the international integration of the New International Division of Labour (NIDL) of Fordism.

These changes in the politics of location are being mirrored by a transition in the economics of location. The 'world-factory' is no longer so viable in the context of declining plant size; flexibility often requires closeness to final markets; and just-in-time production not only requires proximity between suppliers and assemblers but is also biased against the large inventories implicit in the NIDL.

In the context of both these sets of changes, the optimum site of production has begun to move from that of least cost (often involving low efficiency wages) to that of closeness to the final market. The maturation of flexible automation technologies means that the costs of producing near the final market are falling, hence reinforcing further this change in optimal location patterns.

The Changing Social Basis of Industrialisation[21]

Fordist production was based upon the increasing division of labour and the polarisation of skills. The social framework for this labour process involved domination at the point of production. In turn this required a broader pattern of social and political regulation, and complex (and divergent) paths emerged in which work was defined and executed. The major common thread to these varying social regimes was the conception of labour as a cost of production which had to be minimised.

These patterns of social and political regulation are proving to be inimical to the transition to post-Fordist production. Countries such as the UK, which have attempted to reinvigorate industrial growth through an intensification of old Fordist mentalities, have found themselves falling further behind the leading edge of competition. Thus the task facing all countries in the transition to post-Fordism is to construct a new social and political coalition in which production can occur. It is one in which manufacturing occurs through a different 'form of consent' to Fordism,[22] and one in which labour is seen as a resource rather than a cost of production.

IMPLICATIONS FOR INDUSTRIAL POLICY

Constructing a feasible and realistic industrial policy in the context of post-apartheid South Africa is not so much a technical exercise (although there are important technical insights which can be absorbed into policy and which will be considered below) but more clearly lies in the domain of politics. Nevertheless it is possible to identify four major issues which will influence industrial policy. These are the role of the enabling State, the structure of ownership, the development of indigenous technological capability, and opportunities in external markets. These should not be seen as constituting industrial policy itself which will have to be more specific and fashioned on the particular circumstances in which South Africa makes the transition to a democratic status. This discussion of industrial strategy is set in the framework of a global economy in transition from Fordism to post-Fordism, an analysis of the contemporary world economy which is of course contentious.

Industrial Strategy and the Enabling State

One of the more significant developments in recent economic policy in South Africa is the push towards privatisation. A particularly striking feature of post-1945 South African economic history is the capturing of the State in 1948 by Afrikaner nationalists who implemented a concerted strategy in which the State machinery was utilised to allow for the development of (urban) Afrikaner industrial, service and financial capital. Although there are always dangers in teleological explanations of policy, it is clear that the current drive towards privatisation in South Africa represents an attempt by capital (now heavily penetrated by Afrikaner interests) to destroy the enabling State so that black capital will be unable to rise to a situation of dominance in the future.

Hence the first and most important task in the formulation of industrial policy in South Africa is to renew the legitimisation of the State as a key actor in economic activity. This need not necessarily be interpreted as a call for the complete socialisation of ownership, since there is now extensive rethinking of whether socialised policies necessarily require State ownership of productive resources. But at the very least it does require the creation of an enabling State. And almost certainly, given the current structure of ownership in South Africa, it will involve State ownership (or the direction of investment) in key sectors.

But what minimum functions ought this enabling State to perform? First, the major lesson emerging from the experience of successful industrialising countries is the necessity of developing some form of targeting mechanism. The State may either largely assume the responsibility for this task or, as is currently the case in Japan, construct a coalition of industry and State expertise to direct investable resources in a targeted manner. This includes investment in human resource development as well as in technological capabilities. In identifying activities which are targeted for specialisation, it may make more sense to focus on the *filière* than on traditional economic sectors.[23]

Other key functions of State intervention would be to facilitate the networking of small firms and their links with external markets and technology, and construct a relationship between labour and those responsible for innovation and accumulation which allows the full potential of human resources to be tapped. This requires intervention and guidance at a number of levels – with respect to the shop-floor, the structure of industrial relations and the general framework in which 'work' is defined and executed. There is widespread evidence that substantial competitive improvements arise in the transition from Fordist to post-Fordist forms of organisation so that it can be shown to management that the old labour process is no longer the best practice. Moreover, there is also evidence of market imperfections in the adoption of these post-Fordist forms of organisation so that the State has a positive role to play in their diffusion.

The Structure of Ownership

South Africa is a heavily monopolised country, perhaps more so than any other sizeable economy. There are some countries – notably Japan and South Korea – in which rapid industrial growth has been associated with large-scale firms. But even then (and especially in Japan), there has always been a high degree of competition. More pertinently, there are many other countries, and regions within countries, in which small-scale firms have dominated industrial growth. The most prominent examples are Taiwan (whose industrial success exceeds that of Korea), Hong Kong, Singapore and the Emilia Romagnia region of Italy. Moreover, these countries have proved successful in many sectors in which South Africa holds a potential comparative advantage, notably in textiles/garments, leather products and metal- and wood-working.[24] In all of these countries, small firms have proved to be adept at establishing a niche in the market and at flexible specialisation, often facilitated by an enabling State.

In addition to the demonstrated success of countries following the small-enterprise path to industrial development, there are three reasons why such a strategy might prove to be appropriate in an independent South Africa. First, and possibly most important, agglomerations of economic power are most often accompanied by concentration of political power, so a necessary condition for political democratisation and the development of civil society is that the ownership of resources be deconcentrated. Second, there is considerable evidence from many parts of the world that small firms are more likely to utilise labour-intensive and appropriate technologies than large firms. These are important considerations given South Africa's problems of extensive unemployment and its shortage of foreign exchange. And third, it is

clear from the experience of many countries that micro-sized enterprises (that is, those employing less than ten people) hold considerable
potential. Their attractions are not confined to the mopping-up of
employment; they often provide cheap wage goods and services. The
successful facilitation of this sector cannot be pursued independently
of policy towards the large-scale and formal sectors.

Indigenous Technological Capabilities (ITC)

Insights into South Africa's industrial potential can be gained from the
experience of Australia and New Zealand on the one hand, and Korea
and Japan on the other. Australia's exports have largely comprised
agricultural and primary commodities; New Zealand has tended to
specialise in agricultural exports. For many years both countries
followed a policy of protected industrialisation within which markets
were allowed to allocate resources. For most of the post-war period
this policy allowed for high per capita incomes, mostly underwritten by
commodity and agricultual exports. But during the past decade their
terms of trade fell. Moreover, policies designed to enforce manufacturing competitiveness by widening exposure to global competition have
not worked as intended. Instead they have led to significant deindustrialisation, and both countries have begun to experience a fall in real
per capita incomes.

By contrast, Korea and Japan have followed paths of protected
industrialisation within which market forces alone were not allowed to
allocate resources. Instead systematic attempts were made to enhance
ITC.[25] Thus, when their currencies were forcibly revalued during the
late 1980s, both economies were able to sustain high rates of growth
and per capita incomes. Unlike Australia and New Zealand, their
growth rates have not been weakened by the introduction of more
liberalised trade regimes, but this follows many decades of protected
investment in the aquisition of ITC.

There are three major lessons which can be learned from the
experience of these various countries, as well as from that of other
developing countries.[26] First, market imperfections are acute in
technological generation, development and diffusion. An enabling
State is a necessary condition for ITC to occur. Second, the development of ITC is costly. It requires the sustained investment of
significant resources. Finally, it is not possible to buy leading-edge
capabilities. ITC arises as a consequence of an accretion of investments, and takes time.

Policies towards the development of ITC in South Africa thus require careful targeting. They will have to take cognisance of existing specialisation and it is thus very likely that activities associated with the mining sector will play a prominent role, even if they find final expression at the end of the production *filière*, that is, in the production of final goods (including capital goods) rather than minerals. It is here that it is possible to observe a link between policies towards regional integration and the development of ITC. Although South Africa is considerably more industrially advanced than its regional neighbours, there are many respects in which operating and market conditions are similar. This provides potential for the partial targeting of ITC on meeting regional needs.[27] There are dynamic factors in this strategy which bode well for future economic growth, with increased ITC feeding through into greater market penetration and hence the further growth of ITC.

Targeting IAC Markets for Manufactured Exports

A transition to democratic status is likely to provide South Africa with significant opportunities in its international economic relations. In part this will arise from its ability to obtain freer access – and often at lower prices – to imported technology and commodities. But more significantly, it will provide benefits of market access for exports, particularly of manufactures.

Currently there are a variety of mechanisms whereby LDCs gain preferential access to IAC markets. Insofar as SSA is concerned, the most significant of these are the Lomé Convention and GATT's Generalised System of Preferences (GSP) which provides access to North America. Despite the widely-known limitations of these preferential systems (including the growth of sectoral trade limitations such as the Multifibres Agreement), many LDCs have been able to nurture their export capabilities by exporting to IAC markets.

Because of sanctions, South Africa has not been able to take advantage of this opportunity. The relocation by firms to the 'home-lands' has provided access to cheaper labour but not to final markets. Consequently, in recent years a number of South African firms have begun to utilise SADCC production bases, especially in Lesotho and Swaziland. The extent of this relocation, however, is small. Other firms have attempted to gain market access by establishing 'front' companies in Switzerland and Israel, but this route provides only limited opportunity and is aimed at sanctions-busting rather than market access under preferential schemes.[28]

Thus, transition to democratic status is likely to occur in circumstances which offer ambiguous opportunities for South African manufactured exports to the IACs: market access is likely to become generally more restricted although there will be discrete opportunities for preferential access from LDCs. However limited these opportunities are likely to be, they will almost certainly be greater than those which are available currently to South African producers.

POST-APARTHEID SOUTH AFRICA AND REGIONAL TRADE

Transition to democratic rule in South Africa is thus likely to be associated with opportunities in IAC markets. Yet, partly because of the growing regionalisation of trade, partly because of renewed regional growth as apartheid's destabilisation ceases, and partly because South Africa will be able to gain access to sub-Saharan markets previously blocked, it is in regional markets that the major external trade opportunities are to be found.

The degree of South Africa's access to SADCC markets is unlikely to grow significantly, so the growth of exports to these markets will be more significantly affected by the rate of overall growth in this regional submarket. This potential should not be overlooked since South Africa's destabilisation of the surrounding countries has had an enormous opportunity cost on economic growth. The cessation of this destabilisation will thus provide opportunities for regional growth and specialisation. Given the repair of old transport networks and the creation of new infrastructure, however, South African exporters will inevitably face more intense competition.

It is in the wider region – the PTA – that the major new regional trade opportunities are to be found. The PTA now comprises 19 member states, some of which have overlapping membership with SADCC. The PTA only really began to function after 1986 when the first tariff-reduction schedules were published and the currency clearing house began operating. Intra-regional trade is encouraged by reducing tariffs for around 600 commodities which have been defined as having developmental significance. Its distinctive feature has been that these tariff concessions have been limited to firms which are more than 50 per cent locally owned in order to prevent the 'wars of incentives' which have characterised LDC integration in the past, and to ensure that the efficiency benefits of integration are not appropriated by TNCs.

So far the degree of trade integration has been limited and, indeed, the 1980s might more readily be described as an era of regional trade disintegration rather than trade integration. This judgement would, however, be premature, since the PTA has now put in place a series of infrastructural changes which lay the basis for significant intra-regional trade growth. Moreover, the climate within which trade will take place will almost certainly force a greater degree of regional integration. It is instructive here to quote the views of Jacques Pelletier, the French Minister of Cooperation and Development concerning the impact of European integration on SSA:

> The changes in Europe are, to my mind, a model. Without a regional market, sub-Saharan Africa will not be organised on a sufficient scale to become an area of economic growth. Without political co-ordination in all areas – fiscal, social and legal – it will remain too weak in the face of the large groupings which are being established everywhere in the world.[29]

Thus SSA will almost certainly experience a growth in intra-regional trade, if only because of the problems of obtaining access to global markets. But what will South Africa's role be in this regional market? In the PTA the two economies with the largest manufacturing sectors – Kenya and Zimbabwe – command the lion's share of intra-regional trade. Two related problems are thus posed for South African participation. First, to the extent that its manufacturing sector is significantly more developed than those of any other regional econo-mies, it is likely that it will rise rapidly to dominance in this market. This dominance will have to be treated with considerable care in South Africa's policies towards the region. Second, gaining membership to the PTA will not be without difficulty, since exporters in some of the existing PTA member states (notably Zimbabwe) are likely to find themselves displaced by South Africa competition.

These two observations suggest that South Africa's accession to the PTA (or any other sub-regional grouping) is unlikely to be accom-panied by a direct increase in net hard-currency earnings, particularly as PTA member states (with the possible exception of Mauritius) are all facing severe balance-of-payments problems of their own. Benefits to membership will therefore have to be found elsewhere. One possible benefit arises from trade diversion, in that South Africa will be able to obtain inputs from the region which were previously imported from hard-currency countries. On a related front, member states may be prepared to fall into trade deficit with South Africa since, with the abolition of sanctions, they will be able to obtain cheaper imports than those previously obtained from other countries. A second potential benefit arising to South Africa from regional integration is that of trade creation where, although imports and exports may be in balance, this will be at a higher level of trade, thus enhancing both production and goods availability within South Africa. A third benefit which may emerge is that arising from greater capacity utilisation in South African manufacturing as a consequence of access to larger markets.[30] This may enable enterprises to travel down the cost curve of production, and perhaps even make possible investments which would otherwise not have been feasible. And, finally, regional integration is likely to be associated with a growth of indigenous technological capability – this subject has been treated in greater detail earlier.

CONCLUSIONS

This chapter represents a first attempt to grapple with the problems of industrial policy formulation in South Africa. It is much less concerned with the specific directions which this strategy might take than in charting the evolution of South Africa's manufacturing sector and in identifying the starting point for the formulation of an effective strategy. Only when this has been done will it be possible to think through some of the implications for wider regional trade growth.

In general, it would seem that the prospects for South Africa's manufacturing future are not bleak. The major policy issue which will have to be confronted concerns the balance of resources to be allocated to welfare expenditure and industrial development. To some extent this dilemma will be reduced because there are some respects in which labour-intensive industrial growth aimed at the production of cheap wage-goods and simple capital-goods may be simultaneously growth- and welfare- maximising. But there will inevitably be limits to this virtuous circle of development and growth.

A clear conclusion emerging from the experience of other industrialising economies is that the grasping of industrial opportunities will not arise through market allocation of resources. As many countries – including those in Europe and North America – have found, market failure is endemic in industrial restructuring, especially in relation to the acquisition of ITC. Related to this is the legacy of concentrated asset ownership in South African industry, and it is thus inconceivable that a democratic State intent upon grasping industrial and developmental opportunities can allow current ownership structures to remain unchanged. (This may or may not involve State ownership of productive assets.) Most significantly, this conclusion is based on efficiency considerations rather than on normative policy objectives.

The recent experience of the more dynamic economies has shown that the maximisation of economic growth is associated with more democratic social relations than those which have previously represented best practice in capitalism. But the adoption of these new patterns of social relations is difficult, since they represent significant changes with past practice. Hence, a purely technicist approach to industrial policy – aiming to maximise economic growth 'without political interference' – is simply not feasible. Political legitimacy, which includes shop-floor politics as well as the wider sphere of social relations, is a thus a key component of any realistic and efficient industrial strategy.

Once these social relations are in place (allowing for the renewal of industrial growth in South Africa) and the regional destabilisation by South Africa is brought to an end, there seem to be positive prospects for an expansion of regional trade. Some of this might occur within the SADCC region, although here it is not so much that post-apartheid South Africa will obtain a greater degree of access to local markets, but rather that local markets will grow more rapidly after the end of apartheid. However, the more attractive long-term prospects lie in an expansion of trade with the non-SADCC PTA economies, facilitated by a generalised global increase in regional integration.

Notes

Thanks are due to Laurence Harris for his comments on an earlier draft.

1. The phrase 'industrial strategy' is used loosely in this paper to refer predominantly to a strategy for the manufacturing sector. Technically, 'industry' includes not only manufacturing but also utilities, construction and mining. Whilst there are important positive linkages between these various subsectors, there are also areas of conflict, as is pointed out below

in respect to the impact of the 'Dutch Disease' on the manufacturing sector.

2. For details of this change in trend, see A. Maddison, *Phases of Capitalist Development*, Oxford University Press, 1982, and *World Development Report 1989*, Washington, DC: World Bank 1989.

3. D. Kaplan, 'The South African Capital Goods Sector: Prospects for Development in the Post-Apartheid Era'. Paper presented to Lausanne Colloquium on the Future of the South African Economy, 1989.

4. The concept of efficiency wages incorporates both wage rates and labour productivity.

5. Marx characterises this shift in production structure from a period of manufacture (in which profitability depends upon the ability to intensify work) to that of 'machinofacture' (in which machinery and technical change are the prime sources of productivity growth).

6. Because of my concern with economic issues, I will not consider possibly the most significant type of sanction – that directed against military hardware. The loss by South Africa of aerial supremacy in Angola was possibly the single most important factor leading to the independence of Namibia. But other types of military sanctions have also played a key role in removing the military option for the defence of white rule.

7. Commonwealth Committee of Foreign Ministers on Southern Africa, *South Africa: The Sanctions Report*, London: Penguin, 1989.

8. For a discussion of the use of alternative mechanisms for the transfer of technology to South Africa – and for case studies of the automobile and telecommunications sectors – see R. Kaplinsky, *Sanctions Against South Africa*. Report Prepared for United Nations Centre on Transnational Corporations, New York: UNCTC, 1989.

9. It is of interest that these countries also reduced their exports to South Africa by $0.88 billion in the same period. See Commonwealth Committee, op.cit., p 39.

10. D. Kaplan, 'Machinery and Industry: The Causes and Consequences of Constrained Development of the South African Machine Tool Industry', *Social Dynamics*, 13 (1), 1987.

11. For a discussion of South Africa's relative capabilities in the capital goods sector, see D. Kaplan, 'The South African . . .', op.cit. For electronics and automobiles, see A. Black, 'The Crisis in South African Manufacturing Growth: Issues and Alternatives for the Future', paper presented to Lausanne Colloquium on the Future of the South African Economy, 1989, and J. Chataway, 'The South African Motor Industry' and 'The South African Electronics Industry', in J. Hanlon (ed.), *South Africa: The Sanctions Report*, London: James Currey, 1989.

12. Cited in Commonwealth Committee, op.cit.

13. World Bank, op.cit.

14. S.R. Lewis, 'Economics and Apartheid: The Impact of South Africa's Economic Policies', Institute of Development Studies, University of Sussex, 1987.

15. For a review of the literature on the Dutch Disease, see D.E. Evans, *Comparative Advantage and Growth: Trade and Development in Theory and Practice*, Hemel Hempstead: Harvester/Wheatsheaf, 1989.

16. J. Riedel, 'Economic Development in East Asia: Doing What Comes Naturally?', in H. Hughes (ed.), *Achieving Industrialization in East Asia*, Cambridge University Press, 1988.

17. R. Kaplinsky, *The Economies of Small*, London: Intermediate Technology Press, 1990.

18. Taylorism refers to a form of work organisation in which conception is divorced from execution, direct labour is distinct from indirect labour (which is responsible for tasks such as maintenance, quality-control and machine set-up) and where information predominantly flows down from management to production workers.

19. The reduction in optimum plant size is not the case in all sectors, however. Moreover, it does not necessarily imply a reduction in firm economies of scale. See Kaplinsky, *The Economies of Small*, op.cit., for a discussion of these changing principles of scale.

20. As Maddison, op.cit., shows, the growth in trade between 1953–73 (a period which he refers to as 'The Golden Age') was almost double that of the growth in output.

21. For a more detailed discussion of these trends, see R. Kaplinsky, 'The Role of Labour in South Africa's Economic Future', paper presented to Lausanne Colloquium on the Future of the South African Economy, 1989, and for an application to South Africa, see R. Kaplinsky, 'Restructuring the Capitalist Labour Process: Some Lessons from the Car Industry', *Cambridge Journal of Economics*, 12 (1988).

22. For a description of the 'consent' implicit in Fordism, see the description for the USA in M. Burawoy, *Manufacturing Consent: Changes in the Labor Process under Monopoly Capitalism*, University of Chicago Press, 1979 and the extension of this discussion to the Third World in J. Henderson and R. Cohen, 'Capital and the Work Ethic', *Monthly Review*, November 1979.

23. The concept of the *filière* (literally meaning 'thread') is drawn from French planning. It refers to a chain of linkages which enable a particular sector to become competitive. For example, a sectoral target might be wooden furniture; a *filière* approach would identify the need to also upgrade forestry, sawmilling, woodstocking and marketing.

24. These are not of course the only sectors in which South Africa possesses potential comparative advantage – mining equipment and food processing are others.

25. For a summary of Japan's experience, see C. Freeman, *Technology Policy and Economic Performance*, London: Frances Pinter, 1988.

26. For a discussion of recent Brazilian experience, see T. Hewitt and H. Schmitz. 'Learning to Raise Infants: A Case Study in Industrial Policy', in C. Colclough and J. Manor (eds), *States or Markets: Neo-Liberalism and the Development Debate*, Oxford University Press (forthcoming).

27. An example of this similarity arises with respect to the role of maize flour in diets. Through most of the region the staple food is ground maize flour – few other parts of the world show similar specialisation. The milling of this maize is therefore subject to the development of regional ITC, not only in respect to medium- and large-scale roller mills, but also in relation to the small-scale hammer mills used by peasant farmers. Similar

opportunities arise in respect to oil-seed pressing and the provision of small-scale energy in rural areas.

28. The use of false country-of-origin documents only materially assists sanctions-busting trade, rather than that occurring under preferential agreements. This is because most of these preferential agreements have local-content provisions.

29. 'Africa ill-prepared for challenge from Europe', *Financial Times*, London, 16 November, 1989.

30. These scaling factors occur despite the general tendency towards decreasing economies of scale observed above. Scale economies are thus generated, albeit at lower levels than might have previously been thought necessary.

7 Economic Development in the SADCC Countries

Anthony M. Hawkins

SADCC entered its second decade knowing that far-reaching policy decisions on its future structure could not be long delayed. From its inception in 1980, it has been portrayed as an institution established to foster economic development, but the rationale for its creation has always been more political than economic, and this, together with its emphasis on coordination rather than integration, has given rise to a 'debating society' image, unlikely to be appropriate to the challenges of the 1990s. Its economic performance has been a disappointment, not just because of environmental variables beyond its control but also due to inappropriate policies and weak economic management, and there is little evidence to suggest that its existence has cushioned, let alone reversed, economic decline in the region.

SADCC IN A CHANGING REGIONAL AND GLOBAL ENVIRONMENT

Towards the end of the 1980s the environment changed radically, both within SADCC and internationally. Key assumptions held dear by African policymakers in the 1970s were discarded, while pressure for policy change within SADCC mounted. At the start of the 1990s, the validity of the assumptions underlying SADCC's creation is increasingly questioned as developments in the region suggest that a more hospitable geo-political environment is replacing the confrontation, destabilisation and sanctions of the 1980s.

Much is made of SADCC's achievements in transport integration, food security and agricultural research, but if SADCC were to be disbanded tomorrow, it would leave behind little of any permanence other than a large new secretariat building in Gaborone. Most of the regional infrastructure attributed to SADCC pre-dates it and would have been developed and rehabilitated even without SADCC. Its main contribution has been as an umbrella organisation through which

Western and multilateral donors channel aid to member states – aid justified by the region's poverty and underdevelopment, by its suffering at the hands of South African destabilisation and, above all, by Western desires to promote a group of viable economies as a counterweight to South Africa. Western nations such as Britain, West Germany, the United States and Japan, which oppose 'punitive' sanctions against Pretoria, have championed aid to SADCC as their contribution to the future stability of the region.

After a decade and more of falling living standards, SADCC states have adopted new economic strategies, some of which flatly contradict the objectives outlined in SADCC's initial policy document. Increasingly it is recognised that the 'reduction of external dependence' is both meaningless and fruitless. The active pursuit of foreign private investment, the shift towards outward orientation in economic policy, and the recognition of the region's aid dependence, reflect this realisation. The rhetoric of the past decade, economic as well as political, has been overtaken by events, notably the changed political mood and promises of reform within South Africa itself, Namibian independence, the advent of peace talks in both Angola and Mozambique, and open intra-regional co-operation with Pretoria. All these point to a new realism within SADCC and a partial rejection of the original objective of reducing economic dependence on South Africa.

Potentially even more important is the changed international environment. Southern Africa is no longer a playground for superpower rivalry, while the collapse of communism in Eastern Europe, and the Soviet Union's preoccupation with its own internal and regional problems, have radically altered the strategic climate within the region. At the same time, international interest in Africa continues to ebb. Transnational companies, many of which have burned their fingers in Africa, see potentially exciting new investment and market opportunities opening up in Eastern Europe. The reluctance of foreign firms to invest in sub-Saharan Africa is readily explained by comparisons between the rapidly growing Asian economies and their sluggish African counterparts.

Meanwhile, the demands on the aid community are growing as political and economic change gathers pace in Eastern Europe. There will be less capital, official as well as private, to go around. For SADCC, which has basked in the support of Western aid donors to the tune of $2.6 billion annually, the adverse implications could be far-reaching. With the commercial banks reducing their African exposure, and the probability of stagnant or declining aid and private investment inflows, SADCC will have to give priority to the mobilisation of domestic capital resources.

The evolution of large trading blocs in the world raises problems and challenges for SADCC too. Like the European Community, it must grapple with the problems of broadening and deepening. The scope for broadening would seem to be limited; the issue of deepening is much more challenging, especially in light of the region's past unhappy experience with economic integration.

ECONOMIC PERFORMANCE, 1980-8

The 1980s were a decade of stagnation for SADCC. Given the poverty of the data base and the difficulties of making cross-border comparisons and aggregations, the figures in Table 7.1 must be treated with caution. Nonetheless, the message is clear. In the region as a whole, economic expansion failed to match the rate of population growth, and per capita incomes fell 13 per cent between 1980-8. In only two of the nine member states, Botswana and Swaziland, were growth targets achieved, while in a third, Zimbabwe, real incomes showed a modest gain.

Table 7.1   Economic growth

Country	GDP (US $ million.)		Growth rate % p.a.
	1980	1988	
Angola	6 307	6 112	−0.40
Botswana	903	1 805	9.10
Lesotho	382	433	1.55
Malawi	1 250	1 455	1.90
Mozambique	2 414	2 045	−2.00
Swaziland	542	746	4.10
Tanzania	5 138	6 011	2.30
Zambia	3 885	4 082	0.60
Zimbabwe	5 355	7 021	3.40
Total	26 176	29 710	1.50
Population	60 million	77.7 million	3.30
Income per head	$436	$383	−1.60

Source: World Bank *National Economic Indicators* and national estimates (for 1988).

While the region's weak growth performance is partly explained by environmental variables – severe drought in some years and floods in others, war and civil unrest in Angola and Mozambique with severe spillover effects on Malawi, Zimbabwe and Zambia, depressed primary product prices (until 1987), sluggish world economic growth during the first half of the decade, and South African destabilisation – most member governments acknowledge that inappropriate economic policies were also to blame. As a result, all SADCC states except Botswana and Swaziland are either committed to IMF/World Bank structural adjustment programmes or have introduced their own market-oriented reforms.

The Changing Policy Environment

Economic policy change in Southern Africa had its origins in five main influences, four of them external:

1. The impact of Reaganomics and Thatcherism on donor strategies, reflected in the diversion of aid funds towards the private sector and the support for privatisation programmes.
2. The 'demonstration effect' of the success of the Asian rim economies during the 1970s and 1980s.
3. The growing importance of conditional, policy-based lending by the international agencies and some of the leading Western donor nations.
4. The impact on policymakers in Africa of the economic reforms adopted first in China, and the subsequent collapse of communism and the ideology of the command economy at the end of the 1980s.
5. Recognition by African governments themselves that their dirigiste policies emphasising State planning and ownership and import-substituting industrialisation, had failed to achieve the sustained improvement in living standards that was the central objective of economic strategy.

Agriculture

Agricultural production per capita declined in all SADCC countries between 1980 and 1986–8. For the region as a whole, farm output rose 1.3 per cent annually, which meant that agriculture's share in regional GDP fell marginally and production per head fell 11.5 per cent over the period. Output in Swaziland virtually kept pace with population growth, while in both Zambia and Zimbabwe per capita output fell only slightly, but elsewhere there were steep declines.

Agricultural stagnation has had three main adverse effects on the pattern of economic development in the region. First, because approximately three-quarters of SADCC's population is dependent on agriculture, stagnation in this sector implies static or declining real living standards. Second, agricultural failure has given rise to a high degree of dependence either on food aid or on imported foodstuffs with adverse consequences for the balance of payments. Third, a healthy and expanding farming sector is the *sine qua non* for industrial development since, in the absence of a sound domestic market, manufacturing industry is unlikely to develop.

Manufacturing Industry

Manufacturing industry, which ought to have been a lead sector in the SADCC economy during the 1980s, instead lagged behind. By 1988, industry's share of GDP had fallen to 12 per cent from 13.1 per cent in 1980, while SADCC's share of sub-Saharan Africa's manufacturing-value-added (MVA) fell from 17.5 per cent in the mid-1970s to only 9.3 per cent in 1984.

Industrial stagnation was the consequence both of demand and supply-side influences – international, regional and national. With per capita incomes falling, domestic demand for manufactures weakened while industrial growth was also constrained by severe shortages of foreign exchange and of technical and managerial skills. Very few regional manufacturers – with the exception of Zimbabwean firms – managed to break into export markets, reflecting the acute foreign-currency crisis in the region (excluding BLS) and the lack of complementarity between member states. Industrialists were unable to produce goods that could compete both in quality and price with those available internationally, and manufactures accounted for less than 10 per cent of regional industrial output.

Manufacturing's weak performance during the 1980s is largely explained by industrial stagnation in Angola, Malawi and Zambia, sharply-reduced output in Mozambique and Tanzania, and a slowing of Zimbabwe's industrial growth rate after the initial post-independence boom. In only two countries, Botswana and Lesotho, both starting from a tiny base, did manufacturing expansion exceed population growth. The steep decline in industrial output in Angola and Mozambique was attributable to the exodus of skilled personnel and subsequent closure of factories after the wars of independence, while slower growth in Malawi, Zambia and Zimbabwe reflected the severe foreign-exchange constraint resulting in shortages of imported inputs.

Industrial activity is highly concentrated in Zimbabwe and Zambia, which account for two-thirds of regional manufacturing-value-added in 1988, while six member states contributed 23 per cent and Tanzania the balance of 12 per cent. Concentration has increased during the past 20 years as Zimbabwe's share has grown while those of Angola, Mozambique and Tanzania fell from almost 37 per cent in 1970 to 22 per cent in 1988. Industrial output is highly concentrated also in those subsectors producing lower-technology light manufactures. Only in Zimbabwe, where more than 40 per cent of production represents capital and producer goods, has industrial production moved away from dependence on consumer goods.

Mining

Three SADCC economies – Angola, Botswana and Zambia – are heavily dependent on mining activity. The sector's share of regional GDP (excluding Angola) is estimated at seven per cent, and its strategic importance lies in its export capacity. Mining's share of exports by value is 93 per cent for Zambia, 84 per cent for Botswana, 90 per cent for Angola (almost entirely oil) and more than 40 per cent for Zimbabwe.

Mining activity in the region is heavily dependent on world market conditions, and the decline in output during the 1981–6 period was caused by depressed demand and prices for base minerals. The industry was sustained during this period by rapidly-growing diamond production in Botswana and a steady improvement in the value of gold output in Zimbabwe. Zambia was the chief regional casualty of the depressed world copper market, with output falling from 713 000 tonnes in 1976 and 609 000 tonnes in 1980 to little more than 400 000 tonnes in 1988. Indeed, such was the deterioration of the Zambian mining industry in the first half of the 1980s that it was unable to exploit record prices and buoyant demand conditions in 1988–9.

A feature of the industry is its external dependence. It relies heavily on foreign capital, expertise, supplies and markets. Intra-SADCC trade in minerals is tiny, mainly comprising limited coal and coke exports by Zimbabwe, Mozambique and Zambia, and there would seem to be only limited scope, in the medium term, for substantially increasing the degree of domestic processing and value-added.

In the 1990s, the heavy investment needed in processing activities will have to come from joint ventures between member governments and transnational corporations, possibly with financial assistance from international donors and commercial banks. In the recent past – with a few exceptions – international banks and corporations have been reluctant to undertake major new investment in extractive activities in the SADCC countries, though this may now change with the peace initiatives in the region and the improved outlook for metal prices.

For the immediate future, SADCC states have little choice other than to continue to exploit the export potential of their mines, while at the same time seeking to establish both forward and backward linkages and diversifying their export base to reduce dependence on primary commodities. This imperative is most apparent in Zambia where copper production and exports will fall drastically towards the turn of the century and which at present has no viable alternative export sector. Given the limited life of its mines, copper-processing activities are no solution for Zambia which must instead concentrate on the development of an entirely new export base.

Foreign Trade and the Balance of Payments

After a sharp decline in exports in the first half of the 1980s, SADCC's foreign trade situation improved in 1987–8, reflecting improved commodity prices on world markets. Exports fell 23 per cent from $6.6 billion in 1980 to $5.1 billion in 1986 before recovering strongly to $7.9 billion in 1987. Export volumes suffered as a result of drought, serious transport congestion, and weak world demand and prices for much of the period.

Botswana's exports increased 170 per cent between 1980–8, mainly reflecting rising diamond production and prices, while in Angola they rose by 50 per cent as oil output expanded. Elsewhere, export growth was only modest – less than 10 per cent – while revenues declined sharply in Mozambique, Tanzania and Zambia. The strong recovery in 1987–8 was largely the result of higher copper and oil prices which boosted exports in Angola and Zambia.

In this situation, almost all member states were forced to reduce imports which declined 30 per cent in dollar terms to $5.4 billion in 1986 from $7.7 billion in 1980. Import repression was a major contributory factor accounting for slow economic growth, depressed levels of investment and industrial stagnation. Imports subsequently recovered to $7.7 billion in 1988, but remained below their 1980–1 levels.

Despite import controls, SADCC incurred a trade deficit of $5.2 billion during the 1980–8 period and, when invisible transactions are taken into account, the current account deficit exceeded $14 billion. Capital inflows – foreign borrowings and direct investment – were $8.6 billion, leaving a financing gap of some $5.5 billion to be funded by IMF borrowing of $1.75 billion (58 per cent of which was lent to Zambia), debt relief and rescheduling agreements, the accumulation of arrears and some reduction in reserves.

The regional capital account position deteriorated over the period from a peak inflow of $2.15 billion annually in 1981–2 to net outflows of $250 million a year in 1987–8. This was both a reflection of worldwide trends following the Mexican debt crisis in 1982 and a measure of the region's relative unpopularity with foreign investors. Indeed, the bulk of the direct investment inflows were for oil and mining ventures in two countries – Angola and Botswana.

Whatever its origins, SADCC's poor export record during the 1980s was probably the major factor responsible for the region's disappointing economic performance. Exports, accounting for 25 per cent of regional GDP in 1980, were traditionally the engine of economic growth, and their subsequent decline to 17 per cent of GDP in 1986 robbed the regional economies of their main growth stimulus. By 1988 the export ratio had recovered to 26.5 per cent.

The problem was compounded by the resultant strategy of import compression which, in light of the high import-intensity of growth and especially of investment, became a major supply-side constraint on economic activity. Import ratios fell from almost 30 per cent of GDP at the start of the period to 18.5 per cent in 1986 before recovering to 26 per cent in 1988. Two longer-term adverse effects of import constraint are often overlooked: the deterioration in the quality of the capital stock, including the transport and energy infrastructure, and the degree to which technological advance and efficient investment in human capital are undermined by a prolonged period of foreign-exchange scarcity.

Inward investment was minimal. If Angola and Botswana are excluded, foreign investment inflows totalled a mere $130 million during the eight-year period, while Zimbabwe registered an outflow of more than $200 million. Botswana received $600 million in new foreign capital, reflecting its pragmatic and outward-oriented economic strategy, while such were the attractions of oil investment in

Angola that it attracted capital inflows of $300 million despite the joint deterrents of war and Marxist economics.

According to a SADCC study, the region's debt burden has reached crisis proportions, having virtually doubled between 1980–8 (Table 7.2). Angola, Mozambique, Tanzania and Zambia are the largest debtors, accounting for almost 80 per cent of the regional total. The study, using 1986 statistics, classifies Mozambique, Tanzania and Zambia as debt-distressed countries where debt-service obligations exceed 30 per cent of foreign-exchange earnings.

Table 7.2   Debt-service ratios, 1980 and 1988 (percentage of exports of goods and services)

Country	1980	1988
Angola	21.4	40.0
Botswana	1.9	4.8
Lesotho	11.0	38.1
Malawi	27.7	31.8
Mozambique	51.6	540.0
Swaziland	4.0	6.4
Tanzania	23.5	23.6
Zambia	25.3	13.7*
Zimbabwe	3.8	29.0

* = actual
Source: World Bank *Debt Tables* 1989–90 and IMF.

The seriousness of the foreign-debt situation is underscored by the build-up of arrears of unpaid debt. Four member countries rescheduled their foreign debt during the 1980s – Malawi, Mozambique, Tanzania and Zambia – while Angola undertook a partial restructuring of its external debt in 1989. During the early 1990s at least two countries – Mozambique and Zambia – and possibly also Malawi and Angola, will need substantial debt-relief, while the severe regional debt-service burden will continue to constrain imports for the rest of the century with ominous ramifications for growth, investment and industrialisation.

SADCC received net aid inflows of $18.7 billion between 1981–7 with Tanzania (27 per cent), Zambia (16.7 per cent), Zimbabwe (14 per cent) and Mozambique (13 per cent) together accounting for nearly three-quarters of the total. Net aid flows exceeded nine per cent of regional GDP during the this period – a further indication of the degree of external dependence.

Economic Policy

The impact of national economic policies in member countries has tended to be dwarfed by international and regional influences or by exogenous variables such as drought or civil unrest. Furthermore, policy initiatives are constrained in most member countries by infrastructural and market deficiencies. Given underdeveloped money and capital markets, there is little scope for active monetary and interest-rate policies in the SADCC region, though Zimbabwe is an exception to this. Member states resorted to direct controls to curb inflation but, with lax monetary policies and negative real interest rates, all countries experienced double-digit inflation.

Fiscal policy has been largely restricted to the financing activity of matching funding with public-sector expenditures rather than seeking to influence domestic demand or the pattern of incentives in the economy. Most countries incurred substantial fiscal deficits, partly attributable to high levels of spending on security, refugee programmes and social services, especially education.

In contrast, exchange-rate policy has been an active variable, especially since 1985, and every country except Angola devalued its currency substantially during the 1980s. In the nine years to 1989, a weighted index of SADCC currencies (using 1980 GDP weights) fell more than 70 per cent against the US dollar.

If market-based economic policies had limited application – and limited appeal – direct controls were very much in vogue. All countries except Botswana operated tight exchange and import controls, though both Tanzania and Malawi have sought to liberalise these controls. Price controls, regulations governing the employment of expatriates and the dismissal of workers, and minimum wage regulations, were also the norm, though in the late 1980s several countries, including Malawi, Mozambique, Tanzania and Zambia, lifted the control on some prices.

THE SADCC PROGRAMME OF ACTION: AN ASSESSMENT

The Lusaka Declaration in April 1980 identified four broad development objectives for SADCC.[1] These were: the reduction of economic dependence, particularly, but not only, on South Africa; the forging of links to create genuine and equitable regional integration; the mobilisation of resources to promote the implementation of national, interstate and regional policies; and concerted action to secure international cooperation within the framework of the strategy for economic liberation.

Much of the rhetoric of the Lusaka Declaration has been overtaken by events. The nine countries which in 1980 complained of policies that 'enriched externally-based firms and hampered national planning', have since actively courted private foreign direct investment. Similarly, the statement that 'Our trade arrangements should not be at the mercy of free market forces or foreign companies' has also been at least partially overturned by the economic reforms of the late 1980s.

The Lusaka Declaration emphasised production rather than trade, focusing on *regional* import replacement as the vehicle for reducing external dependence. Whilst member states rejected economic integration, they were not opposed to preferential arrangements designed to increase regional trade; however such trade should be 'planned so as to flow from and serve the needs of coordinated national and regional development . . . coordination of production is perhaps what distinguishes SADCC from previous experiments of economic cooperation among African countries'.[2]

The SADCC Programme of Action identified transport and communications as the key to regional cooperation while also listing food and agriculture, energy, manpower development, industry, mining and tourism as priority areas. By 1989 a total of 617 projects had been identified, but it is impossible to assess performance because, as noted earlier, many projects classified as SADCC operations would have gone ahead without the organisation's intervention.

Dependence

Ten years after its establishment, SADCC has made little progress towards reduced external dependence but this is hardly surprising given the nature of the development process. Dependency reduction is a mirage in backward economies whose development necessitates infusions of capital, technology, expertise and foreign exchange. The accumulation of external debt, the increased dependence on expatriate personnel throughout the region, and the extent to which economic growth has depended on foreign trade (mainly with the OECD countries but also with South Africa) and on investment and aid inflows from abroad, underscores the crucial importance of international economic links with the industrialised North.

Indeed, the whole strategy of reduced dependence was ill-conceived, based on the assumption that 'planned trading flows' within regional markets would replace imports from OECD countries and, of course, from South Africa itself. It ignored the crucial role of foreign trade as the engine of economic growth, and the region's inability to supply imports of sophisticated capital equipment.

'Planned trade' failed to get off the ground, partly because the necessary basic complementarities didn't exist, but also because the region's economic decline for much of the 1980s implied narrow and restricted trading opportunities. This failure is illustrated by the fact that intra-SADCC trade, calculated in Special Drawing Rights, declined by 30 per cent from a peak of SDRs 548 million in 1981 (4.7 per cent of total trade) to SDRs 384 million (4.2 per cent) in 1986.

The fact that cross-border business by visitors – not captured in the official trade statistics – is large and growing, reflects scope for increased intra-regional trade once import and exchange controls are dismantled. Such unofficial trade is particularly marked between Zambia and Zimbabwe and, to a lesser extent, between Zimbabwe and Botswana.

Not only did intra-SADCC trade decline over the period but the figures suggest some increase in the concentration that the Lusaka Declaration had been so anxious to avoid. Thus Zimbabwe's share of regional exports rose from 44.5 per cent in 1982 to 48.5 per cent during the 1983–6 period, while Zambia's share rose from 13 per cent to 16.4 per cent and Malawi's from 8.3 per cent to 10.9 per cent. While Zimbabwe's growing dominance of intra-regional trade was only to be expected given its far greater industrial sophistication and its estimated 41 per cent share of regional manufacturing value-added in 1988, it demonstrates both the failure of the planned trade policies enunciated in 1980 and the enormity of the challenge during the next decade if further increased polarisation is to be avoided.

South African Links

Little progress was made, too, in reducing dependence on South Africa. Here also, data deficiencies and the deliberate efforts of all parties involved to avoid publicising economic links, make objective assessment impossible.

Trade
Despite the above, it is clear that trade with South Africa far exceeds
intra-SADCC transactions. SADCC's imports from South Africa were
estimated at $5.5 billion during the 1983–6 period as against exports of
less than $1 billion.[3] This trade flow – in both directions – exceeded
intra-SADCC transactions by more than three-to-one. The bulk of the
trade is carried out by members of the SACU – Botswana, Lesotho
and Swaziland – estimated at more than $4 billion during the four-year
period. Zimbabwe's imports were put at $900 million and exports at
$555 million, while Zambian and Malawian trade exceeded $800
million, almost entirely imports.[4]

Although there is some evidence of a decline in trade dependence on
South Africa between 1982 and 1986 (the proportion of SADCC's
exports to South Africa fell from seven per cent of the total to 4.5 per
cent, while South Africa's share of total SADCC imports declined
from 30 per cent to 24 per cent),[5] these official figures almost certainly
understate the level of trade. In 1989 the South Africa Trade
Commission in Harare issued 16 000 visas monthly to Zimbabweans
to visit South Africa. More than 15 000 of these were estimated to be
'shoppers' rather than genuine tourists or business visitors. On the
basis of this, it was estimated that unrecorded imports from South
Africa exceeded Z$100 million annually (or more than 20 per cent of
the official import figure). Such cross-border business also occurs,
though on a smaller scale, in the BLS countries, Mozambique, Malawi
and Zambia.

Whatever the magnitude of the trade links between SADCC and
South Africa, their strategic importance is undeniable. Manufactured
goods make up 95 per cent of imports in most SADCC countries, the
sole exception being Zimbabwe. South Africa routinely supplies more
than a third of the region's imports of manufactures, with a significantly larger market share in spares, intermediate goods and some
capital equipment, notably for the mining industry in Zambia and
Zimbabwe.

Only one member state – Zimbabwe – has any capability in the
producer and capital-goods field. Its capital-goods exports to partner
states have been increasing at South Africa's expense though, as yet,
the impact has been only marginal. Because of its scale-economy and
experience-effect advantages, the South African capital-goods sector
has a very real competitive edge over Zimbabwean manufacturers. Its
transport costs are lower, it has advantages, too, over foreign suppliers
in respect of delivery times and after-sales service, and its management

has far greater and more intimate knowledge of market opportunities in the region. In the past, too, South African firms have had the benefit of closer technological links with Western industrialised countries, while South African banks are able to provide medium-term supplier credits to buyers on a scale not possible for other SADCC firms.

Transport
Traffic statistics validate the conclusions drawn from trade statistics. The Southern African Transport and Communications Commission estimated in 1988 that 62 per cent of SADCC's total export trade by volume was with countries outside Africa, while 16 per cent went to South Africa, 15 per cent to partner states within SADCC and the balance of seven per cent to other African countries (Table 7.3).

Table 7.3   Distribution of SADCC traffic volumes, 1986–7

	SADCC	SA	Other Africa	Overseas	Total
Exports (tonnes '000)	788	801	371	3 155	5 115
Imports (tonnes '000)	790	3 170	37	5 014	9 011
Exports (%)	15	16	7	62	100
Imports (%)	9	35	–	56	100

Source: SATCC Preliminary Traffic Forecasts, 1988.

Transport dependence is inevitable given the imbalance between exports of 801 000 tonnes to, and imports of nearly 3.2 million tonnes from, South Africa. The BLS countries accounted for 57 per cent of the total traffic with South Africa, while Zimbabwe with 1.2 million tonnes in 1986–7 was responsible for 31 per cent, Malawi for 5.5 per cent and Zambia for 3.7 per cent. Botswana and Lesotho use South African ports exclusively for their exports, while Swaziland typically ships half of its overseas exports via South Africa.

However, SADCC ports handled 81 per cent of all its trade in 1987. Transport dependence on South Africa is therefore seen to have two main elements, namely:

1. The four million tonnes of traffic representing exports to and imports from the south. This is trade dependence rather than transport dependence.

2. The 1.9 million tonnes of overseas traffic transiting South Africa and using its ports, which is less than 20 per cent of the total.

Taken together, these two elements mean that nearly 5.9 million tonnes of SADCC traffic – about 40 per cent of the total – utilised the South African transport system in 1987. Dependency reduction has occurred in two main respects. First, the switch of Zambian copper traffic from South African ports to Dar-es-Salaam and Beira, though the Tazara Railway has increasingly been unable to handle the volume of copper traffic on offer due to shortages of locomotives and wagons, while the inability of the National Railways of Zimbabwe to cope could mean that Zambia will be forced to return to utilising the lengthier and more costly South African route in 1990.

Secondly, Zimbabwe's usage of Beira has increased substantially, reducing dependence on the South African ports from more than 90 per cent in the mid-1980s to 50 per cent by 1987–8, of which 30 percentage points represented trade with South Africa and the balance overseas trade using South African ports.

Further dependency reduction will be achieved through rehabilitation work at Dar-es-Salaam and Beira which would increase the capacity at these two ports, as well as by the reopening and rehabilitation of the Maputo line, and also of the Lobito corridor later in the decade. Eventually only Botswana and Lesotho should rely on the South African system for transit traffic (although in theory Botswana could, if all routes were operational, switch to Maputo which is a distance of 1030 km from Gaborone as against 1170 km for Durban).

However, as the 1989 experience on the Tazara railway and on the National Railways of Zimbabwe has shown, there is far more to dependency reduction than rehabilitation of the ports and railways. Tazara's traffic volumes in 1988–9 were lower than in 1978 due to foreign-exchange-related shortages of spares, locomotives and wagons – a situation exacerbated by the scarcity of technical skills on the system. Similarly, the NRZ has been unable to handle the traffic on offer, including Zambian copper diverted from Tazara, because more than half its locomotive fleet was off the rails due to shortages of imported spares. As a result, the NRZ has on several occasions been forced to hire locomotives from South Africa.

Energy
Dependence in this field is not a major issue except in the BLS countries and Mozambique. The latter should be a major exporter

of electricity to South Africa; instead, with the sabotage of the transmission line from Cahora Bassa, it is a net importer, relying on South Africa for 54 per cent of its total electricity in 1986.[6] It has also been forced to import coal from South Africa because of the deterioration of its railway system. The BLS countries are almost totally dependent on South Africa for petroleum supplies and an important proportion of their electricity. Zimbabwe also obtains an unspecified proportion of its petroleum imports either from, or via, South Africa.

SADCC IN THE 1990S

SADCC has been bound together more by the cement of anti-South African sentiment than economic common interest. In the 1990s, important decisions will have to be taken concerning the *broadening* and the *deepening* of the organisation. Indeed, membership has already been broadened through the accession of Namibia in 1990.

Deepening

This will be far more controversial. Deepening decisions imply a willingness on the part of member states to cede autonomy to a supranational body. To date, SADCC has set its face firmly against such an evolutionary path, but so long as this attitude persists, it will be unable to exploit the full benefits of economic integration.[7] Furthermore, as the South African threat recedes and new political relationships develop, so SADCC's political *raison d'être* will fall away, making deepening imperative if the organisation is to exploit its full potential.

Not only does deepening involve highly technical issues – witness the controversy within the European Community over such matters as the Exchange Rate Mechanism – but also intensely political and emotive issues, such as those implicit in the proposed EC Social Charter, and the European debate between 'Centrists' and 'Federalists'. There are four reasons for believing that deepening will be a very slow process in SADCC.

1. There is little to suggest that member states accept the need for such deepening, though there is evidence that the SADCC

Secretariat itself, in a manner not dissimilar to that of the EC Commission in Brussels, is increasingly anxious to take the lead in deepening the union.

2. Member-state reluctance reflects their determination to keep firm control over the levers of economic power. There is no constituency within SADCC for the surrender of this far-reaching economic authority to a supranational body.

3. As already noted, deepening is a technically complex process. One clear lesson of recent economic performance in SADCC is that the quality of economic leadership and management has been inadequate. The scarcity of managerial, administrative and technical skills is a powerful argument – in the eyes of national politicians – against the creation of what they would see as additional bureaucracies at regional level. There are doubts over the region's capacity to provide the extra economic expertise necessary for successful integration.

4. Divergent policies and different levels of economic development will make it very difficult to achieve policy consensus although an element of policy convergence is evident in the structural adjustment programmes increasingly adopted by member states.

The starting place for a deepening strategy must be coherence in trade, investment and industrial policies, which are closely inter-related. At present, there is no agreed SADCC policy on any one of these issues.

Trade

On the trade side, the existence of three different regional groupings – SADCC itself, the SACU and the Preferential Trade Area (PTA) – forced SADCC to adopt a largely passive role. Trade has been seen as a 'PTA responsibility' though the creation of the Trade and Industry Sector Coordinating Unit in Tanzania in 1985 heightened the latent tensions between the two organisations. For its part, the PTA's proposed investment bank was interpreted within SADCC as an infringement of its regional functions.

Economic development is synonymous with industrialisation, and industrial growth is a necessary, though not a sufficient, condition for economic development. The failure of industrial growth to take off in the SADCC region is attributable to environmental factors, inappropriate policies and the severe foreign-exchange constraint, but it can also be traced to the region's lacklustre trade performance. An essential counterpart of a coherent industrial strategy is a compatible international trading regime. It is this challenge that SADCC must tackle in the 1990s.

Continued reliance on the import-substitution strategy advocated in the Lusaka Declaration raises the spectre of a trade-diverting union in which member states are forced to purchase high-cost, low-quality, SADCC-manufactured items rather than being able to obtain their requirements in markets with the most advantageous price-quality ratio. In such a union, regional welfare losses outweigh the national welfare gains and, as a result, threaten its political survival. This was one of the lessons of economic integration in East Africa and the Federation.

The gains from trade creation in developing-country unions are held to be dynamic in character. The earlier the customs union or free trade area is established, the less the disruption and the greater the gains from intra-regional trade. The short-run gains from freer regional trade are unlikely to be substantial where intra-regional trade is tiny, as in SADCC, or where the bulk of the region's exports are primary products to industrialised economies while imports are sophisticated capital, intermediate and consumer items in which the region has little productive capability.

Regional trade growth is stifled by the import and exchange controls necessitated by the foreign-exchange crisis in most SADCC countries. The quickest way to expand intra-regional trade is not by reducing tariffs or creating regional preferences but by expanding non-regional exports, thereby generating additional foreign exchange to finance expanded intra-regional trade. It is only when this stage has been reached that regional trade preferences would make a positive contribution.

The fastest-growth economies in the 1980s were not those within large trading blocs like the EC or Comecon but those of East Asia which succeeded in penetrating large markets both within and outside the major trading blocs. The belief that SADCC states can grow rapidly on the strength of intra-regional trade – within SADCC or the PTA – is unrealistic given market size.

Furthermore, the experience of intra-regional trading schemes – such as the PTA Clearing House – suggests that trade deflection is encouraged with member states preferring to sell outside the area for hard currency rather than to regional importers for payment in regional currencies. Net balances are settled in hard currency but Zambia's insistence that it be paid in US dollars for its electricity exports to Zimbabwe underscores this rational preference for extra-regional sales.

The positive arguments focus on rationalisation, scale economies, the avoidance of duplication and, of course, the exploitation of regional competitive advantage. There is a strong case for integrating sooner rather than later, thereby avoiding the creation of inefficient capacity as in the Latin American car assembly industry in the 1950s. But the evolution of SADCC into a customs union or free trade area is inhibited by the existence of rival organisations as well as by cumulative causation fears flowing from diverging levels of economic development within the region. The disparities between industry in Lesotho or Swaziland, on one side, and Zimbabwe or even Zambia, on the other, are just too great for the establishment of a free-trade area.

Investment and Industrialisation
The linkages with investment and industrialisation arise from the attempts of member states to foster foreign investment in industry via competitive investment codes. The harmonisation of such codes – consistent with a deepening strategy – would exacerbate cumulative causation pressures, favouring Zimbabwe ahead of Zambia, and so forth.

The inescapable conclusion in respect of trade and industry is that some form of centralisation will be necessary whereby new investments are allocated to those countries which, in a free- market regime, would be starved of investment other than of a location-specific nature (mining, oil) or where large consumer markets justify a new factory. At the same time, history demonstrates that such centralisation is unlikely to succeed unless it is *broadly* in line with market realities.

It will not be possible to achieve a level playing field, nor, in fact, would that be desirable given differing levels of development among members. In the medium term – which means for the foreseeable future – a second-best option of market-oriented intervention is indicated, always providing that comparative-advantage disparities between rival locations are not too great. In the longer term, investment in infrastructure and training, designed to level out the regional playing field, would be needed. Clearly, this poses enormous problems for the more industrialised leaders, faced with the requirement to mark time while the laggards catch up.

The Post-Apartheid Situation

It has been argued above that dependency reduction in the general sense was based on a misplaced enthusiasm for import-substituting industrialisation, while in the South African context its rationale was essentially political. While this latter position can be expected to change with majority rule, SADCC states may still find undue reliance on South Africa an irksome burden in the next century, though for economic rather than political reasons.

Much will depend on two broad sets of factors: first, SADCC's progress, in the run-up to the post-apartheid era, towards closer economic ties, that is, how far and how fast those ties are deepened; and second, the cost-benefit calculations of the different SADCC members as and when majority rule is achieved in South Africa. The greater the progress towards closer economic ties prior to the post-apartheid era, the more likely is it that SADCC will survive that far-reaching change in regional geopolitics. At present there are few structures serving to bind the member states together.

In the 1990s SADCC must strengthen its regional strategy, not so much because its members want to create the solid structure prior to the post-apartheid era in order to ward off alternative forms of regional cooperation, but more because of a general acceptance that the gains from membership hitherto have fallen well short of expectations. The debate over regional industrial policy illustrates the conflict between the loose-knit coordinating approach favoured hitherto and a more activist drive towards regional policy harmonisation – the case for deepening the organisation.

Broadening

An economic integration scenario whereby South Africa joins SADCC after majority rule is the most ambitious, but also the least likely, post-liberation configuration. The tiny SADCC states – BLS and Namibia – are already in a customs union with South Africa, but Angola and Tanzania, with no economic ties with South Africa, would gain little, while Malawi, Mozambique and Zambia would find it extremely difficult to establish viable manufacturing enterprises within a barrier-free union that included South Africa. Because of its relatively sophisticated industrial and financial sectors, Zimbabwe would have the greatest difficulty in becoming part of an economic integration scheme. While Zimbabwe might have the capacity to compete successfully at consumer goods level, its embryonic capital and producer goods sector would face annihilation unless substantially protected from South African competition. Furthermore, both the country's ability to move upmarket into the production of more sophisticated industrial goods and the deepening of its financial and services sectors would be threatened if full-scale integration with South Africa was undertaken.

These considerations do not rule out closer economic cooperation between SADCC and South Africa, or South Africa joining SADCC, but there are very real limitations to economic integration where one of partners is both much larger – in terms of population and GNP – and much more developed. Cumulative causation would apply, and it is difficult to envisage such an arrangement being acceptable to the larger current members of SADCC – Angola, Tanzania, Zambia and Zimbabwe. It would be less of an economic integration than a core state – South Africa – surrounded by satellites.

On the ground of size disparity alone, economic integration is therefore ruled out, except for the SACU. For those SADCC states that do not seek integration with South Africa, there are two main options:

1. Expanding SADCC's present membership, possibly to include Zaire, Uganda and Kenya, in an effort to establish a regional counterweight to South Africa.
2. Retaining the existing SADCC membership, but seeking a *modus vivendi* with South Africa in the form of sectoral coordination – especially in transport, energy, and possibly also tourism. This second option would sit well with SADCC's present strategy of coordination, while not precluding trading links with South Africa, though these would have to be limited to arrangements that protected the infant industries and infant sectors within SADCC itself.

Significance of Capital Flows

South Africa has long been a major foreign investor in the region, and its firms are represented in most SADCC economies, excluding Angola and Tanzania. In Zimbabwe an estimated 25–30 per cent of the privately-owned capital stock is South African though there has been a significant degree of disinvestment since 1985.[8]

The Bank of Botswana estimates that 40 per cent of registered industrial enterprises are owned by South Africans, and substantially higher ratios apply in both Lesotho and Swaziland. In Zambia, South Africa owns key mining engineering firms and dominates the freight and forwarding business throughout the region.[9]

In a post-apartheid situation cross-border investment is likely to decline, at least initially, since there would be no sanctions-breaking motivation for setting up front companies in Botswana and Swaziland, though depending on how SADCC's trade strategy evolves, there could well be a tariff-penetration motive for such investment. Immediately after a resolution of the apartheid crisis, South African firms are likely to be preoccupied with refurbishing and extending their domestic operations in what is likely to be an intensely competitive economy. Given the neglect of the infrastructure and the diversion of funds into non-productive security operations, there will also be a substantial backlog of public sector and parastatal domestic investment to be made good.

In this situation, a medium-term decline in cross-border investment is probable, but once the first phase of economic restructuring in South Africa itself has been completed, South African-based transnational corporations can be expected to resume their traditional policy of market penetration by way of direct foreign investment. How welcome such foreign investment will be will depend on the trade and investment regime adopted by SADCC states in the post-apartheid environment.

If SADCC were to respond to post-apartheid South African foreign economic policy by retreating behind tariff and non-tariff barriers to repel South African imports, barrier-jumping investment might result, though opposition to this from existing SADCC firms, including State-owned enterprises, could shut out foreign investment from South Africa.

Much will depend on the success or otherwise of SADCC policies designed to increase investment, output and growth during the 1990s. If these are seen to be working well, there will be a reluctance to allow South African investors to regain the dominance of some SADCC markets enjoyed in the 1960s and 1970s.

On the other hand, South African capital could well assume a far more dominant role than in the past. This is because far-reaching political and economic changes in Eastern Europe and the Soviet Union could change very substantially the pattern of international capital flows. If this does occur, the region – including South Africa itself – could be starved of foreign investment inflows, thereby underlining the importance of increased domestic savings generation of regional as distinct from international foreign investment flows. The longer sanctions persist, the greater will be the post-liberation demand for capital in South Africa itself. In such a scenario, the role not just of

South African capital but of the Johannesburg capital market assumes even greater importance.

Capital Market Development

Until recently, SADCC states have paid little attention to capital market development. Zimbabwe's ability to finance a budget deficit, averaging 10 per cent of GDP with little resort to both foreign borrowing or bank-created credit, underlines the value of an active and sophisticated capital market. Botswana has now established a stock market to widen the range of financial instruments available in its capital-surplus economy.

The Johannesburg capital market ranks ahead of those in several OECD countries in terms of activity, breadth and sophistication. In a regional common market, with free capital movement across national borders, it would act as a magnet drawing savings away from SADCC states, which would not be desirable, though such an advanced stage of economic integration would be unlikely to be reached until well into the twenty-first century.

A more positive scenario would be if the Johannesburg market were to act as a regional capital market where SADCC entities, private and public sector, could raise risk capital. As a transitional stage, a variation on the Rhodesian model of the 1950s and 1960s, whereby foreign companies were listed and traded on the Salisbury Stock Exchange, could be established, thereby building confidence amongst small and institutional investors within SADCC and creating the climate for domestic flotations and listings.

Recent economic research in developing countries emphasises the crucial role of domestic capital markets in financing investment and, in the 1990s, SADCC will have to increase its activities in the field of stimulating first national, and subsequently regional, capital market institutions.

Development Strategy

Developing economies have followed divergent paths in the past 30 years. At one extreme are the dynamic, newly industrialising, economies (mainly in Asia) while at the other are the retrogressing economies of sub-Saharan Africa. These divergent patterns are closely linked to domestic policy regimes, with the successful economies being those which achieved high investment ratios as well as appropriate and stable incentive systems, and which were able to exploit strong market demand in OECD economies.[10]

The SADCC economies need a combination of:

- externally-generated capital inflows to reverse the long-run trend of economic decline;
- increased levels of domestic savings and investment, especially since the probability is that the external capital flows will either fall well short of what is required (given the likelihood of a diversion of foreign investment to Asia and Eastern Europe) or take the form of debt relief and reduction rather than new inflows of funds;
- increased emphasis on agricultural self-sufficiency in those economies – Angola, Zambia, Mozambique and Tanzania – where the potential exists to raise food production and reduce food imports, thereby de-emphasising the regional role of food security;
- the development of new export sectors and products reflecting the region's competitive advantage in labour-intensive manufactured goods, base metals, gold and agricultural exports (tobacco, beef, cotton, coffee, cashews and so on);
- renewed emphasis on manpower development, especially in the vocational, technical, financial and managerial fields;
- reduced public-sector deficits, and increased emphasis on domestic savings generation and efficient investment through the development of indigenous capital and money markets;
- a broad-based strategy of import liberalisation designed to gradually increase the region's import capacity.

While none of these policy priorities can be said to be ideologically determined, the general strategic thrust is toward a more market-influenced economic structure. SADCC's experience during the 1980s highlights the dangers of excessive State intervention and of circumscribing, and even undermining, private enterprise activity. The imperatives in the 1990s include opening up economies, lifting price, interest and exchange rate controls, and liberalising existing regulations, thereby giving the enterprise sector, whether under private or public ownership, the room and resources it needs to generate output, exports and employment.

The immediate challenge for SADCC is to cement the existing relationship in preparation for the second stage of regional restructuring after the attainment of majority rule in South Africa. Clearly, convergence *is* a major problem. It doesn't and won't exist during the

1990s which means that a laissez-faire integration is out of the question. The pitfall SADCC must avoid is that of special arrangements that may have political, but no economic, logic.

Investment projects will have to be shared out to hold the organisation together by ensuring that there is a more equitable distribution of benefits. The danger is that a sharing-out process could undermine the growth prospects of the more advanced member states, sapping the organisation's economic vitality. A top-down dirigiste approach will work no better at regional than at national level unless integration follows market signals.

SADCC will have to attempt to deepen its activities. A number of possibilities exist:

Tourism
At present there is negligible cooperation in this field but substantial gains could be achieved at little political cost. There are scale economy and rationalisation benefits in tourism promotion, the organising of tours and the creation of a regional airline. It is time to market SADCC, or parts of it, as a single tourist area.

Education, Training and Research
Some, very modest, progress has been made already but the existing programmes need to be urgently extended and broadened, with particular attention paid to technical, vocational, administrative and managerial training.

Market Research and Project Identification
The statistical base is extremely weak, and it is virtually impossible to obtain reliable SADCC-wide statistics. In part this is the consequence of weak statistical services at national level, but even where national statistics are available, there is no attempt to compile and publish them on a regional basis. This would not be a costly exercise and could be handled by the private-sector Business Council secretariat.

Investment Promotion
This is closely linked to the previous item on market research and project identification. It is also a task better handled by the Business Councils than by the public sector.

Investment Code Harmonisation
This is a very divisive issue and is best handled concurrently with the development of trade and industry strategy.

Trade
This must be the top priority for the 1990s. It requires a rationalisation of existing organisations (SACU and the PTA); the gradual reduction of non-tariff and tariff barriers within SADCC; the establishment, over time, of a common external tariff; the adoption of a regional export promotion strategy; agreement on investment code harmonisation; and the sharing out of new industrial projects. Such a programme would have to be undertaken by stages over a prolonged period, but the sooner a start is made, the less the likelihood of disruption of existing productive capacity.

Capital Market Development
Desirable though this may be, it is a technically complicated process. Ultimately, it implies harmonisation of fiscal, monetary and exchange-rate policies.

An Exchange-rate Union
This exists already in the form of the Common Monetary Area. There are obvious problems in extending it, but the smallest states (Lesotho, Swaziland and Namibia) may find that the benefits of exchange-rate harmonisation exceed the costs of trying to operate autonomous currencies.

CONCLUSION

Balanced development and reduced dependence have been described as SADCC's two guiding principles. Neither has been achieved. Ten years on, it can legitimately be argued that the whole concept of reduced dependence was misplaced, while development, and not just balanced development, has proved elusive.

Assuming that SADCC does deepen its union during the 1990s, the stage will be set for very controversial and divisive negotiations over the restructuring of regional economic inter-relationships in the twenty-first century, though the timing and nature of this process will be governed by the speed and character of political and constitutional change within South Africa itself.

At the start of the 1990s the region is in the throes of ideological ferment. Apartheid is collapsing while African governments search for a new philosophy not just to replace the discredited dogma of central planning and State intervention but also the criticism that regional unity will not outlast the demise of apartheid.

Notes

1. SADCC, *Macro-Economic Survey 1986,* pp.1–2.
2. Ibid., p.2.
3. Ibid., p.228.
4. Ibid.
5. Ibid.
6. Ibid., p.73.
7. For detailed discussion of the different types of integration, see Maasdorp's chapter in this volume.
8. SADCC, op.cit., p.229.
9. Ibid., p.230.
10. See Robert Lynn and F. Desmond McCarthy, *Recent Economic Performance of Developing Countries,* Policy Planning and Research Working Papers, WPS 228, Washington: World Bank, 1989.

8 Trade Relations in Southern Africa – Changes Ahead?

Gavin Maasdorp

Economic relations between South Africa and the rest of the region have been influenced by two factors: (i) a fear of South African dominance, and (ii) apartheid.

The first is not unusual in regions where there is a hegemonic economic power. One may cite periodic Canadian resentment against the United States, the feelings of smaller West African countries against Nigeria, and South-East Asian fear of Japan as examples. The second, however, has made normal diplomatic relations within the region impossible. These two factors have been important in the formation of SADCC, which is concerned about the extent of perceived 'dependence' on South Africa in the fields of trade, transport and employment, and with various political problems stemming from Pretoria's race policies. Now that there seems to be a good chance of the ending of apartheid, the readmission of South Africa to good standing in the international community and the normalisation of its diplomatic relations, the old SADCC vs South Africa stance of the 1980s should be changed early in the 1990s.

The intention in this chapter is to explore the main strands of future South Africa/regional relations in terms of institutional arrangements concerned primarily with trade. Transport is omitted, principally because the use by most SADCC countries of the South African transport network for their overseas trade is artificial and should be overcome if political stability can be restored throughout the region. In such circumstances, shippers would be able to decide on the most efficient routing of their consignments without regard to political or security issues. Other infrastructural fields such as energy are also omitted because of space limitations.

REGIONAL ECONOMIC HEGEMONY

South Africa is the economic giant of the region (Table 1.1), inter alia enjoying a significant balance-of-payments surplus in its transactions with SADCC countries. In 1984, for example, the trade surplus alone amounted to US $1.3 billion.[1] Official statistics, however, under-estimate this surplus because they do not include the large volume of cross-border trade by visitors, especially between Zimbabwe and South Africa (see Chapter 7).

The effect of the presence of one powerful economy in a weak economic region is controversial; does it lead (through 'spillover' or 'spread' effects) to an uplifting of other economies in the region, or does the core–periphery relationship operate, by which the more-developed core economy drains resources from the less-developed periphery? These opposing theories were much debated between the 1950s and the 1970s, but need to be reassessed in the light of recent developments in the international trading system.

One clear lesson from 40 years of development economics surely is that it is macroeconomic policies and management which are the crucial determinants of a country's progress. Hence, if the hegemonic power in a region adopts macroeconomic policies which retard growth, and a smaller country adopts policies conducive to growth, there is no ipso facto reason why the core–periphery effect should operate. If all the countries (core and peripheral) adopt growth-orientated policies, the core–periphery effect could also be weakened. Thus, for example, there is evidence of growing regional interdependence in East and South-East Asia with Japan, the core country, increasing its imports from the rest of the region.[2] In fact, it was the demonstration effect of Japan's spectacular economic recovery after 1945 which influenced policies in the newly industrialised countries (NICs) of Korea, Taiwan, Hong Kong and Singapore as well as in the other countries of the ASEAN grouping. Moreover, it is the transfer of Japanese capital, technology, management and kno-whow which has led to increased production in these countries and to their transformation into economic powerhouses. This is the only region of the Third World which has succeeded in industrialising.[3] It has become competitive in exports through 'hard work, high savings and investment, a premium on technology-oriented education and an open rein to private sector initiative',[4] to which one might add sensible government intervention.

The only part of Africa in which a similar process appears possible is Southern Africa. Is not the role of South Africa similar to that of Japan in East and South-East Asia, and would the effect not be even more emphatic if both South Africa and Zimbabwe were to set the example? There is no other part of Africa with the sophisticated capital markets, financial institutions and manufacturing sectors of these two countries. Their role – and particularly that of South Africa – as regional stabilisers (attracting foreign private investment, reducing the risk rating of the region, and so forth), therefore, appears a critical one. Nevertheless, should these two countries adopt economic policies which do not encourage growth, there is no reason why other countries in the region should not adopt growth-orientated policies – the core need not drag down the periphery. For the region as a whole, however, prospects would appear better if the core were to be attractive. This would increase the competitive ability of the region in a world of growing regional trading blocs and limited investment funds.

Since 1975 economic growth in South Africa has been extremely sluggish. Nowhere is this better illustrated than in employment statistics. The economy has failed to create jobs on a scale sufficient to absorb labour-market entrants and restrict open unemployment to single-digit proportions. In this sense, of course, South Africa is no different from other African countries.

Even under the most favourable circumstances, South Africa will be hard put to meet its own economic challenges. This has important implications for its ability to assist the region, especially with regard to employment, investment and services (such as tourism and education). This brings us to the issue of economic integration and cooperation in Southern Africa, and the future of various regional economic groupings. This is best discussed in the context of the emergence of regional trading blocs elsewhere in the world – what is the appropriate way for Southern Africa to respond?

THE EMERGENCE OF REGIONAL TRADING BLOCS

Recent developments indicate the likely emergence of three large trading blocs in the 1990s. First, the EC is set to become a single market by the end of 1992, and this has prompted several other

European countries to apply for membership of, or to consider some form of closer association with, the EC. Second, the United States and Canada have entered into a free-trade arrangement (which might perhaps be extended to Mexico and parts of the Caribbean). Third, twelve nations have agreed to establish the Asia-Pacific Economic Cooperation Forum (APEC), and this could be extended to include China, Hong Kong and Taiwan. There has been no suggestion, however, that APEC should become a type of economic integration. The US and Canada, interestingly, are members of APEC in addition to having their own free-trade agreement.

It is the concept of 'EC 1992' which has given the impetus to developments in this field. The US, Japan and the EFTA countries in particular are concerned that their products will be less competitive in the EC market, although the EC insists that its organisation will be consistent with a liberalisation of world trade and the requirements of GATT.

Developments in Eastern Europe, with the decline of orthodox central planning and the consequent move towards incorporating the market mechanism, open up scope for a further expansion of European trading arrangements and eventual integration. The EC has stated that it cannot consider any new members until 1993 and, in order to forestall applications from the EFTA countries, has opened talks with EFTA on the formation of an eighteen-nation 'European Economic Area' in terms of which the EFTA countries would have to adopt the 1992 rules of EC but would be consulted on any subsequent new legislation. One vision is of a Europe of concentric circles with the twelve-member EC surrounded by two outer tiers of EFTA and East European associate members. However, since any democratic country in Europe with a market economy is eligible to join the EC, it may be very difficult to turn away Austria, the Nordic countries and those East European countries which successfully manage their transformation to the market system.[5]

It is the transformation of these economies, and their potential attraction to foreign investment from the West (both from aid agencies and the private sector) which has led to much speculation about a diversion of investment funds from unattractive Third World countries and regions (including Southern Africa) to Eastern Europe. It is up to Southern Africa to put its economic and political houses in order if it wishes to prevent this diversion, and one way might be through the presence of efficient regional economic organisations.

ECONOMIC INTEGRATION

It is with the field of trade that international economic relations are mainly concerned. The theory of economic integration provides the analytical framework for trade relations in Southern Africa.

Economic Integration in Theory

The aim of economic integration is to promote trade and economic cooperation among member countries. There are four hierarchical types which are shown schematically in Table 8.1.

Table 8.1   Types of economic integration

	No internal tariff/quota	Common external tariff	Free factor movements	Unified economic policies
Free-trade area	x			
Customs union	x	x		
Common market	x	x	x	
Economic union	x	x	x	x

As the above table implies:

1. A free-trade area involves the removal of quantitative trade restrictions (quotas) and customs tariffs among member countries.
2. In a customs union, the free-trade area conditions are extended to include the adoption of a common external tariff against outside countries.
3. In a common market, the customs union arrangements are extended to include the abolition of all restrictions on the movement of factors of production (capital and labour) among member countries.
4. At the top of the hierarchy is an economic union in which national economic policies, for example monetary and fiscal policies, are harmonised.

Note that the term 'economic integration' is used by economists to denote integration of markets, and should be distinguished from a commonly-used concept of 'planning integration', for example some coordination of development plans, transport projects, and so forth, on a regional basis.[6] In this chapter the term 'economic integration' is used in the economist's sense.

In Southern Africa, only one of these types is represented, namely, a customs union. The Southern African Customs Union (SACU) embraces South Africa, the BLS countries and Namibia, and has antecedents which date back 100 years to 1889.

A view held today among orthodox as well as more radical economists is that there are no particularly strong theoretical arguments in favour of integration. El-Agraa and Jones,[7] Robson,[8] Green[9] and Hughes[10] have criticised the relevance of integration among developing countries and, indeed, the weakness of economic theory underlying integration. For example, Helen Hughes, writing of free-trade areas and customs unions, states:

> While it is still sometimes argued that the problems associated with such arrangements are unique and can be overcome, the evidence suggests that they are inherent.[11]

Green, in his work for SADCC, writes that the 'record suggests . . . that the theory is largely irrelevant to the actual purposes, processes and problems of Third World economic coordination'.[12] He therefore proposes the use of economic coordination to reduce dependence on a particular country or company, and the importance of production-orientated rather than trade-facilitating measures. It is for this reason that Green argued so strongly in favour of establishing SADCC as a loose organisation to encourage economic cooperation rather than as a formal integration arrangement. Ravenhill[13] also finds the SADCC approach preferable.

In general, the history of economic integration has not been a cheerful one. The questions for Southern Africa are: how should it respond to the formation of these regional trading blocs? Is economic integration the answer? What prospects are there for existing economic groupings in the region? In order to answer these questions, we need to consider the conditions necessary for successful economic integration, and this section will perforce have to be more theoretical.

Arguments for economic integration are based on Viner's[14] theory of customs unions which revolves around the relative strengths of trade creation and trade diversion. It argues that economic integration should occur only among countries which are at roughly similar levels of development and, in particular, among those whose protected industries prior to union are competitive. 'Competitive' here means that these countries (call them A and B) are producing similar types of manufactured goods. This competition then leads to trade being created within the union in those goods, but imports from the rest of the world (ROW) in other goods continue so that little or no trade diversion occurs. If, in contrast, the protected industries in A and B prior to union are complementary, but trade is not taking place in their products between A and B, the removal of tariffs will lead to imports of those products being diverted from lower-cost (more efficient) sources in ROW. Efficiency, therefore, will be reduced.

The main problems with economic integration arrangements are:

1. They favour the country (or countries) gaining exports and therefore benefiting from industrial expansion and job creation, and adversely affect those which lose industries.
2. Manufacturing industry tends to polarise in the more industrially advanced country (or countries).
3. Member countries lose their fiscal sovereignty – a major instrument of macroeconomic policy.

In a recent article, however, Wonnacott and Lutz[15] reexamined the traditional theory in the light of present-day trading realities. They believe that the trade diversion argument in particular requires some reassessment. First, integration may lead eventually to economies of scale and consequently to production costs in A and B being roughly equal to, or perhaps even lower than, those in ROW. Second, if it is quotas and not tariffs which in fact provide the major protection in A and B, it is no longer clear that trade diversion reduces efficiency. Third, if A and B are producing complementary goods but are not exchanging them before a union is formed, the reason must be that each can obtain the goods it does not produce itself more cheaply from ROW. But if costs in the union are higher than in ROW, how much of this differential is explained by malaligned exchange rates? If the currencies of A and B are overvalued, goods imported at lower monetary costs from ROW may not necessarily represent the lowest economic (or opportunity) costs.

Despite these insights, Wonnacott and Lutz[16] find from empirical research that economies similar in composition of GDP and structure of manufacturing tend to be one another's best customers. Their conclusion tends to reinforce conventional views that, although economic integration should take place among countries with competitive economies, their economies should have the potential to be complementary. In other words, economic integration should occur among countries which (i) are at similar levels of industrial development, (ii) have competitive industrial sectors, but (iii) have the potential to develop complementary industrial sectors.

Application to Southern Africa

How, then, does Southern Africa rate according to these yardsticks? The countries are not at roughly similar levels of economic development, nor are their economies competitive. The economy of South Africa is by far the most industrially advanced and sophisticated in the region, while that of Zimbabwe is also significantly more developed than the rest. Any form of economic integration would benefit these two countries (but especially South Africa) at the expense of the rest. Thus, the region rates poorly in terms of conventional yardsticks. But this still has to explain two important points.

First, why is it that the SACU, which is marked by such imbalance, has proved so durable and relatively successful? The answer, it seems, must be found in the extreme contrast in economic size between South Africa and the BLS countries.[17] The latter have very small economies (small populations, low per capita incomes, small domestic markets) and hence their potential for import-substituting industrialisation is limited to a narrow range of products only. They consequently have little to lose from South African competition; this disadvantage is more than offset by the fact that whatever industries they do attract would have access to the larger customs union market, as well as by the enhancement and stabilisation factors in the SACU revenue-sharing formula. In contrast, countries in the region with larger populations, and hence greater potential for import-substituting industrialisation, would have more to lose from South African competition and therefore would not find a customs union with South Africa attractive.

Second, why is non-complementarity, that is, competition, regarded in official SADCC reports[18] as a major obstacle to intra-SADCC trade? This view requires both qualification and explanation. First, the qualification. As mentioned above, Zimbabwe is more developed than its SADCC partners. Despite Zimbabwe's dominance (especially in industry) in SADCC, it is nevertheless true that the economies of that grouping of countries are more competitive than are those of the region as a whole, that is, including South Africa. If Zimbabwe is ignored for the moment, the degree of competitiveness within SADCC increases still further. But even then the range of industries is too narrow, for example foodstuffs, beverages, textiles and basic light manufacturing, to provide a solid foundation for economic integration. Second, the explanation, which is that SADCC is *not* an economic integration arrangement and therefore each country can protect its producers from competitors in the other countries. If the economies were complementary and did not produce roughly the same range of commodities, there would be greater scope for trade among them. However a different position would obtain if SADCC were an economic integration arrangement: an individual member then could not protect itself from competition from other members, and hence the most efficient (lowest-cost) producers would gain markets, and trade among members would be created.

If conditions for an all-embracing economic integration in Southern Africa are unfavourable, what can one make of the frequent calls from South African business circles for a 'Southern African Common Market' and from African countries for South Africa to eventually become part of a regional common market? Despite the shaky theoretical foundations for economic integration, the idea still retains considerable appeal among politicians and businessmen (especially those from countries in strong regional positions). Some of the calls appear to be based on the premise that the region ought to get together in the face of the formation of economic blocs elsewhere in the world. Moreover, the term 'economic integration' often is not used in the economist's sense and, where specific calls are made for the formation of a 'common market', it is clear that the speakers are not aware of what a common market actually entails.

Implications for Southern Africa

The prospect of these three trading blocs emerging, together with a predicted growing investment by the West in reformist East European countries, has prompted observers to speculate that other regions might become increasingly marginalised in the world economy. Sub-Saharan Africa in particular is mentioned in this regard: the continent, it seems, has been more or less written off. Its problems – corruption, inefficiency, State interference, mismanagement, poor policies, low productivity, falling per capita incomes and rapid population growth – make its future seem gloomy. If there is one part of sub-Saharan Africa which has the potential to make the grade, however, it is Southern Africa, and this is due in no small measure to the presence of two relatively industrialised economies (South Africa and Zimbabwe), the relatively successful economic performances of countries such as Botswana and Swaziland, and the existence of well-established customs and monetary agreements in the form of SACU and the CMA as well as organisations such as SADCC and the PTA.

Southern African goods might find it increasingly difficult to penetrate the markets of the three world trading blocs, and thus the development of an intra-regional market could become of critical importance. This is not to say that exports to the rest of the world should be downplayed – countries such as the East Asian 'Gang of Four' which have taken the export route have performed markedly better than those which have emphasised import substitution – but it does imply that the regional market should be developed. Southern Africa has a significant population but it is a low-income one, and hence the market is relatively small. The challenge is to develop this market potential, and South Africa's role, it has been argued, is to provide exporters in its neighbouring countries with access to the region's largest market as well as with capital investment for development. How realistic is this argument?

Unquestionably, South Africa has the largest market in the region, but even then it is limited for many goods to no more than perhaps about one-quarter of the population because of inequality in income. The SACU countries aside, if South Africa is to act as a market for the rest of the region, it is important to know what products it can obtain which it does not produce itself, and under what trading arrangements. On the question of South Africa providing the region with capital, South Africa itself has always been highly dependent on flows of direct foreign investment; it would first have to re-establish these flows before it could become a source of capital on any significant scale for the region. True, the Development Bank of Southern Africa and individual companies have invested in some SADCC countries in the last few years, but it is difficult to see post-apartheid South Africa, given its own enormous requirements of capital, being in a position to generate capital for the region.

South Africa has the most sophisticated manufacturing sector in the region; it is the only one which includes a wide range of consumer, producer and capital goods. Competition with the rest of the region's industries is found mainly in basic consumer goods (clothing, textiles, footwear and foodstuffs), light manufacturing and agro-industries. Complementarity occurs in some agricultural products (coffee, tea, cashew nuts), handicrafts and some product differentiation (in terms of style, quality, and so on), but generally South Africa has more to export to the region than it needs to import from them. Zimbabwe, the next most developed industrial economy, also has a significant favourable balance of trade with the SADCC grouping, and South Africa and Zimbabwe together dominate trade in the sub-continent.

One-third of South Africa's manufactured exports, and 20 per cent of non-gold exports, are to African countries. Of the figure for non-gold exports to Africa, the BLS countries accounted for about 55 per cent and the SADCC group as a whole for about 82 per cent in 1985. But Namibia was treated in the statistics as part of South Africa. If account is taken of the fact that Namibia receives 75 per cent of its merchandise imports from South Africa, and Namibia is then included in the SACU, SADCC and Africa figures, it may be calculated that 15 per cent of South Africa's non-gold exports in 1988 went to its SACU partners, 20 per cent to SADCC and 23.5 per cent to Africa as a whole.[19] Even if cognisance is taken of the underestimation of trade, it is clear that South Africa's competitive advantage in Africa is strongest in the southern part of the continent.

Zimbabwe dominates intra-SADCC trade, being involved in 80 per cent of the value of such trade. Of total intra-SADCC trade, one-half is in raw materials and the other half in manufactured and semi-manufactured goods.[20] The growth of intra-SADCC trade is hampered by several factors, principally poor market information, consumer preferences for European and South African goods, foreign exchange shortages in all member countries except BLS, and the requirements of tied aid. Some of these factors also apply to South Africa-SADCC trade, and clearly there is scope for increasing trade flows. But this may be achieved by tackling the constraints, and does not require the establishment of any form of economic integration.

ECONOMIC GROUPINGS

A brief description of the various economic groupings and their overlapping memberships is necessary in order to define future possibilities for integration.

The SACU is the only economic integration arrangement in Southern Africa. It allows duty-free movement of goods in the area comprising South Africa, BLS and Namibia. SADCC is a loose organisation facilitating sectoral and project cooperation but with an increasing emphasis on strengthening trade links among its ten members. Of the SACU countries, BLS and Namibia belong to SADCC. The express purpose of the PTA is to promote trade by gradually breaking down tariff barriers. It is part of an OAU initiative which aims eventually at the formation of a common market for Africa. In other words, the intention is that the PTA will become part of an economic integration arrangement. The total membership is eighteen countries stretching from the Horn of Africa to Lesotho; this includes all SADCC countries except Botswana and Namibia (although the latter is to apply for membership).

A fourth grouping – the CMA – is concerned with monetary, not trade, aspects. It is based on the Tripartite Monetary Agreement of 1986 between South Africa, Lesotho and Swaziland, the terms of which have subsequently been extended on a bilateral basis between each of these three countries and Namibia. It allows free flows of capital and a common capital market. At present there is a common exchange rate; although a member country may change its rate unilaterally, there are certain advantages in having parity. However, monetary integration in the area is not as close as it was under the previous Rand Monetary Area Agreement of 1974 as the smaller countries now have greater autonomy in monetary matters. Prior to 1974 BLS had used South African currency on an informal basis. Botswana opted out of the RMA discussions but continued using the rand until introducing its own currency in 1976.

Conflicting Membership

In a climate of 'normalised' relations, there is no political or economic conflict between membership of the SACU and SADCC as far as BLS and Namibia are concerned. In the past, BLS have at times found their membership of SACU somewhat embarrassing.

In contrast, the obligations stemming from simultaneous membership of the SACU and PTA are difficult to meet because of clauses in both agreements. Member countries of the SACU may not enter into concessionary trade agreements with outside countries unless their partners agree; thus, for example, Swaziland and Lesotho have not been able to grant reciprocal concessions in the PTA because South Africa would not agree to preferential treatment for their imports from PTA countries. On the PTA side, a member country may also belong to another regional organisation provided that the conditions of that membership do not derogate from the provision in the PTA Treaty stipulating most-favoured-nation treatment among members, and this conflicts with membership of any economic integration arrangement. For Lesotho and Swaziland the dilemma was solved by a special Protocol (Annex XII) to the PTA Treaty which allowed them a transition period (later set at five years) in which to phase out gradually the preferences accorded to South Africa under the SACU Agreement.

In December 1988 a further five-year extension was granted. Swaziland's Prime Minister stated that his country and Lesotho had been given a time limit to withdraw from SACU but that Swaziland could not commit itself to doing so: it had to weigh up the 'considerable benefits' from SACU membership against the 'little benefit' thus far from, but 'bright future' of, the PTA.[21] Clearly, it would be *ultra vires* the SACU Agreement for them to impose duties on South African goods. It appears, therefore, that Lesotho, Swaziland and Namibia will by 1993 have to choose either the PTA or SACU. The same decision, presumably, would eventually confront Botswana should it decide to join the PTA.

Future

The next question which needs to be broached relates to the future of these groupings. No conclusions will be reached; rather, questions will be raised which need to be addressed by governments and international organisations. There is no doubt that the emergence of post-apartheid South Africa will open up new possibilities for economic integration and/or cooperation. With apartheid out of the way, the moral objection to associating with South Africa will disappear. Whether the new South African government will regard the country as the natural leader in the region and exert its muscle is another matter.[22] Particular questions will face the BLS countries and Namibia (because of their close historical, ethnic and economic ties with South Africa), SADCC (the *raison d'être* of which will be challenged),[23] and the PTA (with regard to the application for membership by the most powerful African economy).

SACU
It has been argued that it would probably be in the best interests of BLS to be in a common market rather than a customs union with South Africa.[24] This is a higher form of economic integration (see Table 8.1 above) and involves the mobility of all factors of production

including labour. Only two factors stand in the way of the SACU becoming a common market: first, the absence of an agreement on labour mobility, and second, Botswana's non-memebership of the CMA which means that capital is not freely mobile between the rest of the SACU countries and Botswana. Labour mobility could be a crucial point for BLS as it is difficult to envisage how they could create sufficient jobs internally to absorb their rapidly expanding labour forces. In a common market, labour would be able to move permanently to South Africa without the threat of repatriation. The same argument might well apply to Namibia. BLS have had close historical ties to South African labour markets, although this is less true of Namibia. Whether South Africa would welcome an influx of labour is another matter since it has the same problem of job creation. But it seems likely that any South African government would want to retain the long-standing integration with the other four countries unless South Africa perceives membership of the PTA as more important, in which case the SACU would have to be wound up unless the apparent conflict mentioned above can be resolved. Perhaps the PTA countries might be prepared to provide an exception to the most-favoured-nation clause in respect of the SACU countries in order to gain preferential access to the SACU market. But as things stand, the long-term continued co-existence of the SACU and PTA with over-lapping membership seems impossible.

However, winding up the SACU would mean the demise of a successful arrangement and one which, despite certain defects, has been able to ensure the availability of a wide range of high-quality consumer goods even in the most remote rural stores. Some households may not have had the wherewithal to purchase these goods, but the fact is that such stores have a rapid turnover principally because of income flows from urban centres to rural households.[25] The countries of the SACU, in sharp contrast to those in the rest of the region, are short neither of goods nor of foreign exchange. The absence of a foreign-exchange problem is the result partly of the CMA and partly of Botswana's extraordinarily strong foreign-exchange reserves. Despite Botswana having withdrawn from a common currency area, the rand dominates the basket against which the pula is valued, and it is perhaps not impossible that Botswana would be prepared to join the CMA in order to reap the benefits of a higher form of economic integration in a Southern African Common Market (SACM). Since the Agreement which established the CMA allows Swaziland to vary the exchange rate of its currency against the rand, Botswana would not be obliged to realign its currency. Exchange-rate parity could be left to the final stage of economic integration, namely, an economic union.

The SACU has probably also been instrumental in ensuring the same quality of management and service in the commercial sectors of member countries because of the presence of the same retail, wholesale and service enterprises. Standards in these sectors are notably higher in BLS and Namibia than in some other SADCC countries.

Whether an SACM would have scope for expansion is doubtful. The other part of the region most closely tied in with the SACU economies is southern Mozambique which has strong labour, transport, trade and investment (and formerly tourism) links. However, central and northern Mozambique are not oriented towards the SACU region, and Mozambique, with a relatively large population, would find it difficult to achieve its industrial potential in the face of duty-free competition from South Africa. Moreover, South Africa itself would be faced with possible large-scale migration from Mozambique, and this would hardly be politically or economically acceptable. It is for these reasons, too, that an SACM would probably not include Malawi, the other country which has traditionally supplied labour to South Africa.

It is possible, though, that Botswana, Namibia and perhaps even Swaziland might not wish to be in a common market with South Africa. In that case an SACM could embrace South Africa and Lesotho (which is geographically tangential to SADCC but totally surrounded by South Africa) while a customs union could still cover the five countries. It is also possible that Namibia, and perhaps Botswana, might quit the customs union in favour of the SADCC although, perhaps significantly, Botswana has not found it beneficial to join the PTA (its imports are mainly from the SACU while its exports are to overseas countries).

SADCC

A number of issues arise here. First, would SADCC open its membership to South Africa and would South Africa wish to join? Although official statements have made it clear that a 'democratic' South Africa would be welcome provided it adhered to a spirit of cooperation and not dominance, Hanlon perceives that there is 'considerable ambiguity'[26] in these statements. SADCC may not want South Africa as a member – it is aware of dependence on South Africa and the problem of smaller economies unable separately to sustain a viable industrial base. An organisation such as SADCC, therefore, may be necessary in order to provide the ten countries with a power base roughly similar to that of South Africa so that they could bargain as equals, that is, SADCC and South Africa could coordinate development as separate but equal partners rather than South Africa being a (dominant) member of SADCC.

It is difficult to see any economic benefits accruing to South Africa from membership: provided SADCC remains organised along its present lines, it would not seem to make any significant difference to practical day-to-day cooperation on technical and economic matters whether South Africa was admitted to membership or whether cooperation was along the lines of two 'equal' partners in Hanlon's sense. But political benefits might be gained which might justify incurring the annual dues and other expenditure required. If, however, SADCC were to continue to push for reduced trade barriers among members, it could become more attractive to South Africa but the larger SADCC countries might not welcome its inclusion since this would open up their industries to competition from more efficient producers.

As mentioned above, it is possible that the SAC could evolve into a common market. Whatever decision SADCC takes regarding South African membership, and vice versa, the SAC grouping of countries is likely to remain intact (unless South Africa joins the PTA and the conflicting SACU/PTA membership obligations cannot be resolved).

Second, could the present SADCC adopt a form of economic integration? There would appear to be a number of problems. First, BLS and Namibia would have to choose between SACU and SADCC, and would in all likelihood opt for the former. Second, there is the issue of industrial polarisation stemming from Zimbabwean domination. Third, a common market would be ruled out since the free movement of labour would not be acceptable to the receiving countries because of their own problems regarding job creation. Finally, the development of SADCC into an economic integration would not be compatible with overlapping PTA membership (for the same reasons mentioned on p. 143 in connection with SACU). In fact, this is a key point at issue for post-apartheid Southern Africa – how far should the 'region' extend in terms of its economic links, that is, should it embrace the entire PTA membership and include countries such as Zaire and Madagascar as well, or should it be restricted to the present South Africa-SADCC area?

PTA

Post-apartheid South Africa is bound to become a member of the OAU. Now, the PTA is part of a series of regional trading blocs set up under the aegis of the OAU, and it does not seem that any OAU member can be excluded from joining its relevant bloc if it wishes. South Africa might well wish to do so. South African exporters claim that they would gain enormously from membership of the PTA, in the same way that Zimbabwe and Kenya are apparently doing at present. But this might not be welcomed by Zimbabwe and Kenya, and there are likely to be major obstacles in the way of the PTA evolving into an economic integration arrangement if experience elsewhere in the world is anything to go by. Unlike the position in Western Europe where several countries competed for the role of economic leadership and economies contained a substantial degree of competitiveness, the position in Eastern and Southern Africa is so one-sided that the conditions for an economic integration of all eligible countries would not seem to exist. South Africa's application for membership could encounter opposition and thus oblige the OAU to regard the SACU as an additional and separate part in its series of regional trading blocs.

Thus, the emergence of post-apartheid South Africa could well be the factor that leads to a contraction of the PTA (losing Lesotho, Swaziland and Namibia). Whether a smaller PTA could then evolve into an economic integration arrangement is another question. And one should also pose the question as to whether a smaller SADCC referred to above might not convert itself into a preferential-trade area at the expense of the existing PTA, that is, the south-central countries would split from the north-east group. For, if SADCC does not take on a greater trade mantle, what does it really have to offer its members as an organisation that could not be offered by the PTA? Of course, if Green[27] and Ravenhill[28] are correct, then SADCC with its loose framework is the more appropriate organisation for the region. However, the trade activities of SADCC need to be rationalised vis-à-vis the PTA.

But would South Africa in fact gain any benefits from PTA membership which it could not gain from a normalisation of politico-economic relations? Despite sanctions, exports from South Africa find their way into all African countries, and the fact that South Africa is continually opening up new markets indicates that its goods are competitive in terms of price and quality. Its trade with Africa would undoubtedly be far greater were it to be conducted directly and openly, and were African currencies convertible. It is quite possible then that PTA membership might result in little *additional* increase in exports, and that these gains could be offset by the institutional costs which would arise. Post-apartheid South Africa would have to do a careful analysis of the costs and benefits involved.

Some of the possibilities for changes in regional groupings are summarised schematically in Table 8.2.

Table 8.2   Possible changes in regional economic groupings

Grouping	Change	Effect
SACU	Becomes common market (SACM)	Lesotho, Swaziland, and Namibia leave PTA
	SA/Lesotho form common market	Lesotho leaves PTA; SACU remains intact
SADCC	SA joins	SACU remains intact
	BLS/Namibia leave in favour of SACM	SADCC perhaps admits Zaire
	Forms an economic integration	BLS/Namibia leave in favour of SACU; remaining SADCC countries (plus perhaps Zaire) split from PTA
PTA	SA joins	SACU and SADCC wound up
	SA joins	SACU/PTA agree re coexistence

Economic Cooperation or Integration?

The path to economic integration is never easy, and it is a process of evolution. Nationalism is always a factor, and governments are loath to lose their sovereignty over various instruments of political, social and economic policy which inevitably become subsumed by the process of integration. The bargaining which is taking place in the EC with regard to a wide range of matters, including commercial legislation, trade policy, competition policy, basic standards and monetary coordination, will serve as a clear example of the difficulties inherent in integration. There is some division, especially with regard to monetary union which implies a single European central bank and common currency. Economic integration in Africa apart from the SACU has not had a particularly successful history: judging from the metamorphosis of the EC since 1957, the PTA might take a long time to reach the stage of a common market.

An important factor in any economic integration is that member countries should be in some considerable agreement as to economic philosophy. Simple trade groupings such as the PTA are able to contain severe philosophical differences, such as those which existed until recently between Ethiopia and Kenya. In contrast, in conditions of economic integration such differences could not be sustained. The reason is that those countries with policies attractive to investors would develop more rapidly than the others, and thus the benefits of integration would not be shared. Funds, for instance, would move to countries with lower taxation rates, more favourable exchange control policies, and so forth. In a common market, people will move to countries of greater employment opportunity and political and economic freedom, and where consumer goods are available. Bluntly, economic integration is not possible between centrally planned and market economies. It is thus important that any systemic divide be bridged if economic integration is to be facilitated.

In the SACU to date, all countries have followed a market-orientated system, but this has not been true of SADCC. Hanlon, however, believes that there is 'no question that in all SADCC states the next decade will see a much larger role for the private sector, both domestic and foreign'.[29] Indeed, the hitherto Statist economies of Angola, Mozambique, Tanzania and Zambia are moving strongly in this direction.

Nonetheless, the State can play an important and constructive interventionist role in promoting economic growth, good examples being Japan and the South-East Asian NICs.[30] Gibogwe, Ngeno and Sisulu[31] refer to this in a recent article in which they point to the importance of technological transformation in the PTA region. The State traditionally has played an important role in economic enterprises both in South Africa and SADCC, for example in railways and electricity. It would be too much to expect that this role would be diminished substantially in all countries in the region or that they would become mirror images of Western industrialised countries. The challenge, rather, is how to combine a vigorous private sector with an efficient public sector concerning itself primarily with social welfare programmes.

If consensus can be reached along these lines, economic cooperation would be easier. This seems to be a necessary step in the reconstruction of Southern Africa, both politically and economically. Such an accord might be easier to reach in the South Africa-SADCC area than in some of the area covered by the PTA. It is for this reason that it might make sense for post-apartheid economic relationships in the region to proceed as follows:

1. Convert the SACU into a common market. It might, in fact, be possible to take this a step further into an economic union by building on the experience of monetary integration in the Rand Monetary Area and CMA and aligning the currencies of all members.
2. Conclude an association agreement between the new Southern African Common Market (SACM) and the remaining SADCC six (which could be extended to include, say, Zaire, Madagascar and Mauritius) with the aim of gradually reducing trade barriers and increasing economic cohesiveness which is an important ingredient for successful integration. Such an association would resemble the EC/EFTA relationship and could perhaps evolve into something similar to the proposed EC/EFTA arrangement which in fact contains many of the main features of an advanced form of economic integration. At present South Africa has a preferential trade agreement with Zimbabwe which is weighted in favour of Zimbabwe; it is possible that this could be extended to the remaining SADCC countries outside the common market. It might also be possible to bring the various currencies in the region into alignment.

It is not at all clear, however, that Southern Africa needs to respond to EC 1992 through economic integration, or that integration (outside the SACU) would provide any benefits that could not be obtained through other measures to encourage trade flows and economic cooperation. El-Agraa[32] finds that economic integration in the form of a customs union is inferior to non-discriminatory tariff reductions, while Robson emphasises that 'no *a priori* case exists for integration among developing countries'.[33] For any proposed grouping the case must be specifically examined. Arguments for an all-embracing Southern African economic integration certainly require a good deal of further investigation into the economic and political costs and benefits to all countries concerned. A serious problem which should be borne in mind is that it has proved very difficult in practice in economic integration schemes to achieve agreement among partner countries regarding the allocation of new industries. It is probably easier to encourage regional trade through measures such as the establishment of a common fund to provide foreign exchange, a pre-financing facility for exports, and an investment promotion fund.

Whichever process unfolds in economic relations in Southern Africa, there should be nothing to prevent the countries of the region cooperating in a wide range of economic and technical matters, especially in transport and telecommunications, agriculture, science and education, and environmental affairs. For example, there is great potential for a sub-continental power grid and also for water projects. The environment will become of growing concern worldwide in the 1990s, and Southern Africa will be expected to play its part, especially if it wishes to attract aid funds.

CONCLUSION

The aim of this chapter has not been to argue for the economic fragmentation of the Southern African region or of any regional organisation which exists. However, as theoretical arguments have been examined and empirical evidence has been sifted, it has become clear that, as with EC/EFTA or EC/Greater Europe relations, or with East Asia,[34] so too in Southern Africa steps towards closer economic organisation might best proceed on the basis of 'regions within regions', merging in the longer term. It is important that reality be confronted; any regional organisation which arises anywhere is formed for a political or economic purpose, and this purpose may become obsolete over time. It then becomes necessary either to restructure the organisation or to form a new one. In Southern Africa it is possible that political events of the 1990s might necessitate both the SACU and SADCC, as well as the PTA, making substantial changes to their existing formats.

Notes

1. S. Lewis, *Economic Realities in Southern Africa (or One Hundred Million Futures)*, Discussion Paper 232, Brighton: Institute of Development Studies, University of Sussex, 1987, p.5.
2. E.H. Preeg, 'The Growth of Regional Trading Blocs', *Economic Impact*, 69, 1989, p.8.

3. H. Hughes (ed.), *Success in East Asia: A Comparative Study of Industrialisation*, Cambridge University Press, 1988.
4. Preeg, op.cit., p.8.
5. *The Economist*, 4 August 1990.
6. T. Ostergaard, *SADCC Beyond Transportation: The Challenge of Industrial Cooperation*, Uppsala: Scandinavian Institute of African Studies, 1989.
7. A.M. El-Agraa, 'Is There an Economic Rationale for Customs Unions?' in A.M. El-Agraa and A.J. Jones, *Theory of Customs Unions*, Deddington: Philip Allan, 1981.
8. P. Robson, *The Economics of International Integration*, London: George Allen and Unwin, 1980
9. R.H. Green, 'Economic Coordination, Liberation and Development: Botswana-Namibia Perspectives' in C. Harvey (ed.), *Papers on the Economy of Botswana*, London: Heinemann, 1981.
10. H. Hughes, 'Inter-developing-country Trade and Employment' in B. Weisbrod and H. Hughes (eds), *Human Resources, Employment and Development*, Volume 3: *The Problems of Developed Countries and the International Economy*, London: Macmillan, 1983.
11. Ibid., p.434.
12. Green, op.cit., p.180.
13. J. Ravenhill, (ed.), *Africa in Economic Crisis*, London: Macmillan, 1986, pp.211, 221.
14. J. Viner, *The Customs Union Issue*, New York: Carnegie Endownment for International Peace, 1950.
15. P. Wonnacott and M. Lutz, 'Is There a Case for Free Trade Areas?', *Economic Impact*, 69, 1989.
16. Ibid., p.32.
17. G. Maasdorp, 'Economic and Political Aspects of Regional Cooperation in Southern Africa', *South African Journal of Economics*, 54, 1986.
18. *Macroeconomic Survey 1986*, Gaborone: SADCC, 1986, p.42.
19. Calculated from D. Muirhead, 'Trade and Trade Promotion' in E. Leistner and P. Esterhuysen (eds), *South Africa in Southern Africa: Economic Interaction*, Pretoria: Africa Institute, 1989, p.91; B. van Rensburg, *South West Africa/Namibia: Post-independence Economic Implications for South Africa*, Johannesburg: Assocom, 1989, pp.26 and 31; and *EIU Country Profile – Namibia 1989–90*, London: Economist Intelligence Unit, 1990, pp.40–1.
20. J. Hanlon, 'Post-apartheid South Africa and its Neighbours', *Third World Quarterly*, 9(2), 1987, p.61.
21. *The Citizen* (Johannesburg), 6 December 1988.
22. J. Hanlon, 'Post-apartheid South Africa and its Neighbours', *Third World Quarterly*, 9(2), 1987.
23. See Chapter 7 and also P. Vale, 'Integration and Disintegration in Southern Africa', Occasional Paper No. 16, Cape Town: IDASA, 1989.
24. See G. Maasdorp, 'Reassessing Economic Ties in Southern Africa', *Optima*, 30, 1981, and J.H.Cobbe, 'Economic Aspects of Lesotho's Relations with South Africa', *Journal of Modern African Studies*, 26, 1988.

25. M. Russell, 'The Rural Swazi Homestead in its Context' in F. de Vletter (ed.), *The Rural Swazi Homestead*, Kwaluseni: Social Sciences Research Unit, University of Swaziland, 1983.
26. Hanlon, *SADCC in the 1990s*, op.cit., p.12.
27. Green, op.cit.
28. Ravenhill, op.cit.
29. Hanlon, *SADCC in the 1990s*, op.cit., p.110.
30. Hughes (ed.), op.cit.
31. V. Gibogwe, J. Ngeno and M. Sisulu, 'Flexible Specialisation in the Preferential Trade Area of Eastern and Southern Africa?' *IDS Bulletin*, 20, 1989.
32. El-Agraa, op.cit.
33. Robson, op.cit.
34. *The Economist*, 11 November 1989.

9 Labour Flows, Refugees, AIDS and the Environment

Alan Whiteside

One of the main links between the countries of Southern Africa has been the movement of labour. Until recently this involved large numbers of workers moving all over the sub-continent, but today most migrants travel to South Africa. This chapter traces the pattern of migration and identifies it as an area in which changes are likely to occur in the next few years.

The flow of refugees, displaced by civil war, banditry, economic hardship and drought, is also significant. In some countries refugees comprise up to 10 per cent of the population and represent a considerable drain on resources. The changing political climate may well ease this problem.

Southern Africa may also be severely hit by two global crises: the AIDS pandemic and the deteriorating environment. These are examined to evaluate their effect on the development in, and economic and social wellbeing of, the countries of the region.

LABOUR FLOWS

The main regional flows of labour over the past century were from Malawi to Zambia and Zimbabwe; from Mozambique to the sisal farms of Tanzania, the tea plantations of Malawi, and the sugarcane fields of Swaziland and Zimbabwe; and from Malawi, Mozambique, Botswana, Lesotho and Swaziland to the farms, mines and industries of South Africa.

In the days before strict border controls were imposed, it was sufficient for the migrant to believe that he could better his circumstances by moving. He would generally find employment although this was often work that the local population regarded as poorly paid, hard or unpleasant. Mozambicans, for example, moved to Malawi to work on plantations. By doing so they would earn more and enjoy better working conditions than in Mozambique. At the same time, these jobs were available because Malawians had migrated to South Africa, Zambia or Zimbabwe where they in turn could command better wages.

Apart from the economic rationale, the other major determinant of labour flows was the way the colonial power treated its citizens. The harsh Portuguese rule in Mozambique, with its forced labour and high taxes, made the local population enthusiastic migrants. In British-ruled countries, various taxes were imposed and these forced the men to seek work in order to earn cash.[1]

While there was virtually free movement of labour, dependants were strictly controlled. Migrants were prevented from settling at the place of work and from bringing their families with them. Thus, they were forced to move between work and home for varying periods. However there were a few exceptions, for example many Malawians settled permanently in Zimbabwe.

The Changing Pattern of Migration

By the mid-1970s the mass movement of labour between countries, other than to South Africa, had ceased. This was due largely to the rapidly growing domestic labour forces, with associated problems of unemployment and underemployment. It is unlikely that this migration of unskilled labour will ever be resumed.

For the past two decades most migration has been from Botswana, Lesotho, Malawi, Mozambique and Swaziland to South Africa. By 1980 four distinct changes were evident. They are described below, and it is argued that they will be permanent.

Overall Numbers
In 1970 over 500 000 foreign migrant workers were employed in South Africa. In 1973 476 000 were registered, and numbers fell rapidly until 1982 when the lowest level since 1945 was recorded – 279 000. Since then there has been a slight increase, and in 1986, the last year for which there are reliable figures, there were 303 000 migrants (Table 9.1). The expected trend is for numbers to fall.

Sex of Migrants
In 1960 females made up 17.5 per cent of the foreign labour force, but by 1970 this had fallen to 9.5 per cent and by 1985 to 2.1 per cent. This trend will not be reversed.

Table 9.1 Distribution of foreign Africans in South Africa

	1972	1974	1976	1978	1980	1982	1984	1986
Botswana	31 960	33 357	43 159	34 464	23 200	26 262	26 433	28 244
Lesotho	131 749	134 667	160 634	155 623	140 746	140 719	138 443	138 193
Swaziland	10 108	9 984	20 750	14 054	19 853	13 659	16 823	21 914
Malawi	131 231	137 676	12 761	38 525	32 319	27 558	29 268	31 411
Mozambique	121 708	139 993	111 257	79 168	56 424	52 323	60 407	73 186
Zimbabwe	–	5961	32 716	27 494	10 377	11 332	7492	7304
Total	426 756	461 638	381 277	349 328	282 919	271 853	278 866	300 252

Source: South African Yearbooks, 1973–86

Employment by Sector

There has been a major change in the sectors in which foreign migrant labour is employed. In 1964 mining employed 58 per cent, but by 1970 this had risen to 77.4 per cent and in 1986 to 81 per cent. Agriculture was the second most important employer of foreign labour with 30 per cent in 1964. By 1986 this had fallen to 4.6 per cent with domestic service and manufacturing employing 3.6 per cent and three per cent respectively. Labour, other than miners, can only be brought into South Africa with the permission of the government. As unemployment has grown among the local African population, such permission is unlikely to be granted (except where skills are needed or where the work is so poorly paid or unpleasant that South Africans are unwilling to undertake it).

Origin of Migrants

Perhaps the most dramatic changes have been in the origins of migrant labour. Table 9.1 shows that numbers from Malawi and Mozambique have fallen considerably.

Mine Migrants: the 1970s and Critical Changes

Mine recruitment underwent rapid changes from 1973, not all of which were of the mines' making or choosing. De Vletter writes:

> The turning-point in the industry's approach to labour was marked by three events: the steep rise in the price of gold in 1973–74; the decision by Malawi in 1974, following an aircraft crash that killed 74 recruits, not to permit recruitment of its nationals by the Chamber of Mines; and shortly afterwards, with the end of Portuguese colonisation, the danger that Mozambican labour might no longer be available. The higher gold price had some bearing on the sharp increase in mining wages, but the unexpected disappearance of its major source of labour (Malawi provided some 120,000 workers) forced the industry to adopt a policy of 'internalisation' by attracting labour from within South Africa with sectorally competitive wages, while reducing its vulnerability to possible further actions by external supplier states.[2]

Crush concurs with de Vletter on the timing of the changes but identifies other forces at work. He writes:

In the early 1970s, the gold mining industry entered a phase of radical restructuring. Manifestations of change include the halting emergence of a new industrial relations format, a rapidly diminishing role for white mine labour, the demise of longstanding methods and structures of labour recruiting and mobilization, and major alterations in the spatial and temporal patterning of migrancy . . . . South Africa's mine workforce, including its sizable foreign component, is currently being transmuted into a more fully proletarian and professional cadre within the constraints of an enduring but more regimented system of migrancy.[3]

The 1970s saw the beginning of severe unemployment problems in South Africa with rapid growth in African unemployment, especially in the homeland peripheries. For the first time active labour recruitment ceased. It was no longer necessary to offer inducements to labour; rather, it became a process of dealing with the workseekers presenting themselves at the gates of the recruiting agencies.

There was little change between 1980–6. The main trend was a slow increase in the numbers from Swaziland, Botswana and Mozambique. Unfortunately there are no detailed data beyond 1986 as that year saw the abolition of influx control legislation, and thus the offices which registered foreign workers were closed.

Pressures

One of the major problems facing Southern Africa is to provide employment for the rapidly growing population. Employment creation is not keeping pace with the number of new job-seekers let alone absorbing the backlog. In Lesotho, for example, the labour force is estimated to be 700 000 of whom only 40 000 are in local wage employment. In Zimbabwe some 120 000 school leavers enter the labour market each year, but there are formal-sector jobs for only 20 000. South Africa itself faces an unemployment crisis, although the numbers are very much higher than elsewhere in the region. Unemployment in the African population stands at at least 25 per cent and may be as high as 50 per cent in some areas. In 1989 the National Manpower Commission, warned that at least 350 000 new jobs were required each year to absorb job-seeking school leavers. This would be eight times faster than the rate of job creation in the 1980s and would require an economic growth rate well in excess of three per cent.[4]

This regional employment crisis means that there are foreign work-seekers who continue to seek employment in South Africa. At the same time, South Africans believe that they should have preferential access to employment within the country. The end result will be that opportunities for foreigners will be further reduced.

One of the crucial determinants of future migration is the demand for labour in the mining industry. This will be influenced by the technology used and by the growth or contraction of the industry. The role of technology has been exhaustively discussed by Pillay who concludes that the knowledge is available to considerably alter the labour/capital mix.[5] The implementation of such technology depends on the relative prices and the view of how biddable labour will be. The growth of the industry is also dependent on the price of its products, particularly gold, the competitiveness of South Africa in world markets, and the willingness of such markets to buy South African products.

Employment in mining is most likely to remain static or even fall, and the mining industry will not solve South Africa's employment problem. The future of foreign migration will not be determined by the classic supply and demand curves. If it were, foreigners would have no place in South Africa's labour force. Instead, more complex factors have to be looked at.

The most important determinant is employer policy. The Chamber of Mines' policy on its labour mix is that 60 per cent will be South African and 40 per cent foreign. The individual mines like to have a mix of labour to prevent dominant, powerful ethnic blocs developing. Linked to this are mine-management views of labour – 'Basotho are the best shaft sinkers, Mozambicans are the hardest workers', and so forth.

The mining houses have introduced a policy of stabilisation which works against the migrant. This is essentially a process whereby the migrant is assured of his job at the end of each period of leave provided he reports to the recruiting station within a certain time and presents his 'valid re-engagement certificate'. The result is that miners have become more career orientated and the mines have benefited tremendously from having what amounts to a permanent labour force at a lower cost. At the same time, there has also been a move to settle more senior workers in family housing on the mines. This discriminates against the foreign migrant who will not be allowed to bring his family to the mines.

Economics also plays a role in determining migrant sources. Labour should be drawn from where it is cheapest, but the existence of unions has resulted in wages being set above the market-clearing rates, and these wages do not discriminate according to where workers come from. There is, however, a difference in the cost of bringing workers to the mines (TEBA takes responsibility for transport at the beginning and end of every contract, and bears all costs). The nearer the recruitment office is to the mines, the lower the cost. This has resulted in many of the more distant offices being closed with the potential migrant himself now having to bear the cost of the journey from home to recruitment office. Clearly, this works against employment of foreigners, especially those from more remote locations.

Not only do employers play an important role in determining sources of workers but so do the governments. In 1979 the labour-supplying countries formed the Southern Africa Labour Commission (SALC). This was charged with finding ways of eliminating migratory labour, withdrawing labour from South Africa, coordinating policies to achieve the aims of SALC and introducing a Charter of Rights for migrant labour.[6] When SALC was formed, it had some potential bargaining power as foreign workers were a major group in the labour force, but members did not present a united front or make demands. As SALC enters the 1990s it has little power, has achieved virtually nothing, and its prospects are bleak.

The government with the most power to influence the movement of labour is the host, South Africa. Employing large numbers of foreign nationals gives South Africa a hold over the sending governments. Migrants may be hostages in certain circumstances, as was illustrated prior to the 1986 coup in Lesotho when South Africa warned the government of Chief Jonathan that recruitment would be suspended. Migrants can be used as a political tool only while migration is allowed: it is axiomatic that the ending of migration will terminate the value of the weapon.

If South Africa were to reduce numbers or end migration, it would need to consider the consequences for the sending countries. Firstly, there would be even greater pressure for employment in the home countries. Secondly, there would be a loss of deferred pay and remittances. The 1987 TEBA Annual Report noted that mineworkers' earnings totalled R4 billion, much of which was sent home. The money is important for three main reasons: it allows the miner's family to buy consumption goods (this is crucial during bad harvests); it may enable the migrant to invest in capital goods such as housing or farm equipment, thus enhancing rural productivity; and it provides governments with foreign exchange and taxes, and is thus an important source of revenue. It should be mentioned that Lesotho's dependence on migration is unique in the region. It is estimated there are 170 000 migrants employed in South Africa as opposed to 40 000 people in informal-sector employment within Lesotho. In 1988 migrant remittances stood at 43 per cent of GNP.

If repatriation of migrants resulted in political instability and a regional recession, this could have negative effects on the South African economy. South Africa benefits greatly from the regional market and would need to assess how much of the money sent out in remittances returns to purchase South African goods.

Future of Migration

In 1990 the last Malawian mineworkers returned home and TEBA closed its offices there. The reason stemmed from the growing incidence of HIV positivity among Malawian miners: Pretoria insisted on testing them but the Malawian government was unwilling to permit this. The mines have been able to replace these workers from other sources, TEBA has closed its most expensive operation, and Malawi will retain its manpower which, if the AIDS epidemic is as serious as projected, will become a scarce resource.

One clear trend is that the mine labour force is more career orientated. It has been suggested that the new structure of mine labour might be composed of three segments, namely: a minority of skilled, settled workers (South Africans); an increasing number of semi-skilled 'commuter' migrants drawn from areas close to the mines (the homelands and Lesotho) who will make up the bulk of the labour force; and a residual group of 'supplementary' workers to be recruited from traditional catchment areas on an *ad hoc* and irregular basis to make up numbers when normal planning mechanisms fail.[7]

The future of foreign migration is bound up with trends in the mining industry. The trend will almost certainly be that mines will become more capital intensive, thus reducing the labour force. The stabilisation of workers will mean that foreigners will be increasingly excluded.

It is generally accepted by most commentators that the trend towards a post-apartheid democratic South Africa is now irreversible. De Vletter argues that 'the emergence of a democratic government will provide migrant-supplying states the opportunity to negotiate the issue of migrant labour on more sympathetic and conciliatory terms than in the past'.[8] However, he warns that foreign labour will not have the strategic usefulness it offered in the past and, because of the internal employment crisis, there will be no compulsion for the new government to continue allowing employment for these workers.

This view is optimistic. The first priorities of the new South African government will be to provide its citizens with employment, education and health care. One way to increase employment will be to reduce the number of foreigners employed within the country, and it is hard to see how a new government will be able to resist the temptation for such a 'quick fix', except perhaps in the case of the Basotho. The reason is simply that Lesotho is so dependent on migration that there is little chance the country would survive without access to employment in South Africa. It is likely that some form of closer integration might be sought by the Lesotho government but the prospects for the other labour-supplying countries are bleak.

Skilled and Professional Staff

It is not only unskilled and semi-skilled individuals who seek work in South Africa. Many educated and qualified professional staff also cross the borders to take up employment there. (Of course, South Africa has encouraged immigration of European workers for decades.) It is comparatively simple for citizens of Botswana, Lesotho and Swaziland to do this because of their ties with ethnic Swazi, Basotho and Tswana living in South Africa – and the existence of homelands for these groups. If their skills are required, then it is easy to obtain the necessary permits. Skilled workers, especially in the homelands, are drawn from further afield in Africa, and include Ghanaians, Ugandans, and Nigerians.

There are three reasons why skilled workers from other parts of Africa seek employment in South Africa. Firstly, salaries are very much higher for all levels of manpower. An example is the top salary for a university senior lecturer which in March 1989 was R49 914 in South Africa, R28 344 in Swaziland and approximately R39 500 in Botswana. The quality of life and access to the amenities of modern life are often better in South Africa. Secondly, politics is a factor. Although its racial policies are universally known and disliked, South Africa is in a region where authoritarian and undemocratic regimes are common, and it offers individuals a choice to escape from these countries and to live in an environment where they are not expected to hold or put forward political views. Thirdly, in many instances the migrant will be able to use his skills more fully and will have better prospects for advancement.[9]

It would be useful to know how many skilled workers from Africa are working in South Africa, but unfortunately there are no data. One study found that, in one month in 1989 (the only month for which records had been kept) in the Nelspruit area of the Eastern Transvaal, work permits were issued to six teachers, a bulldozer operator, and a refrigerator technician from Swaziland. It should be remembered that most Swazi would choose to go to the Witwatersrand or Durban areas; thus, if these figures were replicated there would be a serious outflow of skills from that country.

There is an urgent need for information on the brain drain to South Africa. The departure of skilled and professional workers has negative effects on their home countries: they have been educated at considerable cost to the home economy, and the higher the level they have reached the greater the subsidy. (If they have had the benefit of overseas training, this will frequently have been provided by donors.) The brain drain means that the jobs the migrants were expected to occupy will often be filled by expatriates at a very much higher cost. Finally, skilled and professional workers will have their families with them and thus will remit little or nothing from their incomes.

If a political settlement is soon reached in South Africa, the situation could become worse for neighbouring countries as skilled manpower will be increasingly needed in South Africa. If settlement is delayed, then white emigration may increase with the same result. On all counts, therefore, the issue of the brain drain needs to be urgently addressed in the SADCC countries.

REFUGEES

Southern Africa is host to about 1 592 000 refugees and is the source of 1 674 000. These are people who have fled their homes and are living in other countries where they are registered as refugees by the United Nations High Commission for Refugees. However, the statistics do not reflect either the millions of internal refugees who have moved to urban areas or the educated and skilled refugees who have managed to reach the West.

The vast majority of refugees have been displaced by civil wars in Mozambique and Angola (as is shown in Table 9.2). The only country that does not have any citizens who have fled for political reasons is

Botswana. All the other countries of the region have oppositions in exile.

South Africa has been blamed for destabilisation in the region, and various studies have attempted to estimate the costs involved. The changing political environment and new approach to the SADCC countries marked the end of government-sanctioned destabilisation. This means that the responsibility for political settlement in the region will rest with the SADCC governments, especially Mozambique and Angola which will have to reach agreements with Renamo and Unita respectively.

Table 9.2   Refugees in Southern Africa: the misery matrix

Host/Source	Angola	Mozam.	S.A.	Other	Total
Angola	–	–	10 000[1]	12 500[2]	22 500
Botswana	–	–	900	500[3]	1 400
Lesotho	–	–	4 500	–	4 500
Malawi	–	720 000	–	–	720 000
S.A.	–	200 000	–	–	200 000
Swaziland	–	64 000	6 700	–	70 700
Tanzania	–	72 000	–	192 200[4]	264 200
Zambia	97 000	20 000	3 200	11 500[5]	131 700
Zimbabwe	–	176 500	500	–	177 000
Other	298 700[6]	–	–	–	298 700
Total	395 700	1 252 500	25 800	216 700	1 890 700

Notes: 1. South African refugees are supposed to have left Angola in terms of the Namibia Accord and are in Tanzania and Uganda.
2. Zairean.
3. Some Zimbabweans and Basotho.
4. Mainly from Burundi, Rwanda and Zaire, a few South Africans.
5. Mainly from Zaire.
6. Mainly in Zaire.
Source: *The Economist*, 23 December–4 January 1990.

Refugees are a tremendous drain on the host countries. They require feeding and housing, take up land which would normally be used for the indigenous population, and strain the existing infrastructure. The position is particularly serious in Malawi and Swaziland where Mozambican refugees now make up 10 per cent of the population.

Not only do refugees represent a drain for the hosts, but their departure also disrupts development in their countries of origin. They represent an outflow of human capital. Since for every refugee who crosses the border there are several who flee their homes to other parts of the country, official statistics represent the tip of the iceberg in terms of disruption and cost.

The disappearance of apartheid will reveal many of the underlying stresses that exist within Southern Africa. Moves towards tolerant democracy would lead to refugees returning home. The move towards liberalisation and tolerance of opposition seems to be taking place rather more slowly in Southern Africa than it has in the rest of the world. Lesotho, Swaziland and Malawi do not tolerate opposition, Zambia and Zimbabwe are reluctantly coming to terms with the concept while Angola and Mozambique are trying to come to an agreement with their opposition movements. It therefore seems that refugees will remain a regional problem, albeit in smaller numbers. It is also possible that South Africa could become a haven for refugees or, if the worst scenario was to transpire, it could be a major source of refugees.

AIDS

AIDS may change the pattern of development on the African continent. The epidemic has been sweeping through Central Africa and is now beginning to affect Southern Africa. In a recent editorial, *The Economist* stated:

> Economists, like generals, too often base their next campaign on the lessons of the past . . . . Today it is possible – put it no higher than that – that economists planning the next stage of the war on poverty in sub-Saharan Africa may be making as big a mistake. They are basing their plans on past demographic trends. What they neglect is the scourge of the age, AIDS.[10]

As *The Economist* goes on to note, this may well result in the population growth slowing to one per cent per annum or even declining.

The Situation in Southern Africa

The most immediate problem in examining AIDS in the region is the lack of information. Cases reported in the region are shown in Table

9.3; the number is comparatively small, with Malawi leading the field with 7160 cases reported up to January 1990. If these were the true figures, then AIDS would not seem to be a major issue on the sub-continent, but official data do not reflect the true picture.

The World Health Organisation estimates that cases in the USA are underreported by 25 per cent and in Africa by 90 per cent. The African underreporting is due to lack of medical coverage and facilities. In some countries there is inefficiency or slow reporting, for example Swaziland did not report to the WHO for two-and-a-half years. Unfortunately, in other instances governments are not prepared to admit the extent of the problem for fear of putting off investors and tourists. Governments also have to face the possible political implications, and in some cases a simple denial of the problem is the easiest response.

An alternative source of data on the problem is information on HIV infection. This is generally of limited value as it comprises surveys of specific areas or groups at a specific time. The survey information is most valuable when it covers a known sample over a period of time as is the case with testing in blood banks.

Data on HIV infection show a great diversity in the positivity levels. Surveys in Mozambique in 1989 found 3.1 and 5.1 per cent of adults were positive in Maputo and Nampula respectively. In Zambia figures for blood donors indicate that 20 per cent of those surveyed were HIV positive, while in Zimbabwe levels as high as 60 per cent in the uniformed forces have been reported.[11]

HIV infection is spreading rapidly in the region. At present the worst affected countries are Zambia, Zimbabwe and Malawi. This is a reflection of when the epidemic reached these countries rather than the behaviour of the people. South Africa, Namibia and Lesotho report few cases of AIDS and low levels of HIV prevalence. This is because the virus only began to spread recently: however, evidence suggests that the rate of increase is alarming.

Implications

What will be the effect of AIDS on the region? As *The Economist* indicates, it is a factor that needs to be considered. How seriously it will affect Southern Africa will be determined by how fast HIV spreads, how many people it eventually infects and how long they live after infection. At worst, it seems the level of HIV incidence may double every eight months, up to 50 per cent of the adult population

Table 9.3   AIDS cases reported to WHO by country as at 1 August 1990

Country	1979–1987 Cases	1988[1] Cases	1988[1] Rate	1989[2] Cases	1989[2] Rate	1990* Cases To date	Last* Report	Cumul.* Cases
Angola	41	63	0.6	0	0.0	0	31.12.88	104
Botswana	36	22	1.7	29	2.3	0	17.01.90	87
Lesotho	2	3	0.2	6	0.3	0	27.04.90	11
Malawi	1002	3034	36.0	3124	37.1	0	08.01.90	7160
Mozambique	4	23	0.1	37	0.2	49	23.06.90	#113
Namibia	19	43	2.3	127	6.8	43	31.03.90	#232
South Africa	106	94	0.3	159	0.5	103	21.06.90	#463
Swaziland	7	7	0.9	0	0.0	0	16.06.88	14
Zambia	709	980	11.6	1173	13.2	193	07.05.90	#3000
Zimbabwe	119	202	2.1	1311	13.5	1502	15.07.90	#3134

Notes: 1. Rate: Reported cases/100 000 population
         2. 1989 reporting generally incomplete

Sources: * WHO Case report up to 1 August 1990; # Updated report.

may be infected, and most will die within eight years of infection. But nowhere has the disease or level of infection peaked, and thus it is impossible to assess with any accuracy how serious the problem is likely to be. The areas of concern are detailed below.

Demographic
AIDS could lead initially to the growth in population slowing and then to an actual decline in population. Work in the UK concludes: 'it appears probable that the disease will have a very significant impact on population abundance over the coming decades in developing countries in which the infection is spreading rapidly in the general population'.[12] One projection is that the population of Zimbabwe would fall from 10 million in the mid-1990s to 7.5 million by 2017.[13]

AIDS hits the sexually active population (generally regarded as the 15–64 year age group) and infants infected during pregnancy or birth. This will result in a change in dependency ratios as working-age adults die leaving children and the elderly.

Economic
Two main costs can be identified, namely, the direct cost of treating the sick and the indirect cost resulting from the premature morbidity and mortality of AIDS victims. The World Bank estimates that up to 80 per cent of the cost associated with AIDS will be indirect, and thus very difficult to measure. The various estimates of direct costs are presented in Table 9.4.

Table 9.4   Direct cost of HIV infection per symptomatic adult (1985 US dollars)

Country	GNP per capita	Direct Cost		
		Low	Mean	High
Zaire	170	132	–	1 585
Tanzania	290	104	–	631
Caribbean Islands	1 000	–	2 723	–
Brazil	1 720	–	2 150	–
South Africa	2 010	–	6 000	–
Mexico	2 080	–	8 500	–
England	8 460	–	10 200	–
USA	16 690	27 571	–	50 380

Source: A. Whiteside, *AIDS in Southern Africa*, Durban: Economic Research Unit, University of Natal, 1990.

The World Bank estimates that in Zaire by 1993 the direct cost of AIDS will require an increase in the national health budget of 58 per cent. It already places considerable burdens on the health care system, for example, 25 per cent of deaths in one hospital in Kinshasa are AIDS-related.

Currently AIDS appears in many African countries as an urban disease. This creates particular problems since the skilled and educated gravitate towards the urban areas. Should the disease spread as rapidly in rural areas, it will cause additional problems as most African countries are largely dependent on agriculture. Already there are indications that labour-intensive agriculture may be hit by the withdrawal from the system of the labour force. Cash crops would be especially hard hit.

Political and Social Impact
It is very difficult to assess the political and social impact of the disease as the response to it and its impact are both dynamic. It has been suggested that AIDS will lead to political conflicts and the creation of power vacuums.[14] Others argue that this is exaggerated and that the continent will respond to the threat in a measured manner.

What is clear is that Africa will suffer uniquely from AIDS: 'The continent certainly suffered tragic misfortune in being exposed to HIV before it made inroads in many other parts of the world. However, it is also indisputable that features of African social life encourage multiple sexual partners and frequent partner change that make Africans especially vulnerable to a deadly sexually transmitted disease.'[15]

The key political question will be: who is hit by the disease? If it is the urban elite, it may mean that key political and economic leaders will be lost. Reports from Zimbabwe suggest that the uniformed forces are particularly vulnerable, and this could lead to destabilisation. If there is depopulation, then political vacuums may be created. If societies turn inwards and blame others, this will create social tension and a siege mentality. The world may see AIDS as yet another crisis facing Africa, and African countries may feel they are being blamed and thus cover up their problems.

The social consequences will also depend on who is worst hit in society and how society responds. At worst, AIDS will lead to discrimination, ostracism and an erosion of civil rights. It could lead to untenable pressures on the family and further marginalisation of already marginal groups. As AIDS kills breadwinners it could lead to the breakup of families. It has been described as 'the grandmother's burden'[16] as it creates orphans.

A major concern for South Africa is that, in a divided society, AIDS could be even more divisive. For example, the press coverage laid emphasis on the likely decimation of the African population, implying that whites may somehow be immune to the disease. The result is that AIDS is perceived by Africans to be a white invention to control the population. A recent pamphlet advised that the cure for AIDS was to have sex with an Indian or white woman. Whites, by contrast, have portrayed AIDS as the solution to 'die swart gevaar' (the black peril). The propaganda and destructive value of the pandemic goes far beyond its medical and economic impact.

How, then, will AIDS affect Southern Africa as it moves through the 1990s and into the next century? It seems inevitable that, in countries from Zimbabwe north, there will be an increase in the number of people falling ill and dying. By the end of the decade these countries could be losing between 100 000 to 200 000 people per year from AIDS. The effect on the economies is hard to imagine. South Africa, Namibia, Botswana, Lesotho and Swaziland are probably three to five years behind their northern neighbours. In all countries the impact of AIDS could be reduced if imaginative and immediate action is taken. If this is not done, then the AIDS factor could affect the region in ways as yet unforeseen.

THE ENVIRONMENT

This chapter has considered a number of issues which may affect the region over the course of the next decade. It would not be complete without mention of the environment as this is also a source of concern.[17]

Southern Africa as a whole is not overpopulated in relation to its natural resources and there is vast untapped agricultural potential. Some areas, however, are densely settled and the land use in many parts is not environmentally optimal. Overstocking and overcropping are leading to gradual soil and pasture degradation. For many people, wood is the only means of cooking and heating, and this results in depletion of forests.

The region has little control over the worldwide use of chloroflurocarbons and resultant depletion of the ozone layer. It will, however, have to bear the brunt of this depletion as the hole of the ozone layer spreads from the Antarctic northwards. This may lead to increasing skin cancer and adverse effects on plant and aquatic life. Global warming is also primarily the result of the activities of industrialised countries, but it too may affect Southern Africa. There could be a decrease in rainfall and increase in desert encroachment. There could also be an increase in catastrophic natural events such as floods and droughts. A rise in the sea level would flood much of the coastal areas and adversely affect ports. The result of all this could be to change the future of the region, and if this should happen at a time when the political and economic prospects at last seem to be brighter, it would indeed be tragic.

Notes

1. See, for example, R. First, *Black Gold: The Mozambican Miner, Proletarian and Peasant,* Brighton: Harvester Press, 1983; and J. Crush, *The Struggle for Swazi Labour 1890–1920,* Kingston and Montreal: McGill-Queens University Press, 1987.
2. F. de Vletter, 'Foreign Labour on the South African Gold Mines: New Insights on an Old Problem', *International Labour Review,* 126(2), 1987, p.200.
3. J. Crush, 'The Extension of Foreign Labour from the South African Gold Mining Industry', *Geoforum,* 17 (2), 1987, p.161.
4. *Sunday Tribune* (Durban), November, 1989.
5. P. Pillay, 'Future Developments in the Demand for Labour by the South African Mining Industry', International Migration for Employment Working Paper 34, Geneva: International Labour Organisation, 1987.
6. *Migratory Labour in Southern Africa.* Papers presented to the Conference on Migratory Labour in Southern Africa, Lusaka, Zambia, 1978, Addis Ababa: United Nations Economic Commission for Africa, 1985.
7. Centro de Estudos Africanos, Universitade Eduardo Mondlane, 'The South African Mining Industry and Mozambican Migrant Labour in the 1980s: An Analysis of Recent Trends in Employment Policy', International Migration for Employment Working Paper 29, Geneva: International Labour Organisation, 1987.
8. F. de Vletter, 'Prospects for Foreign Migrant Workers in a Democratic South Africa', World Employment Programme Research Working Paper 48, Geneva: International Labour Organisation, 1990.
9. J. Cobbe, 'Possible Negative Side Effects of Aid to South Africa's Neighbours', *African Affairs,* 89 (354), 1990.
10. *The Economist* (London), 25 November 1989.
11. This was reported in the leading Zimbabwean business paper, *The Financial Gazette* (Harare), 30 November 1980.

12. R.M. Anderson, 'The Impact of the Spread of HIV on Population Growth and Age Structure in Developing Countries', in A.F. Fleming, M. Carballo, D.W. Fitzsimmons, M.R. Bailey and J. Mann (eds), *The Global Impact of Aids*, New York: A.R. Liss, 1988.
13. *Africa Analysis* (London), 23 June 1989.
14. See, for example, C. Butler, *AIDS: A Darkness over Africa*, London: The Bow Group, 1990; and K. Edelston, *Countdown to Doomsday*, Johannesburg: Media House Publications, 1990.
15. A. Larson, 'The Social Epidemiology of Africa's AIDS Epidemic', *African Affairs*, 89 (354), 1990.
16. C.A. Beer, and R. and K. Tout, 'The impact: AIDS-the grandmother's burden', in Fleming et al. (eds), op.cit.
17. B. Huntley, R. Siegfried and C. Sunter, *South African Environments into the 21st Century*, Cape Town: Human and Rousseau, 1989.

10 South Africa and SADCC: Into the 1990s

André du Pisani[*]

This chapter examines future political relations between South Africa and the SADCC states. The chapter draws on perspectives from dependency approaches[1] as well as from regime theory[2]. It is not, however, intended as a theoretical critique of the strengths and limitations of these approaches. They merely function as an heuristic tool – assisting the exploration of the socio-economic fabric of the region. Past and present patterns of political interaction are briefly surveyed, and this serves as an introduction to the tentative probing of future political relations.

INTRODUCTION

One of the most enduring qualities of the politics of Southern Africa is its cunning capacity to defy regional 'experts'. The uncompromising realism of political elites, recently dramatically illustrated in the transition to independence of the continent's last colony, Namibia; the tenuous cohesion of State structures in countries like Lesotho and Mozambique; the delicate balance between domestic, regional and international dimensions; as well as the low life and gratuitous violence that disfigure the regional landscape – all have to be considered in any projection of future patterns of interaction. Moreover, the cold abstractions of the inquiring mind of the social scientist have to be balanced by the warmth of human needs.

In employing the insights culled from the pioneering scholarship of dependency analyses and subordinate state systems in Southern Africa, the socio-political fabric of the region displays the following salient features:

1. South Africa's regional hegemony finds expression in power asymmetry in both an economic and military sense.

2. Both SADCC and South Africa are structurally linked to an international trading regime – essentially based on the notion of a market economy.

3. In its present form, SADCC displays low economic cohesion and fairly high political cohesion, especially on the question of apartheid and its removal in South Africa.

4. Absolute dependence in the region on South Africa by country and by economic sector is relatively rare.[3]

5. Both South Africa and the SADCC states are to some degree capable of manipulating regional economic and political relations to serve domestic and foreign policy needs. Clearly, much in the region works in favour of South Africa, but its regional hegemony is not without its limitations.[4]

6. Finally, apartheid South Africa constitutes a core problem in the region. In the absence of a legitimate political settlement of this problem – one that would also enjoy the support of SADCC – regional security will remain elusive.[5]

A logical deduction arising from the previous point is that South Africa's foreign and regional policies suffer from a credibility problem in the sense that these are widely seen to represent and enhance minority interests. This, in turn, makes the definition of national interest and security difficult. Internal restructuring would thus become an essential part of any move towards normalising political relations with SADCC.[6]

In addition to these insights drawn from dependency literature and work on subordinate state systems, regime theory offers some imaginative avenues for future research. Employing insights from the work of Young, Krasner, Strange, Puchala and Hopkins[7], SADCC conforms to the definition of a regime. It 'hangs together' in terms of decision-making rules and procedures, shares some common attitudinal expectations and convictions – notably an abhorrence of apartheid and a belief in a future non-racial South Africa – as well as displaying patterns of dependence and interdependence. Moreover, there is (arguably) some convergence of interests while SADCC, in Young's typology, constitutes a 'negotiated', regime.[8]

From its inception in Lusaka in April 1980, SADCC showed convergence of interests around the goals of greater economic independence from South Africa as well as more equitable regional political integration.[9] While it is doubtful whether these goals have been realised to any significant degree, SADCC nonetheless displays regime characteristics.

Finally, Southern Africa is not the exclusive domain of state interaction, as is often asserted by political realists. Liberation movements, notably the ANC and the PAC, have their own agendas and demands for a post-apartheid South Africa, and these will have to be considered, at least to some extent, in mapping out the course of future political relations between South Africa and SADCC.

Multinational corporations play an increasingly important role in the affairs of the region. This seems even more probable in view of the prospect of a decline in foreign (overseas) fixed investment in the region – which in turn would enhance the role of South African-based multinationals.

SOUTH AFRICA AND SADCC: THE POLITICO-INSTITUTIONAL SETTING

The formation of the Southern African regional political economy was spawned by the development of mining from the late nineteenth century onwards, and South Africa and Zimbabwe became its principal industrial centres.[10]

The Southern African political economy enjoys considerable economic and trade relations with Western industrial powers. These powers provide most of the foreign investment in the region, and are responsible for most technology transfers. Thus, foreign financial and development capital is an important element in the regional political economy, and the different states variously rely on it to meet domestic requirements.

Conversely, the regional political economy supplies Western industrial economies with raw materials and agricultural products. South Africa and Zimbabwe are the only real exceptions to this pattern of external dependence, for they have developed their own manufacturing industries and secured markets for their produce in the regional economy.

Within SADCC, transport constitutes a vital artery of dependence and interdependence. This is especially true for land-locked states such as Malawi, Zambia, Zimbabwe, Botswana, Lesotho and Swaziland. In this respect, ports outside South Africa, notably Beira, Maputo and Nacala, are already playing an increasingly important role. Progress made on the rehabilitation of transport routes (vital to the SADCC states), together with foreign donor pressure, is likely to reduce dependence on South Africa even further by the end of 1991. A major research report on SADCC concluded that the Limpopo and Nacala railways should be running normally by 1991, if all goes according to plan, while the rehabilitation of the Beira and Dar-es-Salaam ports should be well advanced.[11] Strands of interdependence are also evident in the intra-regional politico-economic relations within SADCC, with states taking responsibility for specific sectors.

To be sure, relations of 'first-order dependence' do exist between South Africa, Western industrial economies and the member states of SADCC, notably in external trade, foreign fixed investment, economic assistance and debt. Likewise, dependence of this magnitude causes internal dislocations in the SADCC states, especially in the rate of economic growth, employment, income distribution and the general level of social welfare.

Such structural forms of dependence, however, do not automatically imply that SADCC is entirely at the mercy of white minority rule, for South Africa, on its part, needs markets and political readmission to the international community. Sanctions, too, have deepened South Africa's diplomatic reliance on the these states.

Other strands of dependence and interdependence are more institutional. The SACU and its predecessors, for example, have provided an institutional framework for almost 100 years between South Africa and three member states of SADCC, namely Botswana, Lesotho and Swaziland, while Namibia is now also a formal member. SACU provides the framework for a common trading area. Renegotiation of the Agreement in 1969 led to a greatly increased flow of revenue to the BHS countries.

The Common Monetary Area (CMA) constitutes yet another politico-economic linkage between South Africa and three member states of SADCC – Lesotho, Swaziland and Namibia. Botswana also used South African currency until 1976 when it established its own central bank and currency (the Pula) which is linked to a basket of other currencies in which the South African rand predominates.

Another notable feature of the regional political economy is growing interdependence in energy and water. The giant Cahora Bassa Dam on the Zambezi River in Mozambique should supply South Africa with about eight per cent of its power requirements, while the Highlands Water Project in Lesotho, presently under construction, will provide water and some electricity for the region's industrial core – the Witwatersrand.

Trade and labour dependence is also found. In the case of
Botswana, for example, 80 per cent of imports are from or through
South Africa, while 20 000 migrant workers are employed on the farms
and mines of its more powerful neighbour.[12] Significantly, despite the
extent and nature of its dependence on South Africa, Botswana has
consistently refused to enter into a security pact with Pretoria. This is
but one illustration of the capacity of peripheral states to pursue
relatively independent policies and interests.

Finally, the growing international legitimacy of the ANC and its
role in the politics of the region paradoxically give SADCC a stake and
role in facilitating dialogue on the conflict in South Africa.

SOUTH AFRICA AND THE FRONTLINE STATES: THE BURDEN OF HISTORY

Political and economic interaction between South Africa and the states
presently within SADCC pre-dates formal colonisation, and acceler-
ated with the colonial expansion of Europe into Southern Africa. Rich
mineral discoveries, notably diamonds (1867) and gold (1886) in South
Africa, copper in Zambia, and coal, chrome and other base metals in
Zimbabwe and Namibia, deepened the patterns of interaction.

Initially South Africa enjoyed diplomatic representation in various
African countries, including Mozambique, Angola, Kenya, Egypt and
Madagascar. In other cases South African interests were advanced by
special diplomatic envoys on the continent. At the time, South Africa
participated in institutions aimed at improving intra-African cooperation and saw itself as making a contribution to the socio-economic
upliftment of the continent.[13]

Historically, South Africa retained key trade and cultural links with
the West, and attempted to expand its sphere of influence by
incorporating the former British Protectorates – Bechuanaland, Basutoland and Swaziland – and the former German colony – Namibia –
into its territory. More recently, a functionalist strain pervaded
regional policy. It proved to be, however, largely misdirected and
based on questionable premises.[14] In more general terms, South
Africa's regional policy and its political relations with SADCC,
turned on the notion that such relations 'should ensure the survival
of white rule'.[15]

A provisional chronology of South Africa's political relations with Africa, under which relations with SADCC are incorporated, reveals the following:

1950–60: Concerted and aggressive attempts to incorporate the former British High Commission Territories of Bechuanaland, Basutoland and Swaziland, as well as the former mandated territory of South West Africa (now Namibia). South Africa enjoyed diplomatic representation in various African countries as well as being a member of the Commonwealth.

1961–66: The politics of 'assertive incorporation', punctuated by UDI in Rhodesia (1965) and South Africa's military engagement in that theatre. The OAU introduced a new element when, in 1963, it called for the 'total isolation' of the apartheid regime and this, in turn, gave impetus to calls for an arms embargo against Pretoria in the UN.

1967–74: 'Assertive incorporation' remained a guiding strain of policy and found form in the Vorsterism notion of a 'common market' of Southern African states. The political language changed with 'detente' and 'dialogue'. In the absence of a strong domestic policy base and growing State repression, however, 'detente' and 'dialogue' failed to improve political relations between South Africa and the Frontline states. South Africa's military involvement in Namibia and Angola were to usher in a new destructive phase from 1975.

1975–87: This cycle ushered in the politics of 'coercive incorporation' or 'destabilisation', or, put more crudely, the triumph of muscle over diplomacy. In this period the South African military and security establishments – greatly assisted by an imperious president – exerted direct and pervasive influence over regional policy. The misguided doctrine of 'total onslaught' provided justification for military aggression against South Africa's neighbours within SADCC. It was a time when our rare dealings in foreign affairs 'ranged from the unmentionable to the illicit' (to paraphrase exiled South African author, Christopher Hope). While the electoral victory of Robert Mugabe in Zimbabwe in 1980 undermined Pretoria's regional designs, South African destabilisation continued in Namibia, Angola, Lesotho, Botswana and Mozambique. Even after the signing of the Nkomati

Accord with Mozambique in 1984, elements within the South African security establishment continued their support for the anarchic violence of Renamo. This period also saw the formation of SADCC in 1980 with one of its principal objectives being the reduction of economic dependence on South Africa. Following the independence of Zimbabwe in 1980, the linked conflicts of Angola and Namibia dominated the regional equation. Parallel with protracted negotiations on these two regional fractures, South Africa experienced a deep domestic crisis. Limited political reform in 1983–4 evoked widespread popular resistance on a scale previously unseen in modern South Africa. The State reacted with more repression and, in 1985, it imposed a partial state of emergency, soon to be made national in June 1986.

Against this background of escalating internal violence, South Africa faced the imposition of further sanctions, notably in January 1986 with the passing of the Comprehensive Anti-Apartheid Act by the United States Congress. At the same time, its military involvement in Angola and Namibia taxed an embattled and isolated metropole. International trade sanctions, accompanied by a loss of investor confidence, turned the country into a capital exporter with a high inflation rate, mounting foreign debt and growing unemployment. In the words of Marcum, 'economic realities called for geo-political retrenchment'.[16]

From the beginning of 1988 a 'neo-realist' thread became perceptible in the weave of regional policy. Influenced by diplomatic experience gained in complex and protracted negotiations on Angola/Namibia – in which the Soviet Union played a constructive part – as well as a grim definition of the limits of South African power in war-wracked Angola, Pretoria's primitive twin-track regional policy underwent further modification. While much of the earlier functionalist strain remained – notably in an understated emphasis on technical and economic cooperation – the earlier impulse to coerce and incorporate lost its *raison d'être*. Far from helping to perpetuate apartheid at home and assisting international propaganda efforts, destabilisation actually weakened further the already tenuous domestic base of policy and contributed to the country's isolation in the region.

'Rampant realism' was replaced by 'neo-realism'. While the latter notion is premised on the idea of South Africa as the regional power in Southern Africa, it readily recognises limits to that power and relies more centrally on non-coercive instruments of policy, such as diplomacy and economic cooperation.

In the words of one of its foremost architects, Neil van Heerden, Director-General of the Department of Foreign Affairs, the following tenets now form the core of South African policy on Africa and the region:

– South Africa is part of Africa, in and through which our future lies.
– African problems must be resolved by Africans.
– South Africa's international isolation is contrary to African interests.
– The use or support of violence for the promotion of political objectives is unacceptable.
– Joint interests and responsibility in respect of the economic, sociological and ecological welfare of Southern Africa ought to be the basis of cooperation and good neighbourliness.
– South Africa is economically powerful and has the infrastructure and capabilities to be the cornerstone of regional development.
– Southern African states are interdependent and their future peace and stability are indivisible.
– The South African Government is irrevocably committed to the removal of apartheid and participation of all South Africans in the governmental process, up to the highest level.
– South Africa favours a regional conference for the promotion of joint interests in Southern Africa.[17]

Thus, unlike earlier articulations of policy on the region, 'neo-realism' and 'new diplomacy' are sensitive to the domestic base of policy and to certain changes in the international and regional environments. These include, among others:

> The emergence of the Third World as a force in international politics (a process that started in 1955 in Bandung); the role of the United Nations in the international system; the primacy of the North-South divide and salient shifts in international law, notably growing international acceptance of the principle of *sic utere tuo ut alienum non laendas* (utilise your property in such a manner that you do not harm your neighbour)[18].

While the style, articulation and language have changed, South Africa's regional interests have remained remarkably stable. These include: ensuring an adequate labour supply from the region through a system of labour dependence; enhancing transport interdependence in the region; limiting the political space of the ANC and the PAC; developing additional regional markets for South African goods; countering the effects of sanctions on the domestic economy by means of alternative trade patterns and new markets; and enhancing functional interdependence and cooperation between South Africa and SADCC.

'Neo-realism' and 'new diplomacy', however, do not constitute a grand design. Similarly, long-standing security interests still influence policy – the discredited doctrine of 'total onslaught' has not as yet hoisted the flag in doctrinal surrender (since writing, recent developments do in fact suggest that the military/security elements have in fact been persuaded that 'total onslaught' is no longer a saleable commodity) – but politico-economic considerations have arguably become more central to policy. Clearly, the 'battlefronts of Southern Africa', to borrow a phrase from a respected analyst of the regional scene,[19] have not yet fallen silent. In the absence of internal political legitimacy, South Africa's political relations with SADCC 'will remain problematic and volatile'.[20]

THE FUTURE: CHARTING A NEW COURSE

At the time of writing, the political relationship between South Africa and SADCC finds itself groping its way from the new uncertainties of the present to the unpredictability of the future. In historic terms, 1989 marked the beginning of the new century, and for the region the 'whiff of negotiation' culminated in international agreements on Namibia and Angola as well as the prospect of a negotiated end to one of the core problems of the region – apartheid in South Africa.

Namibia's accession to independence and its membership of SADCC will influence politico-economic relations between South Africa and SADCC as well. Much will depend on how South Africa decides to project its power in relation to a SWAPO-ruled Namibia, and in this respect the position of the port of Walvis Bay and the Penguin Islands – to which Pretoria claims legal title – could be especially significant.[21]

What will happen inside South Africa is largely uncharted territory, and the nature and outcome of this process of transition itself will have implications for South Africa's future political relations with SADCC. In the interim period preceding post-apartheid South Africa, there is a strong case for special multilateral mechanisms with a view towards facilitating communication between South Africa and SADCC. A mechanism modelled on the Joint Commission established to monitor and facilitate the implementation of the 1988 international agreements on Namibia and Angola, for example, could conceivably be useful as a trust-building mechanism. Special institutional arrangements involving diplomats and officials from the different states could also be considered during South Africa's transition to a majority-based government. Likewise, existing regional institutional arrangements such as SADCC, the Development Bank of Southern Africa and the SACU could be involved in the setting up of specific mechanisms charged with a variety of tasks such as development, security, trade, investment, ecology and health.

The value of such mechanisms could, conceivably, lie principally in the provision of a useful setting for conflict analysis and learning about the sources of regional conflict and their settlement. Moreover, their potential for the preparation of more comprehensive negotiations should not be underestimated. The informal setting associated with such mechanisms could prove conducive to improving trust and communication among the states of the region.

Broadening future political interaction between South Africa and SADCC beyond that of a functionalist nature, would pose special challenges to the political leadership of the region. In the field of diplomacy, fierce originality could be expected from the governing elites and the diplomats of the respective states. It goes without saying that the eczema of apartheid, which has disfigured the regional landscape for so long, would have to be removed in its entirety. While in itself an essential precondition for normal political interaction between South Africa and SADCC, it would not automatically on its own be a guarantee of a healthy relationship. South Africa would remain the dominant power in the region, and this asymmetry would continue even into the long term. Moreover, grounds for conflict would exist in the marginal existence imposed by poverty, social dislocation and the failure of 'governance'.

In other respects, too, some member states of SADCC might face uncertain political and economic futures. The medium to long-term socio-political implications of IMF and World Bank-induced restructuring for the states of the region, as well as of war and famine, are less than clear. In most cases, one suspects, restructuring could result in deindustrialisation and a weakening of state structures in the absence of the emergence of professionally-skilled, administrative and entrepreneurial strata such as exist in South Africa. The social costs associated with such programmes of restructuring could prove to be particularly destructive.[22]

While the primacy of political settlements of the conflicts of the region is likely to gain more recognition, it could be dangerous to assume that outside powers would commit resources in an attempt to settle the different inter- and intra-regional conflicts. Increasingly the burden will fall on the shoulders of local political leadership.

While post-apartheid South Africa, under a majority-based government, is likely to join SADCC and the OAU, it is unlikely that a common market would be formed soon thereafter. In the case of Southern Africa, levels of dependence, the asymmetrical nature of relations of power and the different resource endowments of the various countries, would – at least for a time – work against economic and political integration characteristic of a common market. Against restructuring of the global economy, however, Africa as a continent might become increasingly marginalised, and this might compel the states of the region to cooperate closely on political and economic questions.

This seems likely in view of recent developments in the Soviet Union and Eastern Europe which in all probability will result in a reduction of assistance to Africa. Moreover, even under the most ideal conditions imaginable, South Africa would be unable to match the West in development capacity – for that it has neither the skilled manpower nor the capital. In addition, higher labour costs (compared to most other newly industrialised economies), low productivity and a relatively slow expansion of the lower-income market, would function as further potential constraints.

Over the medium to longer term, however, political relations between South Africa and SADCC will depend on progress made in negotiations within South Africa. In the absence of internal political legitimacy – which could only be attained if some of the principal demands of the liberation movements, notably those articulated in the Harare Declaration and Programme of Action of August 1989, were met – South Africa's political relations with SADCC will remain acrimonious and problematic.

South African politics might well have turned the corner, however, with encouraging signs that prospects for a negotiated settlement of the conflict have been advanced following the speech on 2 February 1990 at the opening of Parliament by President de Klerk. (See also Chapter 2.) After de Klerk's statement one finds it increasingly hard to believe that apartheid has a permanent lodging in the soul of the Afrikaner.

Finally, even under an ANC-dominated government, South Africa would remain the dominant power in the region. With the strongest economy in the region, its cultural, intellectual and political influence would be disproportionate to its economic role – and this would pose special challenges to political leadership as South Africa competes for influence and markets with the other major sub-Saharan power, Nigeria.

Notes

* The author is greatly indebted to Peter Vale and Carlos Cardoso for their valuable comments on a draft of this chapter.

1. See, for example, F. Baffoe, 'Some Aspects of the Political Economy of Co-operation and Integration in Southern Africa: the Case of South Africa and the countries Botswana, Lesotho and Swaziland', *Journal of Southern African Affairs*, 3, 1978; B. Magubane, *The Political Economy of Race and Class in South Africa*, New York: Monthly Review Press, 1979; and T.M. Shaw and S.R. Msabaha (eds), *Confrontations and Liberation in Southern Africa – Regional Directions After the Nkomati Accord*, Boulder: Westview Press, 1987.
2. See R. Gilpin, *Political Economy in the 1980s*, Princeton: Princeton University Press, 1987; and the following articles in *International Organisation*, 36 (2), 1982: S. Krasner, 'Structural Causes and Regime Consequences: Regimes as Intervening Variables'; S. Krasner, 'Regimes and the Limits of Realism: Regimes as Autonomous Variables'; D. Puchala, and R.F. Hopkins, 'International Regimes: Lessons from Inductive Analysis'; S. Strange, '*Cave! Hic Dragones*: A Critique of Regime Analysis'; and O.R. Young, 'Regime Dynamics: the Rise and Fall of International Regimes'.
3. C.R. Hanson, 'South Africa as a Force for Regional Stability or Instability, Development and Mass Violence', unpublished PhD thesis, Harvard University, 1985, p.60.
4. R.T. Libby, *The Politics of Economic Power in Southern Africa*, Princeton University Press, 1987, p.3; and M.C. Lee, *SADCC: The Political Economy of Development in Southern Africa*, Nashville: Winston-Derek Publishers, 1989.
5. P. Vale, 'SA Militarist disruption: neighbours hope it's over', *Cape Times* (Cape Town), 18 January 1990.

6. I am indebted to Annette Seegers of the Department of Political Studies, University of Cape Town for this insight.
7. For the relevant sources, see note 2 above.
8. This point is well argued in I.L. Lubbe, 'The Southern African Development Co-ordination Conference (SADCC): Part of a Whole or a Cover?', unpublished M.A. thesis, Rhodes University, 1989, pp.4–16.
9. Lee, op.cit., chapters 1–2.
10. Libby, op.cit., p.19.
11. *The Herald* (Harare), 2 October 1989.
12. *Financial Mail* (Johannesburg), 10 March 1989, p.33.
13. C.J. Streeter, 'Regionale samewerking in Suider-Afrika', unpublished D. Admin. thesis, University of Pretoria, 1985, p.84.
14. P. Vale, 'Regional Policy: The Compulsion to Incorporate', in J. Blumenfeld (ed.), *South Africa in Crisis,* London: Croom Helm, 1987, p.176.
15. Ibid.
16. J. Marcum, 'The Interrelationships between South Africa and its Neighbours', in D. Clark (ed.), *The Southern Africa Policy Forum,* Washington, D.C.: The Aspen Institute, 1989, p.6.
17. N.P. van Heerden, 'South Africa and Africa: the New Diplomacy', *ISSUP Bulletin* (Pretoria), 4/1989, pp.7–8.
18. Ibid.
19. C. Legum, *The Battlefront of Southern Africa,* New York: Africana Publishing, 1988.
20. Marcum, op.cit., p.8.
21. A. du Pisani, 'Wither Namibia?', in Clark, op.cit.
22. Zambia is but one case in point. Ghana is another.

11 External Pressure for Change in South and Southern Africa

Peter Vale

It has become a cliche to suggest that international relations are undergoing paradigmatic shifts. And yet, no effort to comprehend contemporary affairs can divorce itself from the hard truth that comfortable assumptions about the world have been overturned by the events which began in Eastern Europe in the Autumn of 1989.

The first draft of this chapter was completed as these events played out. At that time the main issue in international relations was whether the central tenets of the Brezhnev Doctrine would be invoked to stop the haemorrhage of East Germans through Hungary. At the time of its redrafting nine months later, the main issue is whether the united Germany will simply overawe Central Europe.

And yet – as the problems associated with the Iraqi invasion of Kuwait showed – some immutable issues in international relations are seemingly unaffected even by structural changes. One such case – common to Iraq and to apartheid South Africa – is how to effect change in states with recalcitrant domestic polities.

In Southern Africa efforts to transform domestic structures have proved particularly fiendish. Witness, for example, the international community's frustration as it cast about for strategies to end colonial rule in the former Portuguese provinces of Mozambique and Angola, and in Zimbabwe and Namibia. However, the successes achieved and the lessons learnt in these cases proved to be only partially instructive as international insistence deepened that apartheid rule in South Africa itself should be ended.

This contribution ponders upon some of the processes at work within international pressures for political change in South Africa. While its central focus is the long drawn-out question of apartheid, the setting of the argument draws selectively from other experience in the region.

International policy towards Southern Africa now, in its final phase, is increasingly nuanced: pressure on apartheid is mixed and matched

187

with other instruments. The origins and evolution of new policy directions are of interest both to academics and policy-makers: accordingly, they too will engage our attention.

The ripening of apartheid as a core preoccupation of the international community has been well covered in academic literature.[1] In addition, the full dimensions and extent of South Africa's isolation from the community of nations was thoroughly explored.[2] There is no need, therefore, to traverse this ground again.

Two structural strands help explain the obdurate resistance which both colonialism and racism made in South Africa and these need to be understood in their historical setting before any sensible explanation of policy is possible.

The roots of the first are to be found in the nature of the international community in the post-war period, specifically in the enforced division of the world into two competitive blocs. This enabled minority rule (and its two colonial manifestations) to incorporate five cardinal arguments which were used singularly, or together, to resist the forces of change. These contentions had little or nothing to do with the centrality of the race question; they were, in essence, effective decoys which made it difficult to dislodge these objectionable political systems. From this flows the second structural strand: the manner in which the Cold War helped amplify South Africa's power in the region and the protective shield which this provided apartheid.

COLD WAR, WARM COMFORT AND CONTAINMENT

Notwithstanding the immense fillip which the Second World War gave to decolonisation and self-determination, Africa was a neglected area of concern in the immediate post-war years. This did not mean that Africa was off the agenda: its issues – including apartheid – were somewhere between unfinished business and the unknown.

It is important to insert a necessary qualifying clause at this point. It seems clear that South Africa was not regarded as an African issue. It was this which engendered a deepening polarity between South Africans and those who share the continent with them. (This, as will be seen, is focal to the conclusion of this chapter.)

The latent shift in the *status quo* with the onset of the Cold War changed this and – for very particular reasons – Western countries feared for the future of their interests in Africa. In the resulting uncertainty, these same countries valued South Africa for its pro-

Western perspectives and saw it as a stabilising influence in a region (and on a continent) which faced an unpredictable future.

Moreover, South Africa's importance to Western states was entrenched by three factors: the Union (as the country was then known) had fought on the victorious Allied side[3]; the war had endorsed a perception that South Africa's long coastline was of some considerable maritime strategic importance; the white minority were firmly in control and were seen to be upholding Western values in what was, after all, an acceptable form of democratic government. These three conditioning perspectives cast a long shadow over the ebb and flow of Western policy towards Southern Africa.[4]

But just as enabling clauses do not make legislation, so conditioning factors alone cannot shape policy. More concrete forces are needed and these were to be found in five considerations. Firstly, the Union was an enviable pool of prosperity and stability in an otherwise turbulent and, relatively speaking, impoverished world. This, secondly, was bolstered by the concentration of a comparatively sophisticated industrial and technological base. Thirdly, the Unions's anti-communist credentials were impeccable. Fourthly, the Union – notwithstanding the 'colour question' – enjoyed a 'special' relationship with a leading Western power, in this case the United States. Finally, South Africa was very far from any immediate agenda as Western nations went about the business of putting together the world after the events of 1939–45.

Because the currency of these five points are central to this paper, they need closer examination and categorisation.

Economic Prosperity

This has been a cardinal issue in the entire debate about South Africa, apartheid and its elimination. The parameters of the issue have been explored *ad nauseam* in all serious considerations of South Africa's and the region's future.[5]

For our purposes, it is important to recognise that such economic accomplishments as existed in the region were one-dimensional in the sense that the prevailing distributive system directed the riches towards the dominant minorities. This was a not inconsequential political issue in a world in which competing ideological positions drew succour from the very morality of how wealth itself was to be distributed. In addition, the structural dependencies in Southern Africa steered wealth in the direction of the region's richest state, South Africa.

Clearly, economic prosperity is a relative concept. In South and Southern Africa it has been largely predicated on the prevailing price for export commodities, especially mineral products. In addition to the uneven tide of revenue which this generated, the concentration of international economic activity was not constant. So, South Africa's (and by implication, the region's) favourable position in the immediate post-war years swiftly gave way to, initially, the economic power of the major trading blocs and, in more recent years, the locus of economic power in the Pacific Rim.

Industrial and Technological Base

Access to technology is understandably linked to both economic development and the industrial base and, in turn, is a function of the industrial base. Here too the terms are relative: so, for example, modern South Africa is industrially developed against, for example, Mozambique but not against Germany, Taiwan or the United States. Nevertheless, the huge (in African terms) advances which followed both the establishment of the Iron and Steel Corporation (including the secondary industrialisation which followed) and from the war effort, put South Africa in a particular category of semi-developed states. (It might be customary here to use 'nations', rather than 'states'. There has, however, never been a South African nation, which in many ways is what the dispute is all about. Certainly the principal task of the post-apartheid government will be to build a nation.)

In the Cold War context both technological skills and the industrial base were not commodities without their own ideological value. The not infrequent arguments about the inherent strategic importance of Simonstown (especially by American Cold War warriors) rested, to a large degree, on the ability of South Africa's capacity to sustain and repair Western shipping in a prolonged non-nuclear conflict. In a more benign setting, it was more attractive for Western countries to buy coal from capitalist South Africa than from communist Poland, even though the technological level of South Africa's coal mining – the question of low wages set aside for the sake of the point – was the same as that of Poland.

Anti-Communist Credentials

This raises the central ideological consideration: the question of anti-communist credentials. South Africa's were not a cynical function of the eroding position she found herself in during the post-war years. Rather they have a lineage as tangled as the Cold War itself. Let the following two illustrations stand for much of what lies below the surface.[6]

The theme of the National Party's 1945 Conference was 'Save South Africa from Communism'. The Party's leader, Dr D.F. Malan, was scheduled to address a public meeting on the eve of the Conference, but the meeting was disrupted by ex-Second World War servicemen, who may not have objected to Malan's theme – the dangers of 'communism' – but were incensed that the Nationalists were holding a public meeting in Johannesburg!

The Cold War also deeply influenced the thinking of English-speaking South Africans towards communism. Indeed, the continual portrayal of South Africa as a 'bastion of anti-communism in Africa', the mythology of the Cape sea route and, later, the strategic minerals position, was the work of influential English-speakers who had access to military circles in, particularly, Britain, but also in the United States. The logical extension of this was perfectly obvious. To offset the possibility that the Soviet Union and its allies might wrest control of South Africa from 'the Western sphere of influence', successive Western governments – British, American, French, Belgium and Italian – supplied the South African Defence Force (SADF) with sophisticated weaponry upon which a limited, though innovative, South African armaments industry was built.

Special Relationship with the US

The development of this anti-communism into the vulgarity and political paralysis of the 'Total Onslaught' was the unique achievement of P.W. Botha. As an approach to world affairs, however, it had immediate echoes in Reagan's White House. So the Reagan Doctrine – in reality a refinement of Nixon's earlier doctrine – with its emphasis on the 'evil empire', encrusted a relationship of a particular texture between the United States and South Africa in the years 1981–7. This was, of course, 'Constructive Engagement'[7] with its not-so-subtle leaning towards Pretoria: a relationship, to whit, of a special kind with the United States.

Consider, for example, the 'special' links which other minority governments enjoyed with other Western countries. The schizoid – now blows hot, now cold – relationship between the rebel government in Rhodesia and successive British governments provides some evidence of this.

Less well documented is the nexus between the United States and the pre-revolutionary regime in Lisbon which retarded the process of decolonisation in both Mozambique and Angola. In a nutshell, Portugal was both a colonial power and a member of the anti-Communist NATO alliance. Faced with an increasing revolt throughout her Empire, Lisbon sought – and obtained – protection from her NATO partners, especially Washington, in her efforts to stem the tide of decolonisation. Indeed, aircraft and other equipment originally destined for Portugal's role within the NATO system soon found their way into the colonial war effort.

It is important, while considering the rubric of 'special' relations, to consider how easily the behaviour of the patron can be misconstrued, thereby putting further limitations on the capacity to influence policy. Consider how many subsequent times the tone and content of Dr Salazar's 1961 speech to the United Nations was repeated by Ian Smith or South African heads of state. Chilcote (clearly a sympathiser) reports the Portuguese President as reiterating:

> the firm stand of a dedicated ruler determined to overcome the Angola crisis at the risk of the downfall of his own regime as well as of his colonial empire. In what might have been moments of reconciliation to appease the world-wide condemnation of his efforts to crush the revolt in Angola, Dr Salazar attacked both the United Nations and the United States. He accused the UN, which by the overwhelming majority vote of its members has sought to investigate the Angolan crisis of mob rule; and the US of aligning itself with the Soviet Union to condemn Portuguese rule in Africa . . . [as] a policy designed to win UN votes in the Cold War, but which has served Communist subversion in Africa.[8]

The point here is that the patron is simultaneously the greatest source of support and the fountain of the deepest insecurity. This phenomenon has frequently repeated itself elsewhere: in the Rhodesian-British relationship and during the South African-American relationship in the Carter-Vorster encounters.

International Priorities

Finally, contrary to accepted thinking, South Africa (and Southern Africa) was a relatively neglected area of international concern. A quick count of the dominant issues since the war suggest that, if anything, it was low in the pecking order.

As a result, successive external crises provided a shield for the South African question. When it periodically emerged, the question was almost monotonously tackled at the moral level. Now, however comforting and, indeed, necessary it is to approach international questions at this plane, it is seldom a successful strategy to move the headstrong. Here again the Southern African lessons are instructive. It took a coup in Portugal to liberate Mozambique and Angola, and the near-ruinous impact of the war and sanctions to disabuse 300 000 white Rhodesians of the notion that they constituted a nation.

It seems, however, possible to argue that the almost universal condemnation of apartheid – itself a function of the end of Rhodesia and the collapse of Portuguese colonialism – and the mass mobilisation against South Africa, helped emancipate the issue from the moral trap. If anything, the weaknesses in the apartheid chain have been identified and acted upon, both internationally and domestically. As a result, apartheid could no longer rely on a sudden lapse in attention as a crisis erupted here or a currency fell there.

TOWARDS NEW FORMS OF PRESSURE

Comfortable assertions about power relations are shifting in the face of a host of new forces, only some of which are associated with the changing relationship between the Superpowers. As the world searches, in Alistair Buchan's words, for "a new order", it is salutory to remind oneself that the changes now underway blossomed from a period of relative tranquillity. This, however, makes the changes more hazardous as Buchan pointed out in the 1973 Reith Lectures which, in many ways, predicted the world which now beckons. He wrote:

> when the structure of power or the climate of world politics changes in a time of peace and high prosperity . . . [T]here is no *tabula rasa*. We cannot make a fresh start; there are no victor powers to impose a settlement upon the vanquished. We must adjust the perspectives and alter the policies that we already have to meet a changing set of circumstances . . . our situation is much more complex . . . [than post-Bismarck Europe] . . . this time the changing agenda of world politics is not the consequence of a single political development but of multiplicity of causes.[9]

This may seem an oddly rash observation; after all, international relations are accustomed to (more or less) an ordered world or, at least, use a set of precedents which play off in acceptable rituals. So, for example, the United Nations system is drawn into the settlement of disputes in a series of protocols which are, more or less, acceptable.

The necessary underpinnings of the international system in-waiting are, as yet, unknown; as are, parenthetically, the issues which will engage the attention of international relations in the next century. This speculation on the future has a bearing on efforts to effect change on recalcitrant states in the following way. Some existing questions are hangovers from earlier epochs: so, for instance, the complexities of the Falklands issue and, nearer home, Walvis Bay, have their roots in colonial times. These are almost without exception the most obdurate problems because they bring with them the complexities of the memory trap. This is the mirror game of international relations which – almost by definition – defies a solution by clearheaded diplomats or reasonable politicians.

During periods of regular changes (after major wars) in the international system, problems such as these are inescapably tackled during the reconstruction process. In the present instance, however, the change – as Buchan notes – is not standard but prefaced on a multiplicity of factors. Therefore, the fate of particularly troublesome international issues is not certain: South Africa and, by implication, Southern Africa is such a case.

Notwithstanding the plethora of racial questions which plague political systems, the particular guise of the South African variety sets it aside from others. Indeed, the pervasive international pressure to end apartheid follows from precisely this recognition. It seems necessary to reassert this truth lest any hope be held out that, by some miracle, South Africans can hope to escape the necessity to change by pleading the 'special case' clause. Nor, indeed, as Enos Mabuza has recent pointed out, can they hide the continuation of apartheid (in some group-oriented form, perhaps) by the 'non-interference clause of the UN Charter'.[10]

As much as shifts in the tide of international events close off systems or end epochs, so too do they create narrow opportunities. In the present mood some important footholds have appeared to resolve some outstanding issues. Take, for example, the deepening consensus over conventional armaments in Europe, which may help bring about some prospect of a more peaceful future on the Central European plain. This particular example follows from the convergence of Soviet-

American understanding and is helped along by the swiftly eroding circumstances in Eastern Europe.

Of particular importance to the theme of this essay is the growing superpower understanding on regional conflicts. This contrasts sharply with the well-tested credo which divided the world into spheres of influence, both east and west. It was this, of course, which created the space for assertive middle powers – like South Africa – to hide behind the skirts of their Western patrons.

The effects of this on Southern Africa have not gone unnoticed: politicians and analysts have used it as the central point of departure in explaining recent Southern African events. While there is no gainsaying its centrality, the conclusion which can be reached is that South Africa's relative power has increased, rather than decreased, as a result. It remains a testable proposition that the end of both Portuguese and British colonialism actually strengthened South Africa in the region.[11]

In other words, the withdrawal of the Superpowers from the region increases South Africa's margins to influence the direction of regional policy. This is not to suggest that the smaller countries of Southern Africa are without any power of their own. As the Mozambican case illustrates, such states can call foul on South Africa's efforts to re-order their own political or economic direction. This is a veto power which flows from their full, unfettered membership of the international community and the complexity around South Africa's position. There are analogous implications for external efforts to change the political system in South Africa itself. The exiled groups, particularly the ANC, enjoy greater international acceptability than the government in Pretoria. As a result, they – in the name of the country's majority – are able to exercise the same veto or blocking power, internationally-speaking, on South Africa as the smaller states of the region.

What strategic points can be gleaned from this rumination? The simple abandonment of big power interest in Southern Africa amplifies South Africa's power both in the region and at home. More promising, therefore, is an understanding of international accords which heighten, rather than lessen, interest in the region. Of course, there is almost a structural tension here between the urgent need to pay attention to circumstances which are more fluid, more pressing. The immediate foreground suggests that the reconstruction of Europe in the aftermath of the exhaustion of East European-style leadership will be of particular importance. Is this to be a case of the South African question, once again, hiding behind the skirts of a 'wider, more pressing' international issue? Perhaps not. As has been argued here, the near universal consensus over apartheid suggests that this may not be acceptable.

What is needed – to affect long-range stability – is greater interest both in resolving the apartheid issue and in supporting the forces which aim to secure the region. Whether or not this means a 'Marshall Plan' for Southern Africa is a moot point: what is important is the recognition that economic verities suggest that South Africa remains central to a prosperous sub-continent. This reality, however, does not mean that apartheid is the engine of regional opulence: indeed the very opposite – as destabilisation so dramatically demonstrated – is the case.

But economic issues are at the core of the debates over change in South Africa. By a curious set of circumstances, events in South Africa will invariably be influenced by the dramatic shifts in socio-political thinking of the past five years. The foregoing sub-ordinate clause is important and deserves some magnification. The surest warranty – in a world where, frankly, nothing is certain – lies in the flexibility (perhaps pragmatism is a better word) which those who will inherit South Africa have shown. It is ironic, especially in the woeful and deleterious Botha decade, that their flexibility was matched by obduracy wrapped up in free-market packaging!

But the trick remains to find the least painful and most expeditious way to end apartheid. International energy needs to be directed towards the cleavages which have appeared in manifold forms within the country. This is not an easy task: apartheid has impounded a complex social geology with deep-seated economic layers. However, these very strata are the source of its undoing. When students from that font of ideological purity, Stellenbosch, march with university workers in an anti-government demonstration, something is crumbling.

This brings us to the hoary issue of sanctions. However cumbersome they may be to operate, however disfiguring they may be to the economy of the region, sanctions are a means to lever the current rulers of South Africa in the direction of change.[12] Two conditions make it a certain bet that sanctions will continue unabated against South Africa until apartheid is ended. Firstly, they clearly have purchase on South Africa's ruling establishment. A leading banker, Dr C. van Wyk, has suggested that sanctions had left the country R100 billion poorer. He concluded his comments, with a 'scathing attack on the proponents of sanctions' and is reported to have said that:

Through impoverishing and radicalizing the nation, sanctions have raised the chances of political confrontation at the expense of political reconciliation in the 1990s.[13]

It goes without saying that those who support sanctions would draw the same conclusions as Dr van Wyk by substituting the word 'apartheid' for 'sanctions'. And, indeed, Albert Luthuli in 1963 acknowledged the damage which would be done by sanctions but reached a somewhat different conclusion with these remarks:

I shall not argue that economic ostracism of South Africa is desirable from every point of view. But I have no doubt that it represents our only chance of a relatively peaceful transition from the present unacceptable type of rule to a system of government which gives us all our rightful voice.[14]

The second reason why the sanctions regime will endure has to do with the fact that, in many cases, South Africa has become secondary to the issue. Put differently: in many places sanctions have developed a life of their own. It is a sober lesson to recognise that this – for this objective, let's call them the second wave of sanctions – followed on the great ruin and hardship which South Africa inflicted on its neighbours, especially Mozambique.

These are, however, essentially negative pressures; what positive pressures can the international community bring? It is here that the embrace of Africa is needed. South Africans – whatever their colour – are consummate Africans. Their ostracisation by their continent has been amongst the most painful of the hardships which they have had to endure. This has fed a one-dimensional view of the continent: for whites it is met with bravado and the inane and reckless 'Africa is a basket case' syndrome. For blacks it has spawned confusion and unnecessary distress.

The countries of Africa have an obligation to help move the present system. This is not to suggest that they have not been vigilant in their efforts to destroy apartheid, nor that many, like the Zambians, have not paid a huge price for their principles. The conflict must, however, come back to Africa in a meaningful way. It may seem slightly incongruous to raise this point but, twenty years after the Lusaka Manifesto, perhaps what is needed is a restatement of the overall principles of that document. Only an African encounter will ensure that apartheid will not again be caught in the shabby tension between extra-continental powers.

In this spirit the interest of the Organisation of African Unity in the process of transition is central. Their willing endorsement of the ANC's proposals for a negotiated settlement of the dispute is a significant breakthrough, but what is needed now are assurances on the African future which faces all South Africans. There should, finally, be no hiding the fact that this will not be an easy task.

Between the drafting of this chapter and its publication, events in South Africa underwent a profound change: President F.W. de Klerk made his speech of 2 February 1990 which set the country's political process loose. Ten days later, Nelson Mandela walked away from prison and within months exiles began returning to the land of their birth.

What role did external powers play in bringing this about? There are no easy answers, as this contribution has suggested. The end of the Cold War will, one suspects, not ease our understanding of the complex processes which underpin the relations between states. And yet there seems little gainsaying the fact that the collapse of the ideological conditioning which characterised interstate relations for the best part of 45 years does enable quick explanations.

In October 1990 a returning exile caught the sense of this with this observation:

> How much, for instance, do ordinary South Africans, black and white, understand the immensity of what is happening to them? Are they at all able to situate the dynamism transforming their own individual political and economic lives in the context of that global revolution, inaugurated by a little man in the Kremlin with a map-like birthmark on his bald pate – a revolution which has ended the 'cold war' and the mythologies of 'deterrence', 'balances of terror', 'total onslaughts' and 'total strategies' to defeat them?[15]

The Gorbachev 'factor' certainly helped de Klerk to free up the political process, but it also created great confusion, as the often futile debate on a future economic policy showed.[16]

The scars which rigid adherence to the two sides of the ideological divide created promise to visit South Africa again and again as it grapples with the necessity to develop a new society in which all its peoples can live in accord; it will not be easy to overcome this. The youth and the underclass trapped by centuries of uneven economic growth cry out for radical re-distribution; the rich posit their faith in the power of the market. The lesson is, however, that South Africa is not an easy country in which to occupy the middle ground.

But there are, however, a number of wider international lessons which flow – inadvertently perhaps – from external efforts to shape the South African experience. Of these certainly the dominant was the view that conventional international relations weapons were relatively blunt instruments: South Africa may have changed that view. When the calls for pressure against Iraq were made, the first instrument to be activated was financial sanctions. Although these failed to deter the Iraqis (perhaps because of the short period involved), in the case of South Africa the lesson was clear: financial sanctions, more than Gorbachev or anything else, helped bring change.

Notes

1. This is literature drawn together in J.A. Kalley, *Pressure on Pretoria: Sanctions, Boycotts and the Divestment/Disinvestment Issue, 1964–1988*, Johannesburg: SAIIA Bibliographical Series, no 17, 1988, p. 299.
2. See, for example, D.J. Geldenhuys, *Internationale Isolasie: Suid-Afrika in Vergelykende perspektief*, Johannesburg: Randse Afrikaanse Universiteit, 1985, p. 106.
3. In the post-war case, deepening international pressure compelled a relaxed General Smuts and a furtive Dr Malan to hide behind the close British link. The three adjectives are deliberately chosen, Smuts was comfortable with the British and clearly did not recognise that it was the very nearness of this link which may have cost him the 1948 election. For his part, Dr Malan patently understood the ambiguity – to use a euphemism – which his supporters felt towards the British in particular. The closeness of the links, however, is most interesting. The United Kingdom was both anxious about its colonial policy and fearful of antagonising the South African government, especially after 1948. Accordingly, London went to some lengths to protect South Africa in the international community. See J.E. Spence, *The Strategic Significance of South Africa*, London: Royal United Services Institution, 1970, pp. 10–11.
4. The central points here were explored in P. Vale, 'The Atlantic Nations and South Africa: Economic Constraints and Community Fracture', unpublished PhD thesis, University of Leicester, 1980, p. 446
5. See, *inter alia*, S. Marks and A. Atmore (eds), *Economy and Society in South Africa*, London: Longman, 1980, p. 385; B. Setai, *The Political Economy of South Africa: The Making of Poverty*, Washington, D.C.:

University Press of America, 1977, p. 200; A. Stadler, *The Political Economy of Modern South Africa*, London: Croom Helm, 1987.

6. Some of these themes have been explored in P. Vale, 'Generals and the Crisis of White Power in South Africa', *Vierteljahresberichte*, no 112, pp. 171–85.

7. On Constructive Engagement, see for example, S.J. Ungar and P. Vale, 'South Africa: Why Constructive Engagement Failed', *Foreign Affairs*, 64, (2), pp. 234–58.

8. R.H. Chilcote, 'Politics in Portugal and her Empire', *The World Today*, 19 (9), 1961, pp. 376–7.

9. A. Buchan, *Change without War: The Shifting Structure of World Power*, London: Chatto & Windus, 1974, p. 18.

10. 'For decades, while the more gruesome and horrifying aspects of apartheid were brutally implemented, successive National Party (NP) governments hid behind the assumed protection of Article 2 (7) of the UN Charter which supposedly prohibited interference in the domestic affairs of member states. It is pleasing to note that the South African mission at the UN no longer attempts to do this and that the sheer force of international pressure, both diplomatic and economic, coupled with the political initiatives of the liberation movements are at last, we believe, forcing the RSA government to take cognisance of what the outside world thinks and believes. Twenty five years ago, no one would have ever thought that the National Party government could entertain the very idea of abandoning the apartheid policy.' E.J. Mabuza, Presidential Address delivered at the Eleventh Annual Congress of the Inyandza National Movement, 23 September, 1989, p. 5.

11. See, for example, P. Vale, *Integration and Disintegration in Southern Africa*, IDASA Occasional Paper No. 15, 1989.

12. See the contributions to M. Orkin (ed.), *Sanctions Against South Africa*, Cape Town: David Philip, 1989.

13. *The Star*, Johannesburg, 3 November, 1989.

14. Quoted in Orkin (ed.), op cit., p, vi.

15. 'Everything is different – but still so much is the same', *Cape Times*, 1 October 1990, p. 6.

16. See the debate prompted by Joe Slovo's paper, 'Has Socialism Failed?', p. 27 (mimeo); M. Frost, 'Joe Slovo and the Fate of Communism', *South Africa Foundation Review*, 16 (5), May 1990, p. 3; L. Schlemmer, 'Mixed Signals: The Nationalisation Debates', *Indicator SA*, 7 (2), Autumn 1990, pp.17–21; H. Adam, 'Eastern Europe and South African Socialism: Engaging Joe Slovo', *South Africa International*, 21 (1), July 1990, pp.27–35; P. Jordan, 'The Crisis of Conscience in the SACP', *Transformation*, no. 11, 1990, pp.75–89.

12   The 1990s and Beyond

Gavin Maasdorp and Alan Whiteside

Politically and economically, Southern Africa in the 1990s will be
influenced by two main forces – global and national. These will
determine the future of individual countries and of the region as a
whole – whether they will be marginalised and, as a consequence, be
condemned to economic stagnation and backwardness, or whether
they will be able to harness their resources and develop their potential
in such a way as to become a force to be reckoned with in the
international community.

GLOBAL FACTORS

The 1980s were critical years in determining global political and
economic systems. The collapse of totalitarian governments in most
centrally planned economies and the orthodox Marxism-Leninism they
represented, together with the renewed appreciation of the importance
of market forces in the West, have together probably set the standards
by which the developed countries and multinational aid agencies will
judge their partners in the developing world. The ending of the Cold
War means that there will be greater unanimity on these issues among
the developed countries. It also has resulted in the end of superpower
rivalry, particularly in the Third World.

These events have occurred concurrently with a growing disenchant-
ment and cynicism in the West with regard to development aid,
especially that which has been poured into Africa. The economic
and political performance of sub-Saharan Africa (SSA) in the first
three decades of independence too often has been disastrous. In
Europe, there has been talk not of the possibility but of the probability
of 'delinking' SSA from the rest of the world. The USA appears to have
lost much of its interest in Africa and the same applies to its former
Cold War adversary, the Soviet Union. The multilateral agencies
continue to provide support, but they and other donors increasingly
take the attitude that, unless certain preconditions are met, aid will
simply not be given.

The opening up of Eastern Europe signals the entry of a powerful competitor for aid and investment. The human resource base of Eastern Europe is superior to that of Africa in terms of overall education and skills, although its entrepreneurial spirit has been dampened by over four decades of communism. The problems of economic and political reconstruction are formidable, and the process may take a decade or two, but Eastern Europe is probably more attractive to Western investors than is Africa. Certainly, individual countries (notably Czechoslovakia, Hungary and Poland) should attract considerable attention.

The fall of one-party states in Eastern Europe has given the EC an opportunity to reinforce the stress on markets and private enterprise in Lomé IV with an insistence on respect for human rights, the rule of law and ecological awareness. This matches the groundswell of public opinion in favour of multi-party democracy in Africa, which may mean that the continent will meet one of the conditions for foreign aid, namely political democracy.

The EC insistence on markets and private enterprise has its counterpart in the structural adjustment programmes of the International Monetary Fund and the World Bank. Governments have to meet strict conditions which limit their ability to adopt radical socialist policies. A recent development is that the EC stresses a social market approach, whilst the IMF and World Bank are paying more attention to the impact of structural adjustment on the poor. Although these programmes may weaken State structures in Africa by eroding domestic sovereignty, donors do not specify a particular political or economic model for SSA. Many African governments have attempted to initiate economic development but with far less competence than in the case of Japan and the East Asian NICs – the technocrats were simply not there to accomplish the goals. Ironically there has been extensive government intervention in SSA and the bureaucracies are large, inefficient and often corrupt. Development will be successful only if production is left to the market with government providing the services and a macroeconomic policy climate attractive to investment and conducive to growth.

Southern Africa is in a better position than the rest of SSA. Indeed, if there is one part of Africa that could develop successfully, it is the south. If Southern Africa can get its political and macroeconomic policies in order, it could attract investment and aid funds away from the rest of Africa. The absorptive capacity of many LDCs is limited, for example, under Lomé III only 20 per cent of the available funds were used. The EC provides over one-half of all aid available to Southern Africa, and under Lomé IV funds will be available in increasing amounts if the projects are there. Southern Africa has a greater institutional capacity – through South Africa and the SADCC – for absorption than other recipients. The dynamism, management skills and technical knowhow of South Africa are important for the region, and donors and investors might well treat post-apartheid South Africa as the entry point for capital to the region. Southern Africa needs an inflow of investment funds – there is no chance for change if there is no foreign investment – and it has the potential to make this investment a success provided that the South African economy remains intact. Southern Africa will not be given a second chance, at least in the next decade.

The region's development potential, however, must be assessed against the background of global technological change. Two major assets, namely raw materials and cheap labour, have been marginalised, while the nature of technological progress is such that productivity differentials between the OECD/NICs and the rest of the world will widen. The development of biotechnology has serious implications for the future of Africa's exports, as will the age of superconductors. Southern Africa will have to keep up with technological development in order to remain competitive in the world economy: in many cases, for example robotics in some areas of manufacturing, it will mean capital-intensive growth, and this trend would be enhanced if organised labour demands high wages for unskilled work. Technological progress, together with the strong bargaining position of industrial investors, places unskilled labour in an increasingly weak bargaining position, but at the same time makes it difficult for governments to cope with problems of unemployment and poverty.

NATIONAL FACTORS

Although Marxism-Leninism has been rejected in Eastern Europe and in LDCs such as Angola and Mozambique, there is still a residue of support for some type of radical socialism in parts of Southern Africa, notably South Africa and Zimbabwe. In the West and in Eastern Europe today, the old capitalism vs socialism debate is regarded as outdated. In the 1990s more attention will probably be directed at the institutional framework in a country which will allow the market and

State to interact in such a manner as to promote efficiency and equity, perhaps along social market lines. In South Africa and Zimbabwe the debate is still underway, and its outcome will have a powerful effect on the future of the region.

Political Influences

Political stability is a *sine qua non* for investor confidence and hence an inflow of funds to any particular country as well as to the region as a whole. Although the signs in Southern Africa are more hopeful than at any time in the last few decades, almost every country in the region could be subjected to political tension and instability.

Nowhere is this more true than South Africa. Whilst some groups are loath, for political reasons, to acknowledge the irreversibility of the government's reforms, it is now clear to analysts that there is no going back. Furthermore, the constitutional process must be completed by no later than March 1995. This is the last date by which the government, in terms of the present constitution, is bound to call an election. Most analysts now agree that matters could be settled by the end of 1992, and it is significant that groups which were previously unwilling to contemplate participating in negotiations appear to have changed their stance.

Worrying factors at present in South Africa are the activities of right-wing elements, violence among Africans, and the expectations of the younger generation. Opinion polls suggest that the right wing is supported by about 25 per cent of the white population. It is unlikely that this will rise significantly, or that the CP, the main element, will refuse ultimately to join the negotiations. The problem is that there are various extra-parliamentary (often paramilitary) groups, whose members have undergone military training and who possess arms. These groups have both the ability to disrupt the negotiations and the potential to indulge in sabotage and similar actions in the post-apartheid period. A further concern is the presence of such elements in the forces charged with keeping law and order. It is important that they be disarmed, and this clearly is an issue which the government of the day will have to address.

The level of 'black on black' violence during the last few years, especially in the Natal and Witwatersrand areas, has dismayed South Africans as well as foreign observers. The cause of the violence is not easy to assess, but it includes political, socio-economic and criminal components. Again, it will have to be stamped out by a post-apartheid government, but if it has an ethnic element as some observers fear, it has the potential to be endemic unless some type of federal system is negotiated.

The level of expectations among Africans, especially among the youth, has been built up to the extent that it is now impossible for any future government to meet them. Many of the political speeches made in the year since the ANC and related organisations were unbanned have done nothing to disabuse the masses of these expectations; indeed, in many instances, they have merely raised them further. The future government, therefore, will be placed in a very difficult position since a large part of its constituency will consist of persons under the age of 30 years (including the so-called 'lost generation' who have been out of school more frequently than in and who consequently have neither the formal educational qualifications nor the employment experience to be productive income earners). Should the first post-apartheid government not 'deliver the goods' to this constituency, it could conceivably be ousted by a more radical party. This would be a major blow to the prospects of the region as a whole.

A number of other Southern African countries appear vulnerable to political instability, sometimes short-lived but in some perhaps of longer duration. In Mozambique, for instance, a peace agreement between Renamo and the government appears imminent. The new constitution, introduced in November 1990, allows a multi-party system and has a commitment to a market economy. In fact, it seems to have cut the ground from under Renamo's feet. But such an agreement would not guarantee stability: there is evidence that many of the 'bandits' in rural areas are criminal gangs, and Mozambique will have to act with resolve to restore peaceful conditions to the country-side. Prospects for peace and stability appear to be rather better in Angola where the civil war has been contested between two well-defined and organised parties.

In Zimbabwe, the government has relented in its bid to impose a one-party state, and has liberalised its economic policies, but remains unpopular among students and the intelligentsia. Unemployment, especially among school leavers, and inflation with its impact on wages, are factors which could cause turmoil. The likely battle for succession in Malawi after Dr Banda has fascinated observers. The succession could be orderly or turbulent, but will herald a new political style. Lesotho, with its new king, is still ruled by the military amid considerable (if as yet muted) opposition. There is open speculation about the future of the country: migrant workers have apparently joined the unions and signed ANC membership forms. Some observers argue that Lesotho may simply be absorbed into post-apartheid South Africa, while others favour a political confederation. Swaziland also has close ethnic ties with South Africa, and any radicalism in South Africa could spill over into the tiny kingdom where the coexistence of traditional and modern forms of government persists with growing uneasiness. Zambia's reluctant acceptance of a multi-party system could lead to a change of government, while Tanzania (tangential though it might be to Southern Africa) might well fracture into Tanganyika and Zanzibar, in which case the latter might perhaps link up with the Comores in an Islamic island republic.

It is too early to say how stable the newly independent Namibia will be in the 1990s. However, the country seems to have got off to a promising start, and its multi-party constitution and economic pragmatism bode well for the future. Botswana is far and away the most stable country in the sub-continent, and is often held up as a political and economic model.

Economic Influences

The economic system favoured by any one country in the region is, of course, closely bound to politics. The changing fortunes of competing economic systems in the 1980s referred to earlier have had a significant effect on Southern Africa. Various experiments in populist socialism have given ground in Tanzania and Zambia while Marxism-Leninism has been discarded in Angola and Mozambique, the ruling party in Namibia has moved from its pre-independence Marxist-Leninist rhetoric to an acceptance of a mixed economy, and the Zimbabwean government's continued official commitment to 'scientific socialism' is not mirrored in its liberalisation of the economy. Within the SACU the governments are all committed to a market economy, and this is true too of Malawi. Thus, there is greater unanimity at government level on economic systems in Southern Africa today than has been the case in the last 15–20 years. Even the 'post-apartheid economy' debate in South Africa is now characterised by a commitment, at least among the major parties, to a mixed economy, although there remain divergent views over the role of the State in the economy.

In Africa most governments have overstretched themselves and are now trying to vacate areas best left to the private sector. This has resulted in the privatisation of parastatals; in Southern Africa this is most advanced in Zambia and Angola. In Zambia, for example, the

State is selling 49 per cent of its shareholding in each industry to the private sector. Enormous problems have been encountered with the State as an operator – it has not had the appropriate technical or managerial capacity, and it is now acknowledged that its main contribution should be as a regulator. For Southern Africa, and especially for South Africa, the important point will be to prevent privatisation from becoming an ideological issue. The approach in each case should be pragmatic, that is, what will work best? The main problem with privatisation is that it takes time to develop a business class.

The problem of poverty is one which will continue to be uppermost in the minds of governments, and in Zimbabwe and South Africa this is related to inter-racial income inequality. The Zimbabwean experience could be instructive. In order to promote greater equality, the government adopted various controls over enterprises, prices, labour relations, and foreign exchange. This had the effect of repelling foreign investment. Now the government is encouraging investors and the private sector, and realises the importance of achieving an appropriate balance between State activity and incentives and rewards for business. However, recent legislation providing for the nationalisation of white-owned farms (including the estates of multinationals) might reinforce the doubts of foreign investors.

Economic restructuring will be most difficult in Mozambique and Angola although the latter has a more favourable resource base. Both will have to cope with the problems and costs of resettling war refugees, but the numbers are greater in Mozambique where six million persons have been displaced. Mozambique needs to reactivate its rural productive base and invest in education and training. Imports are only feasible with strong international support, which includes emergency food supplies to dislocated families. It is essential that as much aid as possible be invested in production otherwise the country will remain dependent on foreign donors. Some investment has flowed into the major cities, especially in the tourism and transport sectors, as well as into mining and agriculture, and an improvement in the security situation would lead to a spurt of economic growth.

POST-APARTHEID SOUTH AFRICA AND THE REGION

There has been considerable speculation about the nature of future relations between a post-apartheid government and its neighbours.

Observers in those countries are increasingly doubtful that a change of
government would necessarily mean any change in Pretoria's hegemonic designs on the region. Much would seem to depend on whether the
government were to approach the region in a cooperative spirit or
whether it were to attach a relatively low priority to regional relations.
Also important would be the strength of South Africa vis-à-vis region.

A Strong South Africa

A number of arguments revolve around the assumption that South
Africa will remain the strong regional economic power. These are
detailed below.

First, the current ANC and PAC view is that the post-apartheid
government will be committed to genuine regional cooperation without domination. The new government will be happy to be an equal
partner with the region in the spirit of the Harare Declaration. South
Africa will renounce a hegemonic role in favour of cooperation and
regional reconstruction, and will take affirmative action by renegotiat-
ing a number of regional agreements.

Second, a more cynical view is that South Africa will continue to
dominate the region irrespective of its government. The post-apartheid
government will not be less hegemonic in outlook, and the SADCC
countries will become more dependent. If economic growth rates are
favourable, however, Angola and Zimbabwe at least might be able to
resist South African domination.

Third, the post-apartheid government will decide to treat the region
on a bilateral rather than a multilateral basis since it will derive few
benefits from membership of regional groupings such as the SADCC
and PTA that it cannot obtain from a series of bilateral agreements. It
will be so strong that it will be able to call the shots either way. Much
of South Africa's regional policy has been conducted on a bilateral
basis, so the new government would merely continue the policy it
inherits.

Four, South Africa will benefit from an 'apartheid dividend' and will
become the engine of growth for the region. New investment and
resources will be mobilised. In the process, however, South Africa
could well draw skills away from the region, especially from Zimbabwe. Its consultants and contractors, with their expertise and
experience of Southern African conditions, could become involved in

the planning and execution of SADCC infrastructure projects, probably at reduced costs.

A Weak South Africa

Several arguments assume that there will be a decline in South Africa's regional hegemony. First, the new government will be so preoccupied with its internal problems that it will pay little attention to the region. Its economy may in fact decline to the point where its regional economic dominance is severely diminished: this is likely to happen if the country becomes increasingly statist with bureaucratic planning and controls. South Africa would then move in a direction opposite to that of regional integration. Many black groups in South Africa already feel that foreign investment is not important, and thus the West will lose interest both in South Africa and the region at the same time that South Africa itself loses interest in the region.

Second, there could well be a change in the balance of power in the region. Angola and Zimbabwe are militarising and already have superiority over South Africa's outdated aircraft. This, together with South Africa's economic decline, will mean that the country will not be as powerful in the region as it is today. The new government will not be able to guarantee regional security, neither will it have surplus funds or skills with which to assist the region. It will itself depend on an inflow of foreign funds and skills.

In both of these propositions, the post-apartheid government might wish to cooperate but might not have much ability to assist the region.

The weakness of these arguments is that they do not take account of interdependence. It is likely that, whether on a bilateral or multilateral basis, there will be increased interdependence between South Africa and its neighbours to their mutual advantage. For example, Southern Africa has the potential markets as well as the water and energy resources which South Africa needs. However, the new government should handle joint projects with tact otherwise it will be accused of hegemony (as some intellectuals in Lesotho apparently feel about the Highlands Water Project). If South Africa does exert its hegemony, antagonisms will remain in post-apartheid Southern Africa. One point, though, on which most observers agree is that South African aggression, epitomised in regional 'destabilisation', will not be a feature of the post-apartheid future.

CHANGING ATTITUDES TOWARDS SOUTH AFRICA

South Africa has made a remarkable comeback to the international community since February 1990. There is no doubt that changes in the Soviet Union, and the alacrity with which Eastern Europe has established trade ties, have been instrumental in reopening the world to Pretoria. Diplomatic links have been forged with Poland, Czechoslovakia, Hungary, Rumania and Bulgaria as well as with Madagascar; senior politicians from Pretoria have visited various other countries, including Zambia, Ivory Coast, Morocco, Kenya and the Soviet Union; and delegations from Eastern Europe have visited South Africa. Trade with Africa has increased and is now quite open, while in the EC it is common knowledge that the case of sanctions has weakened considerably. In many parts of the world, sanctions have been effectively scrapped; the US, where many local politicians have used sanctions as a means of furthering their careers, appears to be one of the last redoubts.

Two-way trade with Africa was worth R4 billion in 1989, when more than 10 per cent of the country's manufactured exports went to Africa. Project and sectoral cooperation is increasing; Eskom, for instance, has good working relationships with ten countries from the Congo-Zaire-Kenya line southwards, and the World Bank is now prepared to lend for such projects so that financial constraints to regional development involving South Africa are being removed.

It is doubtful today whether, even for those who advocated them, any further mileage can be gained from sanctions. The world cannot go beyond sanctions (applied against South Africa because of its unique race policies) and lay down a particular form of State for the future. For example, the question of unitary vs federal systems is not an ideological one.

What is of urgency now is to create the right psychological climate for further investment in the region. Sticks such as sanctions merely erode the South African economy. Retrogression must be stopped and this requires carrots. This is something which cannot wait until the transfer of power: if a post-apartheid government is to inherit an economic wasteland, it would hardly be liberation in any real sense. This would also make it more difficult for the future government to devise a tolerable balance between an efficient market-based economy and a changing social order. It is difficult to see how South Africa can have political stability without economic progress, and sanctions thus entail a considerable cost not only to South Africa but to the region as a whole.

One constructive development is the rapid disintegration of the academic boycott. It is doubtful whether this boycott, which was never totally effective, produced any tangible results other than a mass of literature based on a sometimes staggering ignorance of South Africa and a disregard for facts. A series of conferences in the last two years has shown just how factually inaccurate outside perceptions of South Africa are. This is particularly so in the case of scholars from the front line states. They have tended to exaggerate the importance of the 'total strategy', and the concept of the Constellation of Southern African States has been elevated to a level of importance it never attained. A more accurate analysis has been impeded by the fact that many writers either would not or could not visit South Africa to undertake research, and therefore tended to paint the country according to their perceptions. Frequently, large bodies of critical South African academic writings were simply ignored and never appeared in bibliographies. One of the most important requirements for future relationships between South Africa and the rest of the world, including the region, is a reappraisal of much of what has been written in the last few decades.

SCENARIOS

A matrix of four scenarios of future development in South Africa and the region may be developed, reflecting various combinations of 'right' and 'wrong'. By 'right' is meant that political stability and judicious economic policies combine to produce high rates of economic growth and a growing role for either South Africa or the region in the global economy. By 'wrong' is meant that political instability and inappropriate economic policies together discourage economic growth and lead to the declining importance of South Africa or the region in the world economy. The matrix is shown in Table 12.1.

These scenarios will now be discussed in turn.

Best Scenario

The best scenario is a representation of an ideal outcome. Politically, both South Africa and the region as a whole would have democratic, multi-party systems with a relatively efficient and honest government

Table 12.1   Matrix of possible scenarios

Scenario		
Best	SA right	Region right
Intermediate (1)	SA right	Region wrong
Intermediate (2)	SA wrong	Region right
Worst	SA wrong	Region wrong

and bureaucracy. Governments would be committed to market-based economies with macroeconomic policy environments which encourage economic growth and attract the support of the international investor community. However, governments are also conscious of social justice, and the economic policies are formulated so as to contain social conflict. The post-apartheid government is committed to regional cooperation, and Southern Africa gains in importance in international trade.

Within this, and indeed the remaining scenarios, there could of course be variations with some countries going right and others wrong, but the permutations are too many to be considered here. Some points, however, are worthy of elaboration.

South Africa would become a powerful middle-income country and, together with Zimbabwe, would act as a regional stabiliser. Southern Africa would become attractive for investors although the lack of skilled manpower would have to be carefully approached. Intra-regional trade would increase on a two-way basis, and greater regional cooperation would be achieved, perhaps with the SACU being converted into a common market (SACM) and some type of preferential trade relationship being negotiated with the remaining SADCC states. By about 2025 Southern Africa could begin to resemble something of a South-East Asian-type 'miracle'.

Intermediate Scenario 1

In this scenario South Africa goes right and the region wrong. For South Africa, and perhaps for its SACU partners, developments are the same as in the best scenario. But in the rest of Southern Africa events either take a turn for the worse or remain about the same as at present. A continuation of political instability, lack of security, weak government and ineffectual economic policies prevent countries such as Mozambique, Angola, Zimbabwe and Zambia from realising their economic potential. Regional cooperation is relatively ineffectual apart from that within the SACU (or SACM), and the remaining SADCC countries become increasingly dependent on the rapidly developing south.

Intermediate Scenario 2

In many respects this scenario, with South Africa going wrong and the rest of the region right, is more interesting than the others because of the questions it raises. Could the region, or some countries at least, hold things together if South Africa goes on the slide? What would happen to Lesotho? What would be the implications for the SACU/CMA?

South Africa's decline could stem from a radical socialist government or from a failure to develop the politics of tolerance. The result of constitutional negotiations and an election would not be easily accepted, and a level of violence sufficient to deter investment and economic growth would exist. The government would be disinterested in its neighbours, and a declining economy and currency could well spell the end of the SACU and CMA. Lesotho, however, would be unlikely to be able to break its ties with the South African economy, and radicalisation or violence could spill over into that country and perhaps into Swaziland. But if Swaziland were not affected politically, it could reorientate its import patterns using its natural port of Maputo. Botswana and Namibia could also do so, while Zimbabwe could well then replace South Africa as the regional stabiliser. The SADCC could have an enhanced role in attracting funds for regional projects. The Southern African economy as a whole, however, whilst gaining in importance in the world economy, would not be as buoyant as it would were the South African economy also to be growing rapidly.

Worst Scenario

The worst scenario would see things going wrong both in South Africa and the region. A failed or highly flawed negotiation process in South Africa would lead to continued economic stagnation and political instability. Alternatively, a radical government could take over and, following policies diametrically opposed to those occurring in the rest of the world, lead the country into political and economic isolation. Political failure in South Africa could spill over into Lesotho and Swaziland with similar results. Other key countries in the region such as Angola, Mozambique, Zimbabwe and Zambia could be afflicted by the same ills as in the second scenario above, and only Namibia and Botswana perhaps could remain as small areas of relative peace and prosperity but without being particularly attractive to the rest of the world. South Africa and Southern Africa would virtually be delinked from the world economy.

An interesting variation of this scenario relates to the implications for the remaining countries should the two major economies, namely South Africa and Zimbabwe, both go wrong. In Zimbabwe, for instance, any pursuit of a one-party state could inflame political opposition and perhaps lead to a radical type of socialism in sympathy with that which could prevail in South Africa (in terms of the previous paragraph). In such a case, the role of the maritime countries would become especially important. Mozambique's transport services to Swaziland and Malawi would help those two countries, while Botswana could perhaps look to Namibia since it might have to reorientate its import trade. Zambia would be forced to rely on Tanzania and Angola and also perhaps on a route via Malawi to Mozambican ports. All these countries would have a tougher time in developing their economies, but it would not be impossible for them to continue operating at a reasonable level of economic growth even though the two major regional powers were in trouble.

CONCLUSION

What is certain is that South Africa and the region are at a crossroads. Decisions taken, and negotiations conducted in the first few years of the 1990s, will determine the future of the region for decades to come. For the first time since the 1950s there is an opportunity for the countries in the region to work for economic growth and to move towards democracy, both individually and collectively. Although the prospects for much of SSA seem bleak, Southern Africa at least has the chance to achieve real development. If settlement is reached in South Africa, and if pragmatic political and economic decisions throughout the region are taken, there is a good chance that Southern Africa might come to be a force to be reckoned with in the world.

Index